Behind the Backlash

BEHIND THE BACKLASH

White Working-Class Politics in Baltimore, 1940–1980

Kenneth D. Durr

The University of North Carolina Press

Chapel Hill and London

Manufactured in the United States of America
Designed by Charles Ellertson
Set in Charter with Franklin Gothic display
by Tseng Information Systems, Inc.

⊗ The paper in this book meets the guidelines
for permanence and durability of the Committee
on Production Guidelines for Book Longevity of the
Council on Library Resources.

Library of Congress Cataloging-in-Publication Data
Durr, Kenneth D.
Behind the backlash : white working-class politics
in Baltimore, 1940–1980 / by Kenneth D. Durr.
p.   cm.
Includes bibliographical references and index.
ISBN 0-8078-2764-9 (alk. paper)
ISBN 0-8078-5433-6 (pbk. : alk. paper)
1. Working class whites—Maryland—Baltimore—Political activity.
2. Working class whites—Maryland—Baltimore—Attitudes.
3. Baltimore (Md.)—Race relations.   I. Title.
HD8079.B2 D87 2003
306.2′086′2307526—dc21   2002006744

Portions of this work have appeared previously, in somewhat different form,
as "When Southern Politics Came North: The Roots of White Working-Class
Conservatism in Baltimore, 1940–1964," *Labor History* 37, no. 3 (Summer 1996):
309–31, and "The Not-So-Silent Majority: White Working-Class Community
Activism in Baltimore, 1967–1975," in *From Mobtown to Charm City: New
Perspectives on Baltimore's Past,* ed. Jessica L. Elfenbein, John R. Briehan, and
Thomas L. Hollowak (Baltimore: Maryland Historical Society, 2002): 222–45,
and are reprinted here with permission of the publishers.

cloth 07 06 05 04 03   5 4 3 2 1
paper 07 06 05 04 03   5 4 3 2 1

For Jean

Contents

Maps, Tables, and Illustrations

Maps

Tables

Illustrations

Abbreviations

AFL	American Federation of Labor
BFL	Baltimore Federation of Labor
CIO	Congress of Industrial Organizations
CORE	Congress of Racial Equality
FBI	Federal Bureau of Investigation
FHA	Federal Housing Administration
GM	General Motors
HUAC	House Un-American Activities Committee
ILA	International Longshoremen's Association
IUMSWA	International Union of Marine and Shipbuilding Workers of America
NAACP	National Association for the Advancement of Colored People
NLRB	National Labor Relations Board
NSRP	National States Rights Party
OFCC	Office of Federal Contract Compliance
PAC	Political Action Committee
PBEA	Point Breeze Employees Association
PTA	Parent-Teacher Association
ROTC	Reserve Officers' Training Corps
SCAR	Southeast Committee against the Road
SECO	Southeast Community Organization
SPFH	Society for the Preservation of Federal Hill, Montgomery Street, and Fells Point
SWOC	Steelworkers Organizing Committee
UAW	United Autoworkers
UDA	Union for Democratic Action
UE	United Electrical, Radio, and Machine Workers of America
VA	Veterans Administration

Behind the Backlash

LOR

Introduction

The post–World War II white working class has long been a cultural and political puzzle. Its members were the core constituents of organized labor, arguably the most powerful social movement in American history, but are often casually characterized as resentful and reactionary chauvinists. The backbone of Franklin Roosevelt's New Deal Democratic coalition, working whites put Ronald Reagan in the White House. But between the eras of Roosevelt and Reagan, in the space of a few short months in 1968, their political sentiments lurched perplexingly between Robert Kennedy and George Wallace. More recently, but no more accurately, liberals have tended to see blue collarites as unreasoning opponents; conservatives, as unreflective followers.

Never before or since was as much attention given to blue-collar America as in 1969 and 1970 when a supposed "white backlash" against racial integration became the issue of the day.[1] Popular culture paid the urban white working class its greatest compliment in creating a television icon, the irascible, though ineffectual Archie Bunker. But left to sift through the conflicting evidence—brutal New York construction workers venting frustrations on political protesters or heroic Lordstown strikers challenging the inhumanity of the assembly line?—screenwriters, man-on-the-street reporters, and social scientists soon moved on, and even Archie Bunker left the loading dock to become the proprietor of a small business by the late 1970s.

Historians have been no more effective at making sense of the life and politics of the urban white working class. Textbook authors place the locus of American family life in the industrial city before World War II and the sprawling suburb afterward. Monograph writers find much to learn from the postwar struggles of minority workers, but with only a few exceptions they cede the world of the white working class almost entirely to the social sciences.[2] When mentioned at all in new left historical accounts, the white working class too often serves as a foil for the less privileged who still fight the good fight that whites supposedly abandoned after the New Deal.

Having found white working people on the wrong side once too often, historians seem finally to have given up, explaining too much and not enough by invoking "whiteness": the discovery that driving political, social, and cultural change in the postwar workplace and community was white working people's attempts to protect and expand their unjustly won "white skin privilege."[3] A corollary to this view holds that the populist arguments put forth by white working people that so startled social observers in 1970 and helped power the Republican resurgence of the 1980s can be best understood as code words for race-based resentments.

This book presents a different picture. It argues that behind the cultural, social, and political events that made up the white backlash were motivations and concerns far too complex to be explained by invocations of whiteness or racism in disguise. As a work of history, it is old-fashioned, taking seriously what white working people had to say and examining the institutions and events that informed those words. Fragments of this portrait of a parochial white working-class world shaken by threats that multiplied so after the mid-1950s have been sketched by journalists like Andrew Levison and sociologists such as Herbert Gans and David Halle.[4] Sociologist Jonathan Reider and historians Ronald Formisano and Thomas Sugrue have taken a more evenhanded look at the "white backlash."[5] But Reider and Formisano focus on brief periods of conflict occurring after the backlash emerged, and Sugrue traces its prehistory of neighborhood politics stopping in 1960. The critical years of its sudden leap to notoriety, therefore, remain unexplored.

This book puts the urban blue-collar world in historical context to make sense of white working-class politics by looking not so much at what was different about white backlash, but what was the same. It argues that the key institutions and fundamental concerns of the urban working class remained relatively unchanged from World War II to the 1980s, and that, throughout, blue collarites fought to protect those institutions. Two very fundamental changes did occur, however. The first was contextual. Over time, threats to the white working-class community changed from being intensely local to profoundly national in scope. Accordingly, white working people reevaluated their problems and refocused their efforts to preserve a way of life. As this took place, a second linguistic change occurred: an older language of race-based protest gave way to a newer one that championed the rights of working people.[6]

It has been argued, most effectively by Thomas and Mary Edsall, that this transformation of language was largely pretense: that race-based resentments were encoded into race-neutral language as "white rights" became delegitimized after the passage of the Civil Rights Act of 1964.[7] This is accurate to some extent, but far too simplistic. The insight offered by Daniel T. Rodgers in his important work on political language should be heeded. "Words come to us in clusters," he contends, "trailing associations and meanings we may not intend. Born into political languages we did not invent, we are never able to talk any which way we want."[8] White working-class people took up the familiar language of segregation because it was the nearest tool at hand. But ultimately race-based claims failed, not just because of external political circumstances, but because they could not encapsulate what lay at the heart of white working-class protest—the realization that liberalism was not going to protect the security of their jobs, the worth of their neighborhoods, and the quality of their lives. Quite the contrary, liberal programs seemed aimed at undermining all of them. In this context, what troubled working whites by 1970—at the height of white backlash—was not so much integration and threats to white rights as it was liberalism and its contravention of the rights of working people.

Every historian must begin with a set of stipulations. In writing about a "white working class" I risk insufficiently attending to the fact that, as many scholars have insisted, whiteness, as well as blackness, is a social construction once made and constantly being remade. It would be a study in itself to look at how whiteness was reconstituted during these years. Instead, I have chosen to use commonly understood contemporary phrases to identify a coherent white working class whose members understood themselves as such. For variety's sake, I use the terms "white working class," "working whites," and "blue-collar" interchangeably throughout this book. I fully realize that there is no racial identifier in the phrase "blue-collar," but in the postwar decades it was used primarily to identify white manual wageworkers, and so I have adopted that convention.

Two other terms that appear in this account are "elite" and "liberal," used often and broadly as they were by the subjects of this book. The elites discussed here generally include the well born, the professional, and the highly educated. Although there was no strictly political implication to being an elite, it was generally understood that by the fact of their position in society the members of this group were exempt from performing routine, mostly unrewarding manual labor for wages and, more important, shielded from the insecurities of urban living. A "liberal" was quite simply someone at the federal, state, or local level who championed inimical social and cultural change through legislation, legal interpretation, or executive order.

Baltimore is hardly typical. It combined a northern industrial economy with a southern segregationist social system and had proportionally fewer ethnics than other industrial cities.[9] But in postwar America, the political importance of ethnicity waned as the electoral implications of race waxed. Baltimore presents an opportunity to study whites who came to terms with blacks earlier and in greater numbers than in any other industrial city. The findings of this work are hardly peculiar to Baltimore, however. Industrial boom, suburban flight, racial conflict, crime, and decline defined the post-war years for working-class urban dwellers across America.

This book is different from most contemporary histories because it studies people whose political views were not always laudable. But in giving those who have shaped American society from the bottom up their due, scholars should not pick and choose their subjects depending on per-ceived virtue. Historians are eager to discover that among the apparently powerless lie great strengths, but they resist acknowledging that between base and erroneous arguments can be found some very important truths.

In listening to working-class voices, this study focuses on two types of political expression: electoral politics and community protest. White working-class votes, as understood by examining returns in heavily white working-class wards and precincts, serve as the most concrete indicators of political change. I chose particular white working-class wards (1, 23, and 24) and black wards (5, 14, and 17) because their socioeconomic traits re-mained relatively stable over time. Wards also overlap with census tracts, making comparisons between racial and ethnic characteristics and voting records possible. In studying instances of working-class protest, I consider triggering incidents, the people who protested, and their sources of sup-port. But for all the attention to white working-class protest, the people in these pages were hardly radicals or reactionaries. Their voices were those of a sizable, though diminishing, urban working class that was, at the out-set of the narrative, the seemingly solid foundation of Democratic electoral politics.

Baltimore was far ahead of the nation when it came to the era's defining conflict—one staged by policymakers but waged by working whites and blacks—over the deteriorating institutions and the economic crumbs left over in the deindustrializing city. But Baltimore was behind the nation in backlash politics; its blue collarites were late and reluctant Reagan Demo-crats. This incongruity suggests that the political views of white working people were—and are—more complicated than most of us would like to admit. Echoes of Archie Bunker still reverberate, largely because the chasm that opened up between the white working class and the professional middle class in the years after World War II has never closed. *Behind the Backlash* is a small attempt to bridge that gap.

In chronicling forty years of challenges to white working-class institutions and documenting the failures and accomplishments of blue-collar people, this book seeks to enlighten as historians do best: by telling a compelling and informative story. It foregoes the statistical models often wielded by those who seek the underpinnings of electoral behavior and discounts the theoretical constructs regularly brought to bear by scholars of culture. But the old-fashioned approach may not be a bad one to as elusive a subject as working-class politics. Social scientist Samuel Popkin contends that for most voters political choices are ultimately "gut" decisions. St. Louis Cardinals manager Tony La Russa has cautioned that "when you trust your gut you are trusting a lot of stuff from the past." We shall see which "stuff from the past" white working-class people trusted and which they did not.[10]

CHAPTER 1

A Contentious Coalition

In early 1944 John Cater submitted some verse written by coworkers at Baltimore's booming Westinghouse defense plant to the *Baltimore Evening Sun*. The paper published the piece, even though Cater disavowed authorship. It was a good thing he did. "Beloved Baltimore, Maryland," written from the point of view of the thousands of migrant defense workers who had flocked to the city for the duration, was a vitriolic attack on everything Baltimorean from its architecture—"your brick row houses should all be torn down"—to its economy. "You make us pay double for all you can sell," the piece concluded, "but after the war you can all go to hell." The *Evening Sun* received more than a thousand angry refutations. A postal worker dragged two bulging bags full of letters into the Sun Building's lobby, reached into his pocket, and pulled out a contribution of his own. Weeks later "Beloved Baltimore" was still the most popular topic of conversation around town.[1]

This incident, characterized by *Life* magazine as "The Battle of Baltimore," was less a fight between enemies than a quarrel between partners in a strained, but strong relationship. The coalescence of the New Deal coalition at large, a process also achieved amid the tumult of wartime, was equally contentious. Natives and newcomers, old-world ethnics and southern Protestants, all came into conflict but ultimately formed a political alliance under the Democratic umbrella. This rift between the New Deal coalition's white working-class constituents was fleeting, but there was a much deeper divide between them and the blacks and middle-class liberals who were also integral to the New Deal Democratic coalition, one that was temporarily bridged but never closed during the war years and the four decades afterward.

The Great Depression laid the groundwork for the New Deal order, based on agreement among urban and rural working whites, blacks, and middle-class liberals that grassroots political activity and an activist state could create a more economically equitable society. But in Baltimore, it was not until World War II that a viable coalition came together. Among the uproar, overcrowding, inflation, and anger, key institutions took shape and fragile alliances were formed. Machine politicians began to respond more to ethnic and working-class concerns and less to old-stock business leaders, liberal political groups—chief among them the NAACP—flourished, and industrial unionism became entrenched in Baltimore's workplaces.

This political transition was driven by three broader shifts. First, working-class Baltimore's "new immigrants" of Eastern and Southern European heritage gained political influence that began to rival that exerted by German and Irish ethnics and native-stock whites. Second, Baltimore's black working people, long restricted to unskilled, low-paid work, began to get better jobs—with and without government help. Finally, although many of the southern migrants who worked in Baltimore's war plants returned home as quickly as possible, many more did not. Instead, southern whites stayed to become members of Baltimore's postwar white working class.

The wartime boom made Baltimore, a relatively placid and culturally southern city, look more like a smoky, congested northern industrial city. Its politics also came to resemble that of other post–New Deal industrial cities. In presidential, state, and local politics a "New Deal" coalition of working-white, black, and liberal voters emerged, although each group understood the legacy of the New Deal differently. The most vocal of Baltimore's grassroots New Deal activists, urban progressives, CIO-affiliated laborites, and black civil rights leaders considered the war a political opportunity. Their conception of "New Deal Democracy" included not only the extension of blue-collar workplace rights but also the expansion of rights for blacks in the community and on the job. For Baltimore's white working people, however, the tumult of wartime was fraught with hazards. They welcomed the economic security that industrial unionism and wartime wages brought but resisted social initiatives that seemed to threaten the blue-collar community.

Economy and Society

Baltimore's roots were in commerce rather than industry; as late as 1881 there were still only thirty-nine manufacturers in the city.[2] By the turn of the century there were two hundred, but within a few years, as the nation-

Baltimore Harbor in 1939. (Courtesy of the Special Collections Department, Maryland Historical Society, Baltimore)

wide tide of mergers swept the city, outside corporations bought up local firms and Baltimore became known as a "branch plant city."[3] Nevertheless, by the late 1930s municipal leaders touted an "industrial community" closely resembling its northern counterparts.[4] Iron and steel dominated the economy. Sparrows Point, owned by the Bethlehem Steel Corporation, was the city's largest single employer, sprawling over two thousand acres where the Patapsco River met the Chesapeake Bay.[5] Although the garment industry sweatshops downtown were closing fast, the textile industry remained Baltimore's second largest employer in the 1930s. Mills built in Hampden, north of the city center, still produced cotton duck as they had for a century.[6]

The transportation equipment industry was more robust. Bethlehem Steel had shipyards at Sparrows Point and along Key Highway in South Baltimore. Maryland Shipbuilding and Drydock was on the southern edge of the harbor.[7] Glenn Martin, built in 1928 at Middle River, eleven miles northeast of downtown Baltimore, was quickly becoming the largest single airplane factory in the world. General Motors (GM) opened plants in South-

TABLE I. Comparative Ethnic and Racial Composition by City, 1940–1960

	Baltimore	Philadelphia	Detroit	Cleveland	Boston
1940					
FB White*	7.1%	15.0%	19.8%	20.4%	23.5%
Black	19.3	12.9	9.2	9.6	3.1
1950					
FB White	5.4	11.2	14.9	14.5	18.0
Black	23.8	18.3	16.4	16.3	5.3
1960					
FB White	4.2	8.9	12.1	11.0	15.8
Black	35.0	26.7	29.2	12.9	9.8

Sources: U.S. Bureau of the Census, *1940 Census of Population, Characteristics of the Population: United States Summary* (Washington, D.C.: GPO, 1943), *1950 Census of Population, Characteristics of the Population: United States Summary* (Washington, D.C.: GPO, 1953), and *1960 Census of Population, Characteristics of the Population: United States Summary* (Washington, D.C.: GPO, 1963).
*FB = Foreign-born.

east Baltimore in 1934.[8] Electrical equipment manufacturers like Westinghouse and Locke Insulator contributed to the city's industrial diversity. The largest of these was Western Electric, built in 1929 at Point Breeze, just inside the city limits on the northern edge of the bay.[9]

Baltimore's population was as diverse as its industry. A leading destination for nineteenth-century German immigrants, the city more closely resembled Cincinnati and St. Louis than predominantly Irish Boston or New York.[10] These old-stock immigrants had to compete for jobs with blacks much earlier and on a greater scale than those in northern cities where the black populations were smaller. Dependence on the port for employment made these unskilled laborers especially vulnerable to market fluctuations, and in hard times native and immigrant workers exploited racial tensions to force blacks out of work and to protect their jobs.[11]

Baltimore had a southern segregationist inheritance that was, if anything, heightened by what one historian has called the "assertive self-consciousness" of its black populace, 90 percent of which was free before the Civil War.[12] As Jim Crow descended on the border city, skirmishes between white and black labor heightened its effects, so that by the 1910s segregation was more pronounced in Maryland than in any other border state.[13] Up to the 1890s, when an influx of black southern migrants began, there had been few exclusively black neighborhoods in the city. After the turn of the century blacks began leaving overcrowded and disease-infested

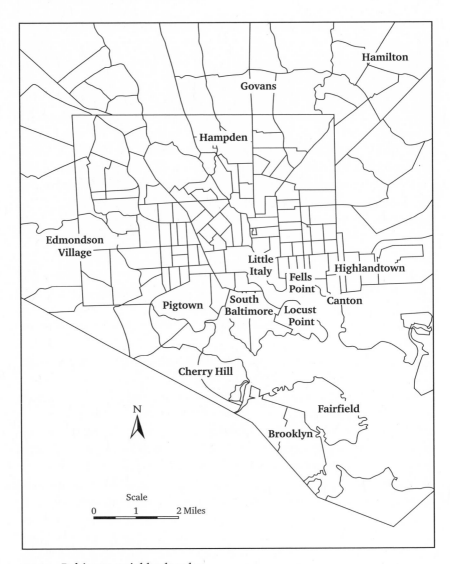

MAP I. Baltimore neighborhoods

alleys, displacing whites in upper west central Baltimore, and by 1910 half of the city's blacks lived there. Whites petitioned the mayor to "take some measures to restrain the colored people from locating in a white community"; this resulted in a 1913 ordinance that made segregated housing legal in Baltimore. So effective was white Baltimore's effort that it set precedent for legislation in other cities.[14] This sanctioned black area, twenty-six blocks centered on Pennsylvania Avenue, became a booming black metropolis by the 1930s.[15]

When Eastern and Southern European immigrants arrived at the turn of the century, ethnic working-class neighborhoods coalesced around the harbor. Outlying industrial suburbs included Brooklyn, on the southern edge of the harbor, and Sparrows Point, far to the east.[16] Fells Point, Baltimore's eighteenth- and early-nineteenth-century shipping and shipbuilding center, occupied the northeastern edge of the harbor along with Canton.[17] Up a gentle slope to the east was Highlandtown, a largely German community.[18] Pigtown, in the near southwest, was named for its early packing houses. South Baltimore lay just below the city center, and to its east Locust Point jutted into the harbor.[19] Only Hampden, home to Protestant textile mill-workers, was largely untouched by the new immigration.[20]

It was at Locust Point that the new immigrants disembarked. Some boarded the Baltimore and Ohio Railroad and headed west. Others, especially the Poles, ferried across the Inner Harbor to Fells Point.[21] A few got off the boat at the foot of Hull Street, walked a few blocks, and spent the rest of their lives in Locust Point.[22] Over the next fifty years many of the Poles moved farther east into Canton and Highlandtown; others resettled in South Baltimore and Brooklyn.[23] Italian immigrants gathered in a neighborhood on the near east side that became Baltimore's "Little Italy" before gravitating west in later years.[24] Czech, Lithuanian, Ukrainian, and Greek enclaves also took shape in South and East Baltimore.

The Catholic Church lay at the heart of these ethnic enclaves.[25] The oldest parishes were Irish and German. A few remained that way, but others, like St. Leo's, which became the center of Little Italy, adopted the nationality of its new congregation.[26] The church served as a bulwark for both the existing social structure and the immigrant community. As these immigrants arrived, Baltimore's James Cardinal Gibbons lauded Catholicism's "tremendous power for conservatism, virtue and industry" among working people.[27] In the 1920s and 1930s Baltimore's Catholics shared Archbishop Michael Curley's faith in the "Catholic Ghetto," emphasizing self-sufficiency and disdaining secular individualism. Curley encouraged them to maintain their ethnic traditions and resist "forceful, improper Americanization."[28]

A building boom accompanied this influx of white ethnics, helped along by the institution of ground rent. Under this system, homes were bought and sold but landowners kept the "ground" and charged rent. This cut initial purchase costs, making housing more affordable for working-class people: Canton resident Bronislaw Wesolowski paid a mere $750 for his

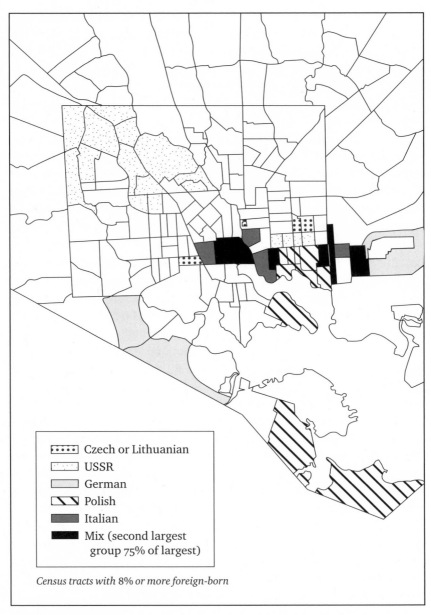

MAP 2. Ethnic population, 1940 (*Source:* U.S. Bureau of the Census, *1940 Census of Population and Housing: Statistics for Census Tracts, Baltimore, Maryland* [Washington, D.C.: GPO, 1942].)

four-room row house in 1910.[29] Of the forty thousand homes built in the 1880s and 1890s, most were the two-story, narrow red brick row houses that came to typify Baltimore's working-class neighborhoods.[30] White working-class Baltimore prospered in the 1920s. Home ownership rates rose, families bought radios, and a few could even afford cars. Social and political clubs multiplied and ethnic institutions flourished as working people enjoyed rising living standards.

But trouble began near the end of the twenties. Unemployment increased, the economy slipped, and by late 1930 the full effects of the Great Depression had set in.[31] As the number of unemployed grew, private relief agencies joined church and community organizations to meet the needs of the jobless. By the end of 1933 their efforts had failed: one in six Baltimore families was on public relief. Blacks suffered the most, but ethnic Baltimoreans were also hard-hit. Nine percent of the city's population, foreign-born whites received 19 percent of the relief, and the insensitivity of city fathers was instructive.[32] Baltimore's conservative, business-oriented Democrats had long cultivated the ethnic vote with little difficulty. But the depression, the New Deal, and World War II hastened the decline of that system.

The Machine, Labor, and the New Deal

Maryland, like its border counterparts, has been called a "three party state" in which a weak Republican Party vied with two wings of a sharply divided Democratic Party.[33] Up to the 1930s these two wings included Protestant "Bourbon" Democrats in the eastern and southern parts of the state and business-led machine politicians in Baltimore. Customarily, according to one historian, the latter bought the votes of ethnic and working-class citizens "with a drink or a dollar bill."[34] The Democratic machine controlled both city and state politics from the 1870s to the 1910s, dispensing patronage and making policy in conjunction with civic and business leaders.[35] An interparty quarrel in 1919 let a Republican into the mayor's seat, but a two-party system never took hold because in segregationist Maryland the Republican Party was widely considered the party of blacks.[36]

As the citywide Democratic machine deteriorated, district bosses became increasingly powerful. William Curran, who grew up in Southeast Baltimore, ran what has been described as an "all-weather constantly functioning organization" in the 1920s.[37] But when he abandoned Southeast Baltimore for upper-class Roland Park, it signaled trouble for the Democrats. Curran was a Catholic, but he was also a well-known and well-compensated criminal lawyer at home with the old immigrant and native-stock businessmen who dominated Baltimore's Democratic Party. He deeply disliked organized labor.[38] In the 1930s Curran shared power with district boss Howard Jackson, who fit the pro-business, southern segregationist mold even more closely.

As the depression set in, the outlines of the national New Deal coalition began to be discernible in Baltimore, but because the business-allied Democrats had a lock on city politics, the pattern first appeared in Republican votes. In 1934 gubernatorial candidate Harry Nice, despite his Republican affiliation, exploited the popularity of the New Deal by promising a "New and Square Deal for All" and campaigned against the machine rather than the Democratic Party as a whole. Nice cut substantially into the incumbent's Baltimore margins and took office to the strains of "Happy Days Are Here Again." The Republican got crucial support from ethnic defectors in the city's eastern working-class wards.[39]

In the presidential races, Baltimore's move to New Deal Democracy was clear. In 1928 the most heavily Catholic wards backed Al Smith, but Protestant working whites supported Herbert Hoover and gave him a slight edge.[40] In 1932, however, Franklin Roosevelt carried Baltimore's white working-class wards by comfortable margins.[41] Four years later the city gave Roosevelt a more decisive victory: turnout was heavy and his margins exceeded even those in other industrial cities like Chicago, Pittsburgh, and Philadelphia.[42] Most important, in 1936 FDR got the black vote in one city ward and did very well in others that had always voted Republican.[43] Overall, from 1930 to 1936 the nature of Baltimore's electorate changed. Working-class ethnics and black voters who had often stayed home were now turning out for "New Deal" candidates, be they Democrat or Republican.[44]

In 1938 Thomas D'Alesandro, a former Curranite with his base in ethnic East Baltimore's Little Italy, broke with the old guard to run for a congressional seat.[45] Distancing himself from the district bosses and their business allies, D'Alesandro waged a pro-labor, pro–New Deal campaign and won.[46] By the 1940 presidential election the shape of the city's New Deal coalition was clear. FDR got 65 percent of the black vote, 96 percent of the ethnic vote, and 97 percent of the vote from people living in substandard housing.[47] A year earlier, conservative Democrat Howard Jackson had retained the mayor's seat by a slim margin. But World War II provided the opportunity, and organized labor the effort, that broke the conservative hold on Baltimore Democratic politics.

In 1939, despite three years of CIO activism, the Baltimore Association of Commerce continued to boast that the city's "labor was notably conservative in its relations with industrial management."[48] In a sense, Baltimore combined the best of two worlds: the heavy industry of the North and the low wages of the South. Since the late nineteenth century the city had been home to dozens of AFL craft union locals, but the Red Scare and the open-shop drive of the early twenties sent them all into sharp decline.[49]

During the 1930s organized labor's dominant institution was the conservative, AFL-affiliated Baltimore Federation of Labor (BFL). There were some outposts of labor militancy, particularly in the garment and maritime trades, but the BFL generally took an accommodating approach toward labor-management relations. Few of the "new immigrants" and even fewer blacks found acceptance in the ranks of its affiliated unions.[50] Organizers who began working in the steel, shipbuilding, automobile, and electrical industries after the founding of the CIO in 1936 met with stiff employer resistance.[51] Some Baltimore employers, such as Bethlehem Steel and Western Electric, were anti-union stalwarts nationwide. But even General Motors, which recognized its Michigan workers after the Flint Strike, held out against the Baltimore Autoworkers until 1940.

Up to Pearl Harbor, Baltimore's reputation as an open-shop town was well founded. Stiff employer resistance had its effect, but labor activists blamed the Baltimore workers themselves for lagging behind other industrial cities in unionization. "In Baltimore," one organizer complained in 1937, "people crawl. Nothing moves, and the earth is still flat." The editor of the independent journal, the *Baltimore Labor Herald,* concurred that "nothing encouraging ever seems to happen in Baltimore."[52] By the time the nation began mobilizing for war, industrial unionism had scarcely a foothold in Baltimore.

White Workers for the Wartime Boom

Glenn Martin and Bethlehem Steel started taking defense orders even before the European war broke out in the fall of 1939. Although recent construction had doubled the plant's capacity, Glenn Martin had a $110 million backlog by 1940. At the same time Baltimore's shipyards had $80 million worth of orders to fill.[53] Industrial expansion swelled payrolls across the city. Glenn Martin's workforce expanded from 3,500 employees in 1939 to a 1943 peak of 53,000.[54] Bethlehem Steel's Fairfield Shipyard, established near Brooklyn to build Liberty Ships for the U.S. Maritime Commission, opened in 1941 with 350 workers. By the end of the year it employed 10,000.[55] Baltimoreans considered defense work a blessing—one called working at Fairfield "wonderful." Albert Arnold worked seven-day weeks his first year there, making $54 per week to more than double his previous income.[56] Fairfield's employment peaked at 46,700 in October 1943.[57] Few reached the gargantuan proportions of Glenn Martin or Fairfield, but nearly all local industries expanded for wartime production. At the end of 1939 manufacturing employment in Baltimore stood at 150,000. By May 1942 it had jumped to 251,000 with four out of five workers in war industries.[58]

Jim Crow's hold on Baltimore ensured that white migrants would fill most of these jobs: employers, state and local employment services, and the Baltimore Federation of Labor were equally uninterested in helping blacks into any but the most menial jobs.[59] The director of the Maryland Employment Service told an investigating congressional staffer that although there were lots of potential black workers in the city, "Baltimore is an old, conservative city with certain traditions to uphold."[60] Denied entrance to the State Employment Service's main office, blacks were directed to an annex where only common laborers were hired.[61] Glenn Martin asserted that the white mechanics at Middle River would walk out if blacks got high-paying production jobs and thus confined its black employees to a small plant in Canton.[62] Martin, like other Baltimore industrialists, felt no responsibility for solving the city's "social problems."[63] Local businesses were also reluctant to employ women in nonclerical work.

The combination of racial discrimination and industrial boom transformed Baltimore socially. Companies began advertising in southern states, and the Maryland Employment Service assured its counterparts in the South that it would take workers trained there.[64] Baltimore's population grew from 859,000 in 1940 to 1,250,000 by late 1942.[65] Within another year, about 150,000 to 200,000 migrants had arrived, and most were from the mountain South: Virginia, North Carolina, West Virginia, Pennsylvania, Kentucky, South Carolina, and Tennessee, in that order.[66] Many of the migrants came to stay, but others soon left, unable to find housing. Still more grew disillusioned by working conditions, transportation problems, and cold weather. More than 3,000 war workers quit their jobs and left Baltimore each month during 1942. Others "shopped around" for better work, making turnover a major problem.[67]

In Baltimore as in other industrial cities, scarcity of housing was the biggest wartime crisis. Builders erected more private homes than ever before but resisted building low-income rental housing. The federal government and the city built projects like Brooklyn Homes, which provided five hundred apartments near Fairfield Shipyard. The Farm Security Administration set up trailer camps at Middle River and Fairfield.[68] Many of the new defense workers moved into old blue-collar neighborhoods. South Baltimore was an especially popular destination since it was closer to the shipyards and had more rental property available than East Baltimore. In January 1941 South Baltimore's weekly paper, the *Enterprise,* reported that "thousands of workers are pouring into South Baltimore plants daily." One merchants' group, hoping to keep war wages in the community, lamented that apartments were "virtually unknown" and home owners had little room to spare.[69] One common solution was for property owners to subdivide their homes and businesses into apartments and become absentee landlords.[70]

Crowding was the rule. In Brooklyn, for example, thirty men employed at Fairfield Shipyard shared four rooms, sleeping in shifts, and one toilet.[71] The first newcomers established "home base," friends and relatives joined them, and migrant enclaves sprang up. In South Baltimore's "Kentucky Colony" one landlord rented out fifty-six rooms in five row houses to more than twenty-five families—over one hundred people in all. The heads of these families, men like Luzell Nettles and Israel Elkins, worked at Fairfield Shipyard and Revere Copper and Brass.[72]

Migrants from the mountain South were subject to discrimination rooted in a tenacious "hillbilly" stereotype. South Baltimore merchants wanted their money, but most other residents wanted them gone. Some locals resented the high wages they were making.[73] More disliked the leisure activities on which they spent those wages. A Lutheran minister expressed both attitudes when he said that "they are here to make money and have a good time."[74] "This part of town had a bad name," one second-generation Italian woman recalled later; "the bars were lousy . . . all kinds of carryings-on and tearing things up."[75] "Lousy" or not, the bars were also becoming increasingly unfamiliar places to Baltimore natives. During the war, the city's jukeboxes were mostly stocked with hillbilly tunes strange to urban ears.[76]

Working-class home owners were especially distressed at the toll the influx took on their neighborhoods. A South Baltimore woman felt that migrants "didn't give a damn because they were just here for the wartime moneymaking," with the result that "South Baltimore eventually became rundown, beat up." Others saw this as the point when their neighborhoods began to go downhill.[77] Some of the criticism reflected the biases of the observers. Heavy turnover at the plants was reflected in the neighborhoods, and although signs on each floor of the Kentucky Colony buildings said

"Don't throw garbage into the sink," a visiting journalist found the apartments "surprisingly clean." Similarly, in Baltimore County, residents apprehensive about the newcomers reported a crime wave that police could not confirm.[78]

Despite the stereotyping and the hostility from both sides exhibited in the flap about the poem "Beloved Baltimore," most migrants were clearly industrious. One West Virginia native, a ship carpenter at Bethlehem Steel's Key Highway Shipyard, claimed to support his own family of eight, his brother's family of four, and his mother on his wages. He also sent money home to pay off debts.[79] Few could make their earnings go as far. Too often, those expecting "a pot of gold" in Baltimore found instead a high cost of living that consumed most of their earnings.[80]

Migrants resented their hostile reception and longed for respect. Harry Isner, a carpenter from Elkins, West Virginia, appeared before the U.S. House Committee Investigating National Defense Migration in July 1941. During his testimony a congressmen interrupted to expound on the possibility that Isner could be out of work in both Maryland and West Virginia after the war: "He will be floating, like a good many others in the country." Isner respectfully cut the congressman off and said, "well my intentions are, if I can do so, to buy me a home and locate here permanently, if I can get some money ahead."[81]

White native Baltimoreans were only temporarily ambivalent about the southern newcomers. In early 1944 the *Baltimore Evening Sun* concluded that they had been "praised and criticized, but ultimately accepted as part of the local scene."[82] More important, both southerners and Appalachians lived under a distinct color line, as did Baltimore's ethnic working people.[83] A new white working class had united with surprising ease because in the neighborhoods and on the job, everybody was white. But this was not the case at the polls.

Mobilizing Workers and Votes

Before World War II about 35,000 union members lived in Baltimore, most of them affiliated with the AFL. By November 1942 the ranks of organized labor had grown fourfold, not counting the company unions established at Glenn Martin and Western Electric.[84] The city and state CIO fought hard for these gains, but ultimately the war made the difference.

The most difficult of the CIO's unionizing drives was at Sparrows Point. Bethlehem was the cornerstone of "Little Steel" and notoriously anti-union.

The Steelworkers Organizing Committee (swoc) had low expectations, sending only two men to organize one of the largest steel plants in the world.[85] Residents of the company town stood to lose homes as well as jobs and viewed the effort with trepidation, so most of swoc's support came from ethnic Southeast Baltimoreans and blacks consigned to the mill's dirtiest and lowest-paying jobs.[86] Most of the steelworkers, according to Brendan Sexton, one of the organizers, were southern whites who were "anti-black, but not violently so."[87] Accordingly, the company tried to use race to its benefit, warning white workers that they could lose their jobs to blacks if the cio got into the plant.[88]

By 1940 the cio was trying mightily to get into Bethlehem Steel and Glenn Martin because they were huge plants dependent on defense contracts—and federal law mandated that government contractors must bargain in good faith with unions. A strong company union at Glenn Martin helped fend off the cio challenge, but Bethlehem, its Employee Representation Plan outlawed by the National Labor Relations Board (NLRB), resorted to more repressive measures. The company used Pinkerton agents, armed "special police," and even local law enforcement officers against swoc.[89] Even the FBI cooperated, planting an agent in a Highlandtown row house to monitor a swoc organizer's activities.[90]

The next year Sparrows Point and the Bethlehem shipyards—including the mammoth Fairfield Shipyard—recognized the cio under the multiple pressures of continuing worker militancy, mounting defense orders, and threats of federal intervention. GM and Westinghouse did likewise.[91] At Glenn Martin, though, the United Autoworkers (UAW) found it difficult to recruit from among the mostly southern white workers.[92] The aircraft plant was a prize sought by the International Association of Machinists as well as the UAW. It was also fiercely defended by the company union. The UAW got an NLRB election in June 1943, but only 40 percent of workers voted cio whereas 42 percent voted "no union."[93] In September the cio finally prevailed with 49 percent of the vote, but its hold remained shaky throughout the war.[94] The election won, it still faced "the job of making union people of the people in that plant."[95]

By the war's midpoint, a liberal leadership had begun to coalesce in Baltimore. It included officers of the state and local cio, middle-class whites, many of them associated with the Union for Democratic Action (UDA), and civil rights leaders affiliated with the NAACP and the Urban League. Together, they helped make Baltimore politics New Deal politics.

The city's cio unions banded together to form the Baltimore Industrial

Union Council in July 1937. The Maryland and District of Columbia Industrial Union Council was organized shortly afterward.[96] Both groups, recognizing that industrial unionism owed its existence to New Deal support, were avowedly political in orientation. By 1939 the AFL and the CIO routinely mobilized to promote progressive national and state legislation. The city and state CIO councils pushed for wages and hours bills at the statehouse which, despite vigorous efforts, were defeated.[97] But in a few short years organized labor had become a formidable political force. The state CIO's per capita income was a little over $5,000 in 1942, but within a year it had increased 250 percent, and the state CIO mobilized working voters with its own edition of the *CIO News* and a weekly legislative report.[98] Wartime mobilization promised more potential working-class support for liberal causes, yet it also posed a challenge: how to transmit the growing union ranks into votes. Concerned that just such a development might disrupt politics as usual, the Maryland legislature passed a "Declaration of Intentions" law requiring all prospective voters to register one year prior to voting, a measure designed to disenfranchise the thousands of war workers in the state. The CIO fought back and in the fall of 1943 launched a massive campaign to register war workers for the 1944 elections.[99]

The institution that thrust organized labor most forthrightly into liberal politics was the CIO Political Action Committee (PAC). In 1943 the state CIO began creating arms of the PAC in Maryland's congressional districts, beginning with the Third Congressional District covering much of working-class Baltimore. One of the first things that district CIO-PAC officials did was meet with Congressman D'Alesandro, Baltimore's New Dealer.[100] They also sought help from the Baltimore chapter of the Union for Democratic Action. In 1941 anticommunist activists, intellectuals, and trade union officials formed the national UDA.[101] The Baltimore UDA was founded the next year by a similar coalition. Important members included noted liberals affiliated with Johns Hopkins University, government officials, and labor leaders. The group sponsored a series of public meetings aimed at bringing government, business, and labor together to discuss Baltimore's wartime problems and enthusiastically supported the CIO's Declaration of Intentions Act campaign, providing printed materials and working with unions and other civic organizations to help spur registration.[102]

In segregationist Baltimore, the issue that most clearly distinguished the emergent liberal coalition was its support for civil rights. Leading the push was the Baltimore branch of the NAACP. Founded in the 1920s, the Baltimore NAACP languished until the mid-1930s, when energetic leader

Lillie M. Jackson emerged from the city's black middle class and mobilized African Americans around antilynching and "don't buy where you can't work" campaigns to make the Baltimore NAACP one of the most powerful branches nationwide. Jackson's daughter established a dynasty by marrying Clarence Mitchell, a Baltimorean and a national NAACP leader. A second center of power in the black community was the Murphy family, which published the *Baltimore Afro-American,* one of the nation's leading black papers. For the next forty years, black Baltimore's political strength would depend on the state of the alliance between these two families.[103]

Civil rights activists, like labor leaders, saw the war as an opportunity to bring about social change. In 1942 local NAACP official Dr. J. E. T. Camper led a march on Annapolis to pressure the state to enforce equal opportunity in employment and housing.[104] The Baltimore Urban League, run mostly by whites, was less confrontational and worked effectively behind the scenes to open up jobs and training programs to blacks.[105] One small, but ultimately consequential, victory was gaining the abolition of a municipal ordinance requiring segregated toilet facilities in industries.[106]

The chief objective of all these liberal groups, both black and white, was to turn out the vote. The first test of the new activist coalition came in the 1943 mayor's race. The incumbent Howard Jackson, sensing trouble, had entered into an alliance with old rival William Curran, guaranteeing Jackson all the votes that the Baltimore machine could muster. His opponent, Republican Theodore McKeldin, forged close ties with civil rights groups, ran hard against Jackson's "greedy political machine," and won.[107]

It took a Republican—although not the Republican Party, which never really operated as such in Baltimore—to break the old-line Democratic hold on the city. Blacks who had changed parties to vote for FDR and the New Deal in 1936 switched back to vote for the racially progressive McKeldin. Three black wards that had voted 54 percent for FDR that year went 71 percent for McKeldin in 1943.[108] More significant, Baltimore's ethnic and working-class whites broke with the Curran machine and reversed parties to back the liberal candidate. Voters in white working-class wards 1, 23, and 24 voted for McKeldin by a margin of 63 percent, higher even than more reliably Republican outlying middle-class precincts.[109] The importance of the switch is underscored by the fact that although McKeldin beat Jackson decisively, every other Republican candidate lost by a substantial margin.

The major test for labor came the next year, when Franklin Roosevelt ran for a fourth term. Although the Declaration of Intentions Act remained on the books, and city and county election boards made registration as dif-

Amid stories focusing on wartime production, liberal Republican Theodore
McKeldin reads of his victory in the May 1943 mayor's race. (Courtesy of
the *Baltimore News-American* Photograph Collection, Special Collections,
University of Maryland, College Park, Libraries)

ficult as possible for war workers, the Baltimore City CIO-PAC, established
in April 1944, worked hard to get out the working-class vote.[110] There was an
early morning rush to the polls by war workers in East and South Baltimore,
but turnout overall fell from 85 percent in 1940 to 65 percent in 1944.[111]
Roosevelt's margins were also smaller in 1944, but working whites gave
him 70 percent of the vote and Baltimore's blacks went three to two for
FDR.[112] Although middle-class voters in outlying precincts voted decisively
against him, Roosevelt got a plurality in Baltimore and swung Maryland to
the Democrats.[113]

   Although demographic and social shifts meant that it was only a matter
of time, it was a twist in machine politics that made the 1944 election the
pivot on which the Baltimore Democratic Party swung from old line to New
Deal. The district controlled by Boss Jack Pollack was becoming majority
black, and alert to changing political realities, he broke decisively with the
Curran-Jackson machine and allied with the liberals. Curran responded

with increasingly strident attacks on the New Deal, hastening the end of his influence. From that point on, factional bosses who relied on the support of labor and ethnic groups took control over Baltimore's Democratic politics.[114] Previously white working-class votes could be bought cheaply, but the liberal organizations demanded legislation instead of favors, ensuring that statewide, Bourbon-Baltimore Democratic coalitions would become increasingly hard to maintain.[115]

After the 1944 election the president of the Baltimore Industrial Union Council crowed that "the newly won strength that labor has gained by exercising its political rights will now be used to push a program of fully expanded industry, an end to race bias and security at home and the achievement of a lasting organization of world peace."[116] Such overarching rhetoric foundered on the details: local events suggest that a more modest assessment may have been in order.

Race, Housing, and the Limits of Liberalism

Baltimore's working-class whites and blacks may have increasingly been partners on the tally sheets, but they voted in different precincts and working whites preferred it that way. At the highest levels of political and intellectual leadership, Alan Brinkley has observed, World War II marked a period of transition between the reform liberalism of the early twentieth century and the rights-based liberalism that succeeded it.[117] But that was a transition that Baltimore's blue-collar residents were not prepared to make. They supported government efforts to cushion the effects of the free market and modestly redistribute wealth at the polls, but their actions at home and on the job demonstrated that they did not share the racially inclusive liberal vision extolled by social progressives in civil rights and labor organizations.

During the war years blue collarites steadfastly resisted New Deal efforts that even remotely threatened white neighborhoods, and since the residential boundaries established in the 1910s remained largely intact, the battle lines were drawn over public housing. Projects for both white migrants and blacks were proposed by the city and opposed by citizens, but in each case outcomes were quite different, demonstrating precisely where white working-class Baltimore drew the lines of both inclusion and exclusion.

In June 1939, when the city unveiled a federally sponsored project for white families to be built on a Southeast Baltimore site known as "Area D," civic groups from working-class Southeast Baltimore mobilized to oppose the project and found themselves in conflict with a leadership that invoked the New Deal in the name of racial inclusion. A liberal city councilman and a CIO official praised it at a Board of Estimates hearing, but the crowd of three hundred "roared its disapproval."[118] In another confrontation, a proponent's characterization of the project as "a New Deal measure" infuriated opponents from a Czech neighborhood.[119] Nevertheless, there was not enough clamor to stop Area D, and in 1940 the first white migrant war workers moved in. One of the most potent arguments during the controversy had been that despite assurances to the contrary, blacks might be allowed in; but they were not, and that made all the difference.[120] Baltimore residents never succeeded in blocking a single white housing development, and by 1943 there were seven large-scale projects in the city.[121] By mid-1943 over twenty thousand separate units of war housing for whites had been constructed in Baltimore, much of it with federal assistance, but wartime housing for blacks had yet to be built.[122]

Blacks suffered disproportionately from Baltimore's wartime housing crisis. From 1940 to 1942, 33,000 blacks came to Baltimore, half of them from rural Maryland and half from the South. The newcomers squeezed into the ghettos, where rents shot up and housing deteriorated. One 1942 study estimated that the city's black population—then at about 20 percent of the total—was packed into 2 percent of its residential space.[123] But white Baltimoreans steadfastly opposed any relief.

When, in the summer of 1943, a plan for a federally financed black housing project at Herring Run near the Area D site was proposed, citizens mobilized again but this time more effectively. In July, in front of a crowd of eight hundred hostile whites, Mayor McKeldin cautiously backed the plan, but, caught between two key constituencies, he disavowed any responsibility, claiming that final authority rested with the federal government.[124] The Baltimore CIO joined the NAACP and the Urban League in backing the Herring Run plan, but it came at a price since local politicians were much more attentive to white working-class concerns than to the arguments of organized labor.[125] "Politicians with whom we had developed friendly relations took the occasion to launch bitter attacks against the leadership of the CIO," one labor official complained.[126] This contention at the top deepened into a split between the leadership and the rank and file. The leadership of Local 43 of the CIO's International Union of Marine and Shipbuilding Workers (IUMSWA) endorsed the housing plan, but one of its members suspected that Washington was only courting black voters for the 1944 presidential election.[127]

Three city councilmen led the opposition, but among the more vocal opponents to the Herring Run plan were white home owner association leaders, Catholic priests, and even a rabbi.[128] One influential adversary was Lutheran minister Luke Schmucker, who had previously condemned white migrants at the Area D project for not being "interested in anything but making money." But the black housing threat led Schmucker to portray the migrants in a different light. Noting Herring Run's proximity to the Area D site, he complained that "middle class defense workers" would be set upon by blacks "in the streets, in the cars and buses, in the stores and movies, and even in the schools."[129]

The debate over Herring Run took place in the midst of escalating racial tensions nationwide. In Buffalo, a nearly identical controversy was raging, spearheaded by priests representing their Polish and Irish Catholic parishioners.[130] In Los Angeles, white sailors had recently attacked Mexican American zoot-suiters, and only a month earlier, three days of rioting in Detroit left twenty-five blacks and nine whites dead.[131] A number of citizens who wrote angry letters to McKeldin had Detroit on their minds. Most expressed anxiety over property values and personal safety. Some explicitly blamed integrationists for racial tensions, agreeing with one man who warned that "it would not take much to set off another Detroit episode in Baltimore City."[132] The Baltimore NAACP applauded McKeldin's "courageous leadership" on the issue but spoke too soon.[133] Housing for Baltimore's black defense workers was not destined for a white area: McKeldin bowed to the greater pressure and settled on a site at Cherry Hill, insulated from Brooklyn and South Baltimore's white neighborhoods by water.[134]

The Color Line on the Shop Floor

Wartime exigencies brought an even more concerted challenge to racial segregation in industry. In early 1942 about nine thousand blacks worked in Baltimore's war industries; a year later there were twice as many, and by mid-1944 forty thousand black defense workers were on the job in city plants. By the end of the war companies that had once excluded blacks were advertising in the *Afro-American,* although according to the Baltimore Urban League's Alexander Allen, it was "the economics of the situation" more than Roosevelt's "fair employment" Executive Order 8802 that finally cracked Baltimore's segregated shop floors. "Some companies just ran out of workers to hire," he recalled.[135] The big CIO unions backed increased opportunities for blacks, but a public posture in favor of civil rights was easier to assume than enforce.[136] Total exclusion gave way fairly easily, but the white rank and file resisted working closely with blacks and tried hard to prevent them from taking skilled positions. One black member of Local 43 of the IUMSWA warned leaders of the state CIO that "if you are just going to give lip service and do nothing, you are going to be sorry."[137] The largest CIO union in wartime Baltimore, IUMSWA was also the most vulnerable to conflicts between natives and southerners, blacks and whites.[138]

Before the war, native Baltimoreans had used southern stereotypes to denote undesirable labor. A 1938 organizing flyer condemned "plow-jockeys and bean-pickers" willing to toil for low wages. These sorts of workers, the flyer said, constituted a menace to "bona-fide union men."[139] By 1940, however, the union was using southern images to appeal to, rather than to shame, workers. One leaflet, advertising a pipe fitters' department meeting, featured a sketch of an overall-clad worker, pipe wrench in hand, uttering "recken I'll be there."[140] Three years later, candidates for union office appealed to the Appalachian "ex-coal miners" at the Fairfield Shipyard and publicly sympathized with the controversial 1943 coal miners' strike.[141]

In the shipyards, so many workers were southerners that Baltimore natives may have realized that they had little choice but to get along. Still, white workers felt less pressure to coexist with blacks. African Americans were limited to maintenance or unskilled jobs that kept them away from whites, who, in turn, displayed a firm resistance to any further encroachments, regardless of CIO rhetoric.[142] Bethlehem's Sparrows Point Shipyard is a case in point. According to the U.S. Employment Service, Sparrows Point was "an old established plant" with many senior employees—a marked contrast to the turbulent Fairfield Shipyard with its large, undisciplined, mostly southern-born workforce.[143] If experience had been a determining factor, then Sparrows Point would have been peaceful. Instead, an attempt by black workers to surmount barriers of skill set off racial conflict.[144]

In late July 1943 fifteen blacks were admitted to a training school for riveters at the Sparrows Point Shipyard. The news soon spread to the riveting department, and after white riveters walked out in protest, the company removed the blacks from the class. When eight hundred black employees gathered to demand that the company resume the training, management— with approval from union leadership—complied. Meanwhile, white riveters marched through the yard gathering support. Thousands of whites ended up encircling a group of black workers who had to be escorted out of the yard by police. State police and federal troops stood by for eight days;

Workers take a break at the huge Fairfield Shipyard in 1942. (Courtesy of the *Baltimore News-American* Photograph Collection, Special Collections, University of Maryland, College Park, Libraries)

the shipyard workers did not return to work until the company and the union pledged to adhere strictly to seniority in promoting riveters.[145]

IUMSWA leaders were convinced that a violent race riot had been narrowly averted at Sparrows Point. But one union official denied that the membership was in any way responsible. Instead, he said, "non-union men," both black and white, were "the chief agitators."[146] Civil rights leaders, on the other hand, had long known that racial tensions in Baltimore's shipyards were high; the NAACP observed that "the union was not as vigorous as it should have been in aiding the colored members."[147] Whites attacked labor from the opposite side. One of the most powerful arguments the UAW's opponents used at Glenn Martin was that the CIO would allow black workers on the shop floor.[148] One Machinists Union leaflet went further, exploiting the sensitive issue of skilled work for blacks. "If you want a negro boss," the flyer said, "vote for the CIO and get him."[149]

As economic necessity put more blacks in Baltimore's workplaces, white workers became even more determined to enforce the boundaries between skilled "white" work and unskilled labor. By the end of the Great Depression there were few of the company unions left that had been so ubiquitous in the 1920s. Wartime mobilization dislodged Glenn Martin's company union, but still the one at Western Electric hung on. There, as part of an effort to forestall CIO organizing, the Point Breeze Employees Association (PBEA) mobilized southern, ethnic, and native whites against workplace integration. It was so effective in accomplishing both that it ultimately triggered a federal plant seizure.

Before the war, Western Electric had a workforce of 2,500. At its wartime peak it employed nearly four times that number.[150] In late 1941 the company began hiring black workers and segregating its restrooms to comply with the Baltimore plumbing code. In early 1942, after the Urban League got the plumbing code changed, the company desegregated its washrooms. Meanwhile, as the proportion of black employees in the plant rose from 2 to 29 percent, whites became increasingly embittered.[151]

The precipitating event occurred in August 1943, when a black woman was promoted to a supervisory position and twenty-two white women working under her walked out.[152] In response, leaders of the Point Breeze association took up the issue of the desegregated washrooms, circulating petitions and threatening to strike.[153] In October the membership authorized a strike, but the PBEA agreed to postpone it until a December War Labor Board hearing. The War Labor Board backed the company, the union struck, and President Roosevelt ordered the army to take over the plant that produced critical communications cable. When the army finally left in March 1944, Western Electric's restrooms were effectively resegregated, although the company and the government described things differently.[154]

A complex of issues underlay the Western Electric strike, but most important the PBEA was using race to shore up its support. Both the Machinists and the United Electrical Workers had been trying to organize the plant, and at the time the NLRB was investigating the PBEA's reputation as a "company union."[155] Also, as a committee of black employees pointed out, although the union made the integration of facilities the ostensible strike issue, the factor of skilled employment was definitely involved.[156] By making a black woman an inspector, Western Electric had violated the same tacit agreement restricting blacks to unskilled positions that Sparrows Point Shipyard had.

The PBEA had relatively little difficulty getting white workers to draw the line between themselves and their black coworkers. Few other local defense plants had integrated restrooms, and white workers reported being taunted by neighbors who called the plant "nigger heaven." Some whites were also convinced that "the policy of the company [was] to coddle the negro in order to court government approval" and that supervisors favored blacks at whites' expense.[157]

It was easy to blame southerners for the racial strife at Western Electric. One worker accused black women of calling some employees "poor white trash," and during the War Labor Board hearing one army official complained that the "philosophy of legal customary segregation in the South seems to pervade the whole atmosphere of these Western Electric discussions." Segregation could not be challenged in the South, he said, but "when one of these questions arises in the North where there has been a lot of immigration of southerners, we are too prone to want to yield to their sentiments and attitudes."[158]

Although women precipitated the strike, men conducted it. When picket lines formed, they were almost exclusively male. In addition, most of those who crossed the lines were older workers whereas those who manned the lines were younger. Older workers were more likely to have been Baltimore natives, and younger workers were more often migrants.[159] When the army reopened the plant, though, those remaining out were mostly skilled workers, fewer of whom are likely to have been newcomers.[160] This suggests that although southerners readily joined the PBEA's effort, they were relatively quick to desert it. Though initiated by the local union leaders, the strike depended on southerners for critical support. But while the migrants were willing to help others enforce the color line, they declined to do it alone.[161]

When it came to race, the PBEA represented the prevailing attitudes of many white Western Electric workers. Few were moved by the strident condemnations of the Baltimore CIO and its insinuations that they were being manipulated.[162] Furthermore, white determination to enforce the color line can only have been strengthened by the left-led United Electrical Workers' strident denunciations.[163] Good unionists who happened to be Communist Party members were sometimes tolerated in wartime Baltimore, but Western Electric's workers never gave the UE a hearing, despite its persistence.[164] Not surprisingly, the UE had tried hardest to organize Western Electric's blacks: its only full-time organizer there was a black man.[165]

It is telling that the strike at Western Electric was touched off by women. By the war's end, 38 percent of Baltimore's industrial workers were female and the number doing war work had shot up 97 percent from 1940 to 1944.[166] As early as September 1942, Western Electric's workforce was 35 percent female, and by the end of the war over 55 percent were women.[167] Most of this increase came as women replaced draftees or transients, and although some were Baltimore natives, plenty of wartime working women were migrants themselves. Many of these women, like their male counterparts, agreed with the assessment of "Beloved Baltimore" and left town at the war's end. But about half—including a Louisiana man who helped write the poem, yet later married a Baltimore woman—made their peace with the city and its residents and became part of the postwar white working class.[168]

What Was Left Undone

By 1945 Baltimore, like its counterparts in the industrial North, was home to a strong industrial union movement, a growing civil rights community, and a political system increasingly sensitive to the power of ethnic and black working-class voters. In addition, the wartime economic boom provided southern and ethnic blue collarites with their first, albeit limited, taste of the plenitude on which the postwar New Deal order was premised while giving black working people a foothold in the industrial economy. But between working whites, blacks, and urban liberals, intractable problems remained. Baltimore's blue collarites had rewarded the Democratic Party as much for what was left undone as for what it accomplished.

Although New Deal legislation delivered little in terms of civil rights, President Roosevelt's Executive Order 8802, issued well after wartime pragmatism displaced New Deal fervor, marked a decisive first step toward the rights-based liberalism that would hold sway in postwar America. In response, urban liberals, labor, and civil rights progressives most responsible for mobilizing urban voters formulated a vision of racial inclusion that was sharply at odds with that held by urban white workers. White working people had seemingly attained long-sought economic rights and political representation. Liberal leaders in Baltimore as elsewhere, therefore, sought to use the economic growth and expansion of the federal government that began during the war as a platform on which to build a new, more inclusive social order.

Working-class whites were much less ambitious. For them, the New Deal order promised social security rather than social change. And despite the rhetoric of equality nominally embraced by the liberal wing of the Demo-

cratic Party, the workplaces and especially the neighborhoods of Baltimore's white working-class voters remained unaffected by racial change.
Liberals seemed to have delivered much and demanded little, and working whites found few reasons to waver in their loyalty to the party of the
New Deal. But in the postwar years, as programmatic liberalism began to
emphasize civil rights over economic rights, keeping this contentious coalition together would require a real commitment to racial equality, one that
Baltimore's working whites were not prepared to make.

CHAPTER 2

Reds and Blue Bloods

In 1938 Donald T. Appell, a twenty-two-year-old from a blue-collar Baltimore family, got a job helping out with a Maryland congressman's campaign.[1] Although he followed the victorious candidate to Washington, the congressman was gone after one term and Appell wound up as a janitor. Eventually he landed a job as a clerk for J. Parnell Thomas and from there became an investigator for the House Un-American Activities Committee (HUAC). In October 1948 former Baltimorean Whittaker Chambers took Appell to his Carroll County farm, reached inside a pumpkin, and produced five rolls of film implicating Alger Hiss as a spy. In 1951, with the anticommunist fervor of the McCarthy era still building, Appell dismissed the Baltimore Communist Party with contempt. "They started off as a bunch of draft-dodgers from out of town," he said. "They never got much tougher."[2]

In a little over a decade, as the janitor from Baltimore worked his way up to become a $10,000-per-year investigator for HUAC, anticommunism became intrinsic to white working-class politics. But it entered the blue-collar mainstream not through the fiery speeches of national demagogues but during a series of smaller-scale contests over labor unions, schools, and public institutions. The early targets of Baltimore anticommunists—radical unionists and local party activists—were usually nearer the bottom of society than the top. But through the 1940s, as the influence of Communist Party members declined, blue collarites and the political leaders who appealed to them began to view highly placed sympathizers as a much larger threat, not only to local institutions but also to the nation at large. By the time Joseph McCarthy warned of communists in the U.S. State Department in February 1950, Baltimoreans had already learned from experience to associate communism with class.

Working-class whites were far from ready to reject New Deal politics wholesale. On the contrary, they valued a government that for the first time seemed to champion their interests. Newly secure labor unions were beginning to raise wages and improve workplace conditions, and the expanding economy promised plentiful jobs and prosperous communities. But if they did not reject the legacy of the New Deal in the late 1940s and early 1950s, working-class Baltimoreans did begin to discount New Dealers.

The rise of anticommunism in the postwar years spurred the construction of a new populist class politics. In the 1930s blue-collar Americans had targeted elite opponents in corporate boardrooms—"economic royalists," as Roosevelt called them—but by the 1950s they viewed the denizens of universities and bureaucracies—policymakers rather than moneymakers— as the bigger threat to working-class life. This new populism was fundamentally conservative; its adherents could champion existing American institutions while castigating key officials. Although some historians argue that it narrowed the limits of political debate and deflected blue-collar attention away from intractable social problems like racial and economic injustice, to white working-class Baltimoreans beginning to enjoy security and affluence previously unheard of, neither were of much concern.

"Draft Dodgers from out of Town"

Wartime mobilization invigorated Baltimore's radical left. The Baltimore Communist Party had been small and ineffective in the decade after its founding in 1919 but revived with the onset of the depression to champion civil rights, labor unions, and unemployment relief.[3] The Baltimore party was strongest on the waterfront and in 1934 even established what was known as the "Baltimore Soviet," when for a time seamen took control of their own hiring, lodging, and board.[4] New radical talent came in later in the decade with the organizing drives of the CIO. All of Baltimore's UE organizers were party members, and communists were key organizers at Glenn Martin and Bethlehem Steel.[5] That shifted the locus of party power from the port to the new industrial unions like the steelworkers and autoworkers. Of particular concern was the International Union of Marine and Shipbuilding Workers of America (IUMSWA), another CIO affiliate.[6]

Up to the late 1930s, Baltimoreans usually displayed what one historian has characterized as "an amused tolerance" toward party members. There was little sustained anticommunist activity in the city at large and few detractors besides the American Legion and a handful of longtime critics— with one important exception.[7] Nationwide throughout these years, the most consistent and principled opposition to communism came from the Catholic Church, led in Baltimore by Archbishop Michael Joseph Curley.[8] To Catholics, communism was a threat because it was supercharged secularism, placing ultimate faith in human actions and institutions rather than divine guidance. Curley, archbishop of Baltimore from 1921 until his death in 1947, repeatedly voiced this Catholic critique, calling it "a godless, soulless thing."[9]

Anticommunism was an integral part of Catholic social doctrine that stemmed from two papal encyclicals: *Rerum Novarum,* issued in the late nineteenth century, and *Quadragesimo Anno,* appearing at the outset of the Great Depression. These encyclicals condemned unrestrained capitalism and socialism alike and commanded Catholics to fight against class divisions and respiritualize working-class life.[10] *Quadragesimo Anno,* in particular, became a "Magna Charta" for Catholic social activists who fought social injustice and communism with equal fervor.[11] Since the 1910s, the leader of the American Catholic Church's social justice movement had been Monsignor John A. Ryan. Studying under Ryan at the time *Quadragesimo Anno* was issued was John F. Cronin, Baltimore's preeminent labor priest.[12]

In the 1930s Cronin had offered assistance to union organizers in the shipbuilding, aircraft, and steel industries. The work was encouraged by Archbishop Curley, who, although an economic conservative suspicious of American liberalism, supported church social doctrines.[13] In the late 1930s Cronin, like Catholic clergymen in other industrial cities, began organizing labor schools.[14] Assisted by several other priests, he set up "Schools of Social Action" that emphasized the church's social teachings and taught labor history and public speaking.[15] Twenty-five to forty students, mostly industrial workers, attended twelve-week sessions conducted by priests, local CIO representatives, and professors from local Catholic universities.[16] At one point there were schools operating in twelve parishes at once.[17]

These efforts had some unintended results. In 1939 organizers for the Amalgamated Clothing Workers reported "difficulty among the Catholic workers" concerned about communism. Some parish priests, it seemed, were discouraging unionization entirely, suspicious of the CIO's party ties.[18] But communism remained a relatively minor issue for Cronin—he was more interested in organizing Catholic workers than fighting radicals who appeared to have little real influence. Like his parishioners, he confessed to being "more amused than angry" about the party's antics.[19] For a time, communists and Catholics peacefully coexisted.[20] Cronin even delivered the invocation at the 1939 Maryland and District of Columbia Industrial

Father John F. Cronin, S.S.,
Baltimore's labor priest.
(Courtesy of the Sulpician
Archives, Baltimore)

Union Council Convention, an event dominated by party members.[21] But his complacency was shattered in July 1942 after Francis O'Brien, a rigger at Bethlehem's Fairfield Shipyard, sought Cronin's help in fighting a communist faction there.[22]

The dramatic growth of Baltimore's unionized shipyards made them prime targets for communist organization; with few veteran officers and no experienced rank and file to challenge them, party members were able to rise quickly. Their first big success was at Maryland Shipbuilding and Drydock (Drydock), a ship repair yard near Brooklyn organized by IUMSWA Local 31. The union's organizers were not party members—the leader of Local 31's communist faction was a worker named Carl Bradley, a long-time Baltimore member.[23] Drydock recognized Local 31 in the summer of 1939. That fall Bradley got a job at the yard, where he and Norman Dorland, a Minnesota native, started organizing for the party. Bradley and Dorland were resourceful and dedicated union activists; after the local's first business agent resigned under suspicion of embezzlement, the members elected Dorland president. Bradley took the more influential post of business agent.[24]

It is unlikely, however, that more than a few Baltimore shipyard workers approved of Bradley and Dorland's politics. In late 1939 an IUMSWA organizer there had reported that charges against the CIO made by the congressional investigating committee led by Martin Dies had troubled local workers—"good union men" who wanted to know if "the CIO is controlled by the commies."[25] Working-class Baltimoreans who viewed members of the party with bemused tolerance when they led hunger marches were less sanguine when the union was involved: organizer William Smith reported that Local 31's noncommunist leaders resented Bradley and Dorland's using them "to further communist philosophies." The local's vice president was disgusted when they set up a "Peace Committee" to garner support for the Soviet Union's nonaggression pact with Germany. On deciding that he had been duped, the vice president tendered his resignation and told Bradley and Dorland to "stick their Peace Committee up their. . . . [ellipsis in original]."[26]

Communists were powerful at the local level, but the IUMSWA national office was not firmly controlled by the party. Smith, encouraged by the International, began working to unseat Bradley and Dorland.[27] In April 1941 the two were expelled on the basis of an IUMSWA General Executive Board declaration against "any member proven guilty of subverting the real purpose of the organization."[28] The next month the navy, which had contracts with Drydock, ordered that the two men be fired.[29]

This first attempt to "clean up" a communist-dominated union was deceptively simple. This was mostly because it came on the heels of the Nazi-Soviet nonaggression pact, which forced the party to join in common cause with Nazi Germany and bore out Catholic arguments that Nazism and communism were indistinguishable forms of totalitarianism. As Philip Jenkins argues, it was this, rather than revelations of atomic spying, that detonated the midcentury Red Scare.[30] The Baltimore party suffered dearly from the untenable position created by the nonaggression pact and the charges of the Dies Committee. Several unions even pulled out of the state CIO over the issue.[31] None of this concerned Father Cronin, however. It took the 4 July 1942 visit from O'Brien, followed two days later by an FBI request that he help the shipyard workers, to change his mind.[32]

In October 1941 IUMSWA Local 43 won the right to represent the 32,000 workers at Bethlehem Steel's Fairfield Shipyard.[33] In a flyer circulated prior to the election, Cronin urged workers to support the "thoroughly American union" that "deserves the vote of decent American workers."[34] But the party quickly put a number of capable but low-profile members into place.[35]

The communists organized a rank-and-file slate and moved to capture the local in the July 1942 elections. Their opponents, led by O'Brien, appealed to workers' patriotism and perhaps sent a signal that in Baltimore, as in so many localities, union conflict over communism amounted to a fight between locals, many of them Irish Catholics, and party members who were frequently New York Jews. Flyers featured an American eagle and screamed "drive out the invaders."[36]

O'Brien was out-organized, and his slate was roundly defeated. Nevertheless, some of his followers, encouraged by Cronin, formed a "Pleasure Club," began disrupting union meetings, and attempted to oust the elected officers. When the local, backed by the International, expelled the anticommunist "troublemakers," the opposition called a work stoppage. The International's left-wing secretary-treasurer, Philip Van Gelder, credited "sinister forces" and "outside influences" with disrupting the union and the yard.[37]

In contrast to the situation at Drydock, the "communist problem" at Fairfield Shipyard proved to be much more intractable, and the International felt less pressure than formerly to act—in part, because Van Gelder was secretly a party member.[38] It did not help that the caliber of the Pleasure Club leaders was questionable at best. Among them were vicious racists, petty criminals, and opportunists who tried to take the local over to the AFL.[39] Most important, the anticommunists at Fairfield could not draw on the same reserve of skilled, veteran workers that had helped build Locals 31 and 33. The Fairfield Shipyard grew quickly from nothing, and its large, inexperienced workforce was more easily won over by party activists.

By early 1943 Cronin had nearly a dozen priests promoting anticommunist trade unionism in Baltimore's aircraft, steel, and electrical industries who had local party members worried. But Cronin worked hardest to get the communists out of the shipyards and even called on the rank and file personally.[40] He conceded that anticommunism alone was rarely sufficient to win the allegiance of Baltimore workers. Instead, he hoped to offer a "positive" program to counter the communists. The motives of those who followed Cronin were no doubt complex. Some may have agreed with Local 31's vice president that party members subverted the legitimate work-based concerns of unionism. At least a few believed deeply that communism and Catholicism were irreconcilable.[41] But Cronin never made his case in terms of Catholicism, an approach he considered futile with so much of Baltimore's wartime labor force "from the Protestant South."[42] Cronin and his followers appear to have offered little in terms of trade unionism. In-

Local 43

★ ★

AMERICANS

Drive Out the Invaders!

BROTHER MEMBERS OF LOCAL 43:

There has come into our midst a Communistic element which is as deadly to our United and Democratic Union of rank and file as the Axis powers are to our United and Democratic way of living.

Help us drive out this element.

VOTE THE ALL-AMERICAN TICKET FOR A DEMOCRATIC UNION.

➔ "DOWN THE LINE WITH O'BRIEN" ⬅

President............FRANCIS W. O'BRIEN ☒	Rec. Secretary.......LEONARD ZYGMONT.. ☒
Vice-President......CHARLES R. GALL......... ☒	Trustee................FRANK HOPKINS......... ☒
Business Agent....FRANK TESAR............... ☒	Trustee................LACE HYATT............... ☒
Treasurer............DANIEL APPEL............. ☒	Trustee................MELVIN GREEN.......... ☒

LOCAL 43—I. U. of M. and S. W. of A.

★ ★

43

A campaign leaflet issued by the anticommunist faction at the Fairfield Shipyard invokes Americanism against invaders in the workplace, July 1942. (Courtesy of the *Baltimore News-American* Photograph Collection, Special Collections, University of Maryland, College Park, Libraries) stead, they adopted a strategy that persisted in the postwar period. They harnessed anticommunism to two other "isms": anti-elitism and racism.

Before Pearl Harbor, another outspoken Catholic, Father John L. Bazinet, a member of Baltimore's America First Committee, was an aggressive purveyor of the anti–New Deal anticommunist rhetoric popular among small businessmen.[43] Cronin's constituents, however, did not share Bazinet's concerns about an all-powerful government. They, Cronin discovered, more often resented "smart New Yorkers coming in and taking over their organizations."[44] In an important series of articles in the *Catholic Review,* the weekly paper of the Roman Catholic Archdiocese of Baltimore, Cronin described communist infiltrators as people "who had rarely lifted anything heavier than a pen" only to become "welders and riveters in our shipyards and factories."[45] Cronin had hit on a significant weakness. Even Albert Lannon, the head of the Maryland Communist Party, conceded that the "New York influence" had been counterproductive.[46]

Equally effective was the reliance of Cronin and his followers on racial appeals. The communists in the CIO, especially in the shipyards, were among the strongest civil rights advocates in the city, but shipyard workers were firm defenders of racial prerogatives, as they demonstrated in the July 1943 "hate strike" at the Sparrows Point yard. A few days before that event a Cronin supporter known as "Salt Water Smitty" made the case for Local 43's anticommunist slate in anti-Semitic and racist terms. Electioneering near the main gates of the Fairfield yard, he proclaimed "let's make this a white man's union."[47] Smitty's harangue was no doubt the louder part of what the left called "a vicious whispering campaign" that Local 43's right-wingers waged against blacks.[48] Another influential Cronin follower was considered the "focal point" of racism in his department. Despite his commitment to social justice, Cronin's efforts made things worse for black workers.

Cronin consistently overstated the effects of the party's integrationist efforts, both in public and in private. In the *Catholic Review* he wrote that communists "actually seek special privileges for the Negro and discriminate against the white."[49] In a report that he sent to the IUMSWA International office, Cronin claimed that the communists in Local 43 pursued "complete intermingling of races in such a way as to provoke suspicion that they wished to have all white men replaced with negroes."[50] Ultimately, sympathy for civil rights became, in Cronin's view, closely linked with communism. In a 1946 *Catholic Review* article, he presented five tests for discovering whether a union leader was a communist or not. Number one was "attitude toward Negroes."[51]

By January 1945 the anticommunists in Local 43 were strong enough to withdraw the local from the state CIO.[52] After continued sniping between factions, the International finally imposed a trusteeship. By this time Philip Van Gelder was gone and his successor did not share his allegiance to the party. The communists were voted out and eventually withdrew.[53] The fate of Local 43 reflected a clear-cut victory for neither Cronin nor his supporters, because neither side was able to cut through worker apathy. Cronin repeatedly pointed out that communists took control only because small numbers of activists could gain the acquiescence of thousands of workers.[54] Conversely, despite his desire to train a new cohort of unionists in Catholic social principles, the Baltimore labor schools reached too few to have much effect. "It does little good to tell workers that their leaders are communists," he wrote. "They do not have the organization to vote them out of office or the trained leaders to replace them. Nor will they give up the union since it has given them tremendous benefits."[55]

In late 1944 the National Catholic Welfare Council asked Cronin to come to Washington to prepare a report on communism in America. In this document, issued in October 1945, Cronin maintained that "the problem of communism in the CIO will be solved at the local, not the national level" and predicted impending conflict between those on labor's left and right wings.[56] After Cronin left, concern over infiltration of union locals gave way to apprehension over higher-placed laborites who controlled politically powerful city and state labor councils. Cronin was right in predicting conflict, but the arena for anticommunist action had already begun shifting away from the local level.

In early 1945 Ulisse DeDominicis, the president of the embattled state CIO, wrote to CIO president Philip Murray. He denounced the "America Firsters and Christian Fronters" who, by condemning communist influence and withdrawing their support, intended to "murder the State CIO."[57] Curiously, DeDominicis, the socialist leader of the Amalgamated Clothing Workers, had been among the first to denounce communist influence in the local CIO, but he was now in a position of power and was reluctant to turn on those who had helped put him there.[58]

In the state Industrial Union Council a small group of communist unionists—most notably secretary-treasurer Sidney Katz and vice president George Meyers—gained an exceptional amount of power through hard work, knowledge of procedure, and sheer tenacity. But as the war wound down, the left-wing leaders were in trouble. By December 1944 communists were losing their grip on the shipyard unions and party influence elsewhere was dissipating. At that month's state CIO convention, Michael McHale, of UE Local 130, backed by other right-wing unionists who were sure that DeDominicis was being duped, attempted to wrest the secretary-treasurer's office from Katz.[59]

McHale lost by a narrow margin, and the right-wingers, charging "dictatorship and communist domination," began to renounce their unions' membership.[60] IUMSWA Locals 33 and 43 quit the Industrial Union Council, and UE Local 130 voted to "partially disaffiliate."[61] The split within the Maryland CIO was well publicized. DeDominicis claimed that it devastated the state CIO just when it was enjoying credit for swinging Maryland to FDR in the 1944 presidential election. Furthermore, he believed, bad publicity was eroding the CIO's influence in the city and state legislatures.[62] Katz finally resigned in September 1945, only to be replaced by a less public party member, a move that failed to placate the opposition.

Like Cronin before them, the anticommunist labor leaders in the Baltimore CIO, short on ideas and abilities, were ineffective on their own. The turning point came in November 1946, when Philip Murray, a staunch Catholic, abandoned his previous rapprochement with communists.[63] A month later, anticommunists in the state CIO who considered themselves "the real trade unionists" began working to disarm the communists by watering down their influence.[64] In late 1947 the Industrial Union Council adopted constitutional changes expanding the executive board from seventeen to fifty members.[65]

Paradoxically, the communists gained control of UE Local 130 only after the war, when the left's influence was waning elsewhere. There, left-wing leaders used the postwar electrical workers' strike to gain support from workers at a new defense plant that right-wing leaders had tried to relegate to second-class status.[66] In 1948 William Spillane, the local's Catholic right-wing secretary, pinned his hopes on Murray's leadership. Most members supported his criticism of the UE International, he wrote Murray, and "we feel 1000% better since you stated your policy at the CIO convention because we feel we can go higher than our international officers if it becomes necessary."[67]

Raising the Sights

During the war most of the party members active in Baltimore labor could be—despite the brevity of their experience or their New York roots—loosely described as "fellow workers." At this point communists were truly considered subversive—as coming from below. At higher levels, communism looked less threatening. Especially during the 1944 presidential campaign, it was not uncommon for prominent politicians to appear at party-sponsored events.[68]

In the half decade after World War II, anticommunists continually raised their sights to fix on threats appearing from farther and farther up the social scale. Some Baltimoreans, particularly ethnics with ties to countries behind the Iron Curtain, had concrete reasons for concern. Elsewhere, real—if hapless—party members were removed from factory floors and schools. But more frequently, practitioners (especially politicians) seemed more intent on demonstrating their own commitment to anticommunism than identifying and removing real communist threats: communism became increasingly abstract and charges of anticommunism correspondingly easy to make.

For a time, Catholics in Baltimore as elsewhere seemed to be going it alone. As eastern European homelands fell to the Soviets, Catholic groups passed resolutions and adopted official positions in opposition. The Knights of Columbus launched a letter-writing campaign urging Congress to push for firmer opposition to the Soviets and aired radio broadcasts condemning the "evils of communism."[69] But in early 1946, new revelations brought public opinion in line with Catholics' long-held views. In quick succession came news of a Soviet atomic spy ring, George Kennan's "long telegram" identifying the Soviet Union as a malignant state, and Winston Churchill's Fulton, Missouri, speech that gave a name to the Iron Curtain. After that, Mayor Theodore McKeldin and other politicians began stiffing the dwindling audiences at Soviet-American friendship rallies to speak among huge crowds assembled in ethnic Southeast Baltimore for Polish Constitution Day.[70]

During this period, anticommunism retained a great deal of personal relevance among its working-class practitioners. Whether they were union members fighting over their institutions or ethnics apprehensive about relatives and friends in Eastern Europe, most understood exactly why anticommunism was important. Politicians were quick to capitalize on this. The 1946 elections provided the first opportunity for politicians to wield anticommunism without the complication of the wartime Soviet alliance. In his Maryland gubernatorial primary bid, conservative Democrat H. Street Baldwin harnessed anticommunism to attacks on "socialization" and the CIO Political Action Committee. Like other candidates, he put his strongest anticommunist advertisements in the *Catholic Review,* one of which insisted that "communism is the only issue in this campaign."[71] Baldwin lost to William Preston Lane, but in the general election even liberal Republican Theodore McKeldin voiced similar rhetoric, although in more muted tones. During the same election Democrat Herbert O'Conor rode to a Senate seat by promising to root out subversion.[72]

The postwar strike wave brought Baltimore's business community enthusiastically into the anticommunist fray. City business journals again expressed concerns about "communist subversion" of the free enterprise system that they had largely forgotten during the war.[73] Baltimore's Bar Association, the Chamber of Commerce, and the Kiwanis, Optimist, and Rotary Clubs all appointed anticommunism committees, and six local trade associations studied the question. Business supported national groups like the Crusade for Freedom, the Association for the Preservation of American Ideals, and the All-American Conference to Combat Communism.[74]

By early 1947, being anticommunist was becoming as natural as breathing. "Everybody does it now," the *Baltimore Sun*'s exhilarated political columnist Frank Kent declared.[75] One of those doing it in Baltimore was city council vice president William J. Muth from the middle-class Fifth District. Muth, a veteran and a staunch Catholic, began with general and predictable speeches against "Godless" communism before local groups, but by May 1948 he had settled on specific targets in Baltimore's schools.[76] When Muth leveled charges (accurately) of party membership against two Baltimore teachers, the only opposition came from the increasingly marginal Baltimore party itself. In June the school board responded to Muth's charges by adopting a firm anticommunist policy.[77]

This was more than just a witch hunt. As M. J. Heale has demonstrated in his work on anticommunism at the state level, in industrialized metropolitan areas, concerns about communist influence in labor unions and other organizations were well founded. And as Heale pointed out, due to a remarkable confluence of events, Maryland was probably "more than unusually receptive to the anticommunist persuasion" in the late 1940s.[78] In 1948, responding to revelations like those made by anticommunist trade unionists and politicians like Muth, the Maryland General Assembly directed that a program be established "for the exposure and expurgation of subversive activities."[79] Governor Lane appointed Baltimore attorney Frank Ober to head up the committee that drew up a bill bearing Ober's name. The legislation, modeled on the Smith Act, which made it a crime to advocate the overthrow of the U.S. government, required loyalty oaths of all public employees, directed the state attorney general to seek out and prosecute subversives, and made records on subversives available to employers. While the Ober Bill was before the legislature, the *Baltimore News-Post,* a Hearst paper popular in blue-collar Baltimore, published daily statements encouraging its largely working-class readership to "Show Your Americanism" by urging legislators to pass the bill without amendment.[80] The bill, opposed by a lone delegate from rural Washington County, was signed into law in April 1949.[81]

The Maryland Civil Liberties Union, with the support of party activists—among them a few remaining left-wing CIO organizers—launched a petition drive to get the law put to a referendum.[82] The state CIO, having finally recovered from a long bout with communists in its own midst, declined to take part, correctly surmising that working people were either "indifferent or unopposed" to the Ober Law.[83] When the referendum came to a vote in the fall of 1950, 72 percent of Baltimore's voters approved the law.[84] Although some liberal observers despaired over the returns, a majority of Baltimore voters clearly agreed with Alice Oberle, a city fireman's wife, who could not understand "why there is so much ado" over it. "A good American," she said, "has nothing to fear in the Ober Law."[85] Legislators across the country agreed, and within the next few years the Ober Law became the model for legislation in eight other states.[86]

The 1950 elections marked the last time that local and state level anticommunist initiatives overshadowed those on the national level. By then, three national events—the passage of the Taft-Hartley Act, Henry Wallace's 1948 Progressive Party campaign, and the Alger Hiss affair, galvanized Baltimore. Taft-Hartley was aimed at radical unionists, outsiders bent on undermining society from below, but in the cases of Wallace and Hiss, anticommunism was directed the other way—up and at highly placed "insiders."

One of the most important initiatives taken by the Republican Congress that swept into office after the postwar strike wave was the passage of the 1947 Taft-Hartley Act. In addition to putting new restrictions on labor's ability to organize, Taft-Hartley required union officers to sign anticommunist affidavits. The Baltimore CIO's alarm over Taft-Hartley was met with skepticism by workers who felt alienated from the city and state Industrial Union Councils, still left-led in 1947. When the CIO held a rally to protest the legislation then heading for a vote, the *Labor Herald* set attendance far below that reported by the *Sun.* "Union members did not respond in sufficient numbers to voice a thundering protest" against the bill, said the paper. Most in attendance, the paper observed, were from the largest CIO unions, and the rally's complexion was decidedly radical.[87] A reader wrote that "it was plainly a left-wing CIO crowd . . . and we of the AFL who were hoodwinked into going played the game for the Henry Wallace crowd."[88]

After Taft-Hartley became law, UAW leaders at Glenn Martin faced a problem. In 1947 the Machinists Union mounted a serious challenge to the UAW, which had never been secure at the aircraft plant. With a vote set for the fall, local leaders found the UAW days away from being decertified by the National Labor Relations Board (NLRB). Although Baltimore officials had been quick to file noncommunist affidavits, the International— standing on principle for a time—had yet to do so. "We cannot hold our people much longer," the president of Local 738 told the International. "The people in our plant are not old militant union people," he explained. "They are young yet, and they have read the papers, and they want to know the answers to certain questions they have a right to ask."[89]

Even if the Glenn Martin workers had been old and militant, it would likely have mattered little. The Machinists had complied with Taft-Hartley, leaving the UAW little choice in the matter. Neither experience nor militancy could prevail over the law of the land. Most important, the "red issue" had long been a powerful one among Glenn Martin's largely southern workforce. During the war UAW organizers had despaired over the workers' readiness to believe charges of communism "without an honest investigation."[90] Glenn Martin workers were not alone in having questions about communism. Sparrows Point steelworker James Goertz asked Philip Murray "why there is such a contention" about it. "I would like to know why a fellow American should hesitate to sign a non communist affidavit," he said.[91]

Questioning Their Betters

Around 1950, Baltimoreans were equally perplexed that two politicians and a professor could show so much contempt for opponents of communism. For all their differences, Henry Wallace, Alger Hiss, and Millard Tydings appeared to share a credulous tolerance of destructive radicals and a haughty contempt for the wisdom of average people. They also seemed dangerously influential, deriving power not from money, but from ideas—ideas that blue-collar Baltimoreans were not inclined to respect.

Former vice president Henry Wallace claimed to be the true inheritor of the New Deal mantle, but few working whites were impressed. His campaign appeared chimeric and hopelessly tarred with communism. Of the major CIO unions, only the UE refused to accept this judgment, but Local

130's membership was so hostile to the Progressives that the officers refused to even broach the subject.[92] In the 1948 election, Harry S. Truman carried Baltimore's working-class white wards and black wards, but more middle-class precincts defected, leading to a Republican victory statewide.[93] Wallace got 2.8 percent of the Baltimore vote, and local Progressive candidates did only a little better.[94] Autoworker Phil Kulinski got 3 percent in the Third District, steelworker Mike Clifford received 4 percent in the Second District, and NAACP leader J. E. T. Camper took 6 percent in Baltimore's heavily black Fourth District.[95] Local leaders paid a heavy price for allying with the Progressives. Only Camper, a respected African American physician with a long civil rights record, escaped the red label. Kulinski and Clifford, both of whom had been local union pioneers, were ostracized for running on the ticket.[96] The United Steelworkers stripped Clifford of his union office even before the election.[97]

Clifford's wife sensed the importance of 1948 for CIO politics and asked CIO president Phil Murray if her husband's dismissal meant that "a man cannot hold office in the Union unless he is a Democrat."[98] But as the voting returns showed, few of Baltimore's working people considered the Progressive Party a real alternative to the Democrats. The *South Baltimore Enterprise* dismissed it as "a puff of wind" and depicted Truman as a common man who had succeeded on individualistic terms. He was, the paper said, a "self-made man" of "humble means" who "stems from US stock." Wallace, the paper countered, who had been "kicked out of the cabinet because he shot off his big mouth too loud and too often," was apparently none of those things. Most important, working people recognized that the realities of Stalinism could allow no justification for communism, be it on the grounds of integration or internationalism. They well understood, as Robert Zieger has pointed out in his important work on the CIO, that support for communists "was a matter not susceptible to nuanced preferences."[99]

The hypocrisy of the Progressive campaign irritated blue-collar Baltimore above all. To whites, some of whom preferred segregated workplaces and more of whom feared integrated neighborhoods, the party that claimed to champion working people appeared to be staffed by elites and supported by communists and Jews too quick with pro-integrationist rhetoric. For all of these reasons, Henry Wallace did not convey the impression of a 100 percent "American" fighter of humble means. White working-class Baltimoreans seemed to have had much the same opinion of another New Dealer. In June 1948 Johns Hopkins honored one of its graduates, a scion of an old patrician Baltimore family, in a formal dinner. The university recognized

Alger Hiss for his service to the State Department; two months later, Whittaker Chambers recognized Hiss for his service to the Communist Party.

Chambers, an editor of *Time* magazine and a former Baltimore party member, had helped funnel classified government documents to Soviet agents in the late 1930s.[100] He had renounced communism by the 1940s, and one of the first to hear his story was Father John F. Cronin. In the report he produced for the National Catholic Welfare Council in October 1945, Cronin named Alger Hiss as a member of "one of the primary communist cells to infiltrate the early New Deal."[101] Cronin told Richard Nixon about Hiss in early 1947 and subsequently fed him information that he obtained from FBI contacts.[102] In August 1948 Chambers made his charges public, Hiss denied them, and Chambers took Donald Appell to his farm. Hiss's first trial ended with a hung jury. Since the statute of limitations on crimes from the 1930s had run out by 1949, a second jury could only convict Hiss for perjury—it did so in January 1950. Coming after the Progressive Party debacle, the Hiss case even more strongly linked New Deal liberals with communist subversives.[103]

The Hiss case troubled Baltimore's elites; they could hardly believe that, in the *Sun*'s words, "a Baltimorean of such distinguished attainments and of such high promise" could have done what Chambers alleged. But when the *Sun* sought to include working-class Baltimore among those "pained" by Hiss's plight, it was rebuked.[104] A state senator, whose letter to the editor the *Sun* called representative of others received, described most Baltimoreans as "jubilant." "They are given a ray of hope that our democracy will carry," he said, "despite the dastardly effects of trusted individuals to tear us down."[105]

Working-class Baltimoreans who had long since grown accustomed to "red" charges leveled at Jewish labor leaders and left-wing activists were now hearing—and repeating—anti-elitist anticommunism directed at patrician Protestants with connections to the federal government. The government and manipulative elites were becoming one, and, together or separately, both were suspect. Shortly after Hiss was charged the *News-Post* proclaimed that HUAC was the only government agency "either able or permitted to guard the country."[106] Said one working-class Baltimorean, "The Hiss case proved that it is possible to get away with a great deal of prevarication. Washington still has a red face."[107]

In 1950 Maryland was in the eye of America's second Red Scare. In January, the Hiss verdict came in. In February, Maryland senator Millard Tydings was appointed head of a Senate Subcommittee set up to inves-

tigate the charges being made by Joseph McCarthy, who was just beginning his anticommunist career. In March, before the Tydings Committee,
McCarthy named his first "communist": Johns Hopkins professor Owen
Lattimore.[108] He charged Lattimore, an authority on China and sometime
government adviser, with being "the top Russian espionage agent" in the
United States."[109] By this time Baltimore's communists, with the exception
of a few leaders, had gone underground, meeting in cells as small as two or
three. There were few real party members left to attack, but in a political
atmosphere in which proving anticommunist credentials was more important than delivering up subversives, stalking horses sufficed, particularly
thoroughbreds.

In July, the Tydings Committee report charged McCarthy with perpe-
trating a "fraud and a hoax" on the Senate. But the document lacked the
signatures of the two Republicans on the committee who claimed that the
Tydings investigation had not gone far enough.[110] McCarthy took this as a
signal that he had support from the Republican Party, and he immediately
sought revenge. Although he was not up for reelection himself, McCarthy's
newfound notoriety put him in high demand during the 1950 congressional
elections. Though he campaigned in fifteen states nationwide, McCarthy
expended most of his effort in the Maryland senator's race.[111]

Tydings was a pro-business, conservative Democrat. In the past, the only
thing that had kept labor in his corner was party loyalty.[112] In the 1950
primaries, labor had backed another candidate who ran against what he
termed the Tydings "whitewash" of McCarthy's charges.[113] Another primary
opponent, Hugh Monaghan II, was even more McCarthyesque. He claimed
that Tydings had "given the green light to Stalin's agents," had been a pup-
pet of the treasonous Dean Acheson, and had been partly responsible for
the outbreak of the Korean War.[114] Monaghan's rhetoric appealed to Catholics in particular.[115]

Tydings did his best to ignore the "whitewash" issue and won the primary, although by a slim margin. In the general campaign, however, he had
McCarthy to contend with. McCarthy provided Tydings's opponent, John
Marshall Butler, help with speeches, money, scurrilous campaign materials,
and an enterprising staff.[116] Most memorable was a widely circulated com-
posite photograph concocted by McCarthy's people that portrayed Tydings
consulting with Communist Party chief Earl Browder.[117]

Baltimore's labor and liberal groups gave some support to the beleaguered Tydings, but the whitewash charge—the basis of Butler's entire
campaign—hinted at a tendency toward arrogant obfuscation that blue col-

larites were coming to expect from highly placed elites.[118] Tydings's own campaign, complained one Baltimorean, smacked of "smugness, double-talk and demagoguery."[119] Tydings customarily assumed a distant, patrician image that had long before, according to his biographer, "crossed the fine line from aloof to haughty."[120] This helped account for the fact that, according to David Oshinsky, "Tydings was one of the few men in politics whom McCarthy genuinely disliked."[121] Even in the early 1930s, constituents complained that he had "gone Washington"—and Washington was the kind of target that McCarthy liked.[122]

McCarthy's popularity with Roman Catholics has been well documented, and Baltimore's Catholics were no exception.[123] The *Catholic Review* gave what one historian called "muted but unmistakable" support to McCarthy. But it did not go far enough for some Baltimore Catholics. One rebuked the paper's editor for equivocating on the Tydings whitewash. "Whether Senator McCarthy proves his charges before a Fair Deal court is of minor importance," the critic said, "if he can arouse the conscience of the Nation to the dangers that threaten it."[124]

The Maryland Action Guild was Baltimore's principle Catholic anticommunist group in the early 1950s. Father John L. Bazinet founded the group in late 1949. Business leaders were among his strongest supporters, but Bazinet also tried hard to attract working people. From the beginning, the guild's primary work was running labor schools. In the abstract, the guild opposed both secularism and moral decay while propounding Catholic social principles. Its concrete accomplishments, apart from its labor schools, usually amounted to supporting any and all anticommunist measures.[125] In July 1950 the guild, speaking for its one thousand members, demanded, among other things, the ouster of Dean Acheson and the passage of the Mundt-Nixon Bill to outlaw the Communist Party.[126] Baltimore's Archbishop Francis Patrick Keough lent his support to the guild's activities.[127] By fall, the guild's attacks on Tydings joined a growing chorus. The *News-Post* condemned the "Tydings whitewash committee" at every opportunity.[128]

It was in this atmosphere that Joseph McCarthy appeared at a 15 September "Americanism Rally" sponsored by the Maryland Catholic War Veterans. At the rally, McCarthy affected an "above politics" stance, never mentioning Tydings in a radio-broadcast speech before a crowd of two thousand at Baltimore's Lyric Theater. Instead, McCarthy castigated Acheson, Lattimore, and the Truman administration's foreign policy in general.[129] One observer informed Tydings that more than half of those in attendance were women, and most were over fifty years of age. He further implied that there were many ethnics in the crowd, since "a considerable percentage of them spoke broken English."[130] The Catholic vote loomed as a major weakness for Tydings. Another Baltimorean predicted that "the investigation" and Tydings's "hatred of Catholics" would ensure his defeat.[131] Butler accordingly informed local priests that he would fight "communists and their friends within our government" as strongly as he would oppose "atheistic Russia overseas."[132]

Butler won the election by forty thousand votes, gaining 53 percent of the vote statewide. In Baltimore, he received 47 percent to Tydings's 40 percent of the vote. Everybody but Tydings was quick to attribute the defeat to McCarthy, but several other factors helped raise the Republican tide: Truman's own popularity was suffering, which left Tydings bereft of support from above, and a strong primary challenge by Baltimore County contractor George Mahoney split the party in the governor's race. This election has been widely studied. Some attribute Tydings's loss to the labor, liberal Democrat, and black vote; a few give McCarthy no credit at all; but even the most skeptical credit Catholic opposition.[133] Whether McCarthy's personal intervention dethroned Tydings or not, Catholic anticommunism was never more pronounced or powerful.

Most important, however, is the phenomenon of the campaign itself. It ranks among the dirtiest in the nation's history and was fought almost exclusively over the issue of communism. No one suggested that Tydings himself was a communist, but anticommunism appears to have easily borne a host of resentments stirred up by the "country club" Marylander, who had married into an elite Washington family and contemptuously dismissed McCarthy and his charges. Tydings's character as much as his politics helped McCarthy's charges stick.

Turnout was highest in middle-class North Baltimore, where Butler won 56 percent of the vote. Baltimore's blacks, still leaning toward the party of Abraham Lincoln in state and local elections, gave Butler impressive margins, but even in the Democratic white working-class wards he got 48 percent of the vote—better than his showing citywide.[134] The *Baltimore Evening Sun* was impressed that wards "which never in history deserted their Democratic bosses" could give a plurality to the Republican.[135] At the crest of Maryland's Red Scare, McCarthyite anticommunism was now conducted, in the words of Richard Gid Powers, "on the level of symbolic politics." To working-class voters, two familiar symbols, the "silk stocking" elite and the treacherous communist, had become one. If their "betters" could do this, what else might they be capable of?[136]

The Demise of "Class War"

On May first 1947 Baltimore-area Catholics fifty thousand strong gathered at Memorial Stadium to pray for the conversion of Russia from "Godless communism" to Christianity. Students from every parochial school in the city were there. Clad in their various colored uniforms, the children "stood out like flowers in a field," noted the *Sun*. Catholic veterans organizations fielded bands and drum and bugle corps. The featured speaker, Bishop Lawrence Shehan of Baltimore, lamented the compromise by the United States and the United Nations that had led to the "abandonment" of Eastern Europe. But Russia, Shehan observed, was not entirely lost. Its people, he told the crowd, long subjected to autocratic rule, had simply been reduced to "full slavery by a more powerful and immeasurably more clever dictatorship." Shehan hoped that a "change in those at the top" might bring freedom to the East.[137]

The 1947 event was large and well publicized, but it was only one of many such services dating back to March 1930, when the archdiocese inaugurated regular prayers for "bleeding Russia."[138] In 1947 the majority of Catholics were working-class people who most likely found Shehan's emphasis on the spiritual over the material appropriate. But two points are of further importance. Russia's people, as Shehan noted, were not to be vilified. Instead, a small group of clever and powerful leaders were to blame. Equally important, the bishop concluded, "this country and every country in the world needs a reconversion to God. As individuals and as a nation we have often wandered far from God's law." The implied corollary is clear: if Russia could be enslaved by a godless elite, then so could America. In the three years after this rally, Baltimore's Catholics acted—and voted—out of similar convictions.

The anti-elitist strain that is readily detectable in Shehan's speech became more pronounced as the targets of anticommunist wrath shifted from labor unions to the halls of government. In World War II and the early Cold War, blue-collar anticommunism was shaped by experience, as working whites witnessed the escapades of left-wing laborites at home and Stalin's occupation forces abroad. By the 1950s, though, anticommunism had been wedded to anti-elitism, reinvigorating and redirecting the populism that had long characterized white working-class political thought away from economic and toward political elites.[139]

Although public confidence in the government remained high during the 1950s, anticommunism helped cut the rhetorical grooves through which later antigovernment critiques would run.[140] As the 1950s progressed and the actual threat of domestic anticommunism grew ever more dubious, anticommunism fixed on Soviets rather than senators. But the populist anti-elitism cultivated by the Red Scare took firmer root in the soil of racial and social upheaval than in ideological debates. In the 1950s and 1960s Baltimoreans outraged by neighborhood transition, school desegregation, attacks on school prayer, and urban crime began to see some familiar faces behind the problems. Liberal elites, once taken in by communists, now seemed to be at the service of other menacing forces.

The anticommunist episode demonstrated just how evanescent the class-based populism of the New Deal was. In December 1949, an illustration on the front page of the *Enterprise* lauding the revival of Smith Act prosecutions showed the boot of federal law stomping out tiny radicals carrying signs marked "criminal conspiracy" and "subversive activities." A third tiny radical, carrying a sign saying "class war," was also destined for destruction.[141] The class politics of the New Deal perished in the postwar period, not so much stomped out by the boot of federal law as left to wither by working people newly content with their jobs and neighborhoods and increasingly wary of the plans of liberal policymakers. But the populism of the New Deal endured, borne along by postwar anticommunism until the perils of racial change and urban decline overshadowed the threat from subversives within.

CHAPTER 3

You Make Your Own Heaven

In the late 1970s Grace DiMartino, who had come as a child from Italy, re-flected on her life in Highlandtown. Her attitude, seemingly out of place in a time of deindustrialization and urban decline, opens a window to a view of citizenship built on the values and actions of the postwar white work-ing class. DiMartino, the wife of a Sparrows Point steelworker, prized her neighbors for "the way they think. The way they do things." "We got heaven here and don't know it," she said. "Of course, you make your own heaven."[1] By then, growing numbers of Baltimoreans were losing the sanguine view that Mrs. DiMartino retained. The measure of their unease, however, was determined by a sense of white working-class citizenship constructed in the two decades after World War II.

The meaning of citizenship, as understood by Baltimore's working whites in the postwar decades, revolved around community as an arena where family, ethnic, religious, and sometimes workplace-related endeavors could be carried out. Every community was defined by boundaries, and within them working-class citizenship emphasized obligations over opportunity and responsibility over rights. Blue collarites safeguarded their institutions by closely observing and diligently enforcing those boundaries.[2] Ethnicity and religion served as important benchmarks, but they crosscut the white working-class community. The most clearly defined boundaries were racial and geographic, and in Baltimore, as in most postwar industrial cities, these were perfectly aligned; to be working class was to be white. The church, clubs, the workplace, and the union were all important working-class institutions, but the latter two—because they lay outside of commu-nity geographic and racial boundaries, and because the workplace was largely beyond the control of working people to shape—were far less im-portant than more traditional community institutions.

"Working" nevertheless remained at the heart of white working-class citizenship. Blue-collar whites recognized differences with those below and above them in society. They had an identity based on work—a class identity. But it was more actively expressed in the neighborhood than in the workplace. Working whites did not see the job as having a higher social purpose: the workplace and the union had specific rather than general implications. It was in the community where working could matter because the community was theirs. For blue-collar whites the expression "working class" usually fit within an economic context, describing income and type of work. The term "working" operated in a cultural domain. Income and occupation were starting points, but allegiance to neighborhood institutions and faith in a constellation of values centered around responsibility to the community, narrowly defined, were most important. This is key to understanding the political implications of white working-class citizenship.

In the urban setting, and increasingly during the postwar years, in the national arena, working whites did not hesitate to make rights-based claims; they had a keen sense of particular responsibilities and limits. They felt strong communal obligations, but these did not foster a sense of broader societal responsibilities. For some, certainly, this worldview was shaped and sustained by the basic Roman Catholic principle of subsidiarity. This held that society was best understood as a hierarchy extending from church and state at the top to neighborhood and family at the bottom, and, what is most significant, no higher level entity was expected to undertake a responsibility properly belonging to a lower-level association.[3] Regardless, both Catholics and Protestants recognized that there were responsibilities and obligations incurred by every citizen, but they were best met within rather than without the community. Thinking otherwise bordered on arrogance. Heaven was something you had to make: but you made *your own*—and no one else's.

The Working Class Ascendant

On Tuesday night, 6 May 1947, thousands of blue-collar Baltimoreans gathered in Little Italy for a celebration replete with confetti, honking car horns, and people screaming from the rooftops. At age forty-three, neighborhood boy Thomas "Tommy" D'Alesandro Jr. was mayor of Baltimore.[4] During D'Alesandro's three terms (1947–59), times were mostly good for white working-class Baltimore. In the past, pro-business Democrats had managed to obtain working white support while making few concrete concessions.

Thomas D'Alesandro Jr., "East Baltimore's Mayor," is sworn in, May 1947. (Courtesy of the *Baltimore News-American* Photograph Collection, Special Collections, University of Maryland, College Park, Libraries)

But in the late 1940s and the 1950s, with a New Deal Democrat in the mayor's office, blue-collar Baltimoreans began to feel represented rather than just appeased. D'Alesandro's election confirmed to working whites that the sacrifices of depression and war had been rewarded and that their voices were being heard. When D'Alesandro stepped from his car to greet the throng that night, it seemed, said the *Baltimore Sun,* that "he knew them all." "East Baltimore's got a Mayor," declared a voice from the crowd.[5]

If D'Alesandro's victory signaled a new beginning, it also emphasized a link with the liberal past. Since his election to Congress in 1938, D'Alesandro had been Baltimore's preeminent New Deal politician, and he benefited from the association. White working-class residents remembered one important thing about the New Deal: it ensured a "decent" hourly wage. "When Roosevelt went in he put the NRA [National Recovery Administration] in," said Joseph Sergi from Little Italy. "They had to pay 40 cents an hour . . . it was a big raise."[6] A Hampden man recalled that "they put that NRA through and it put people to work and they cut out that fifty-five hours a week work for eleven dollars."[7] With government support, industrial unionism provided higher wages and helped ensure better working conditions.[8] Some Baltimore unionists saw the 1947 mayoral race as a chance to repay a long-standing debt. "Tommy always voted for labor, one union leader said, and today it was labor's turn to vote for Tommy."[9]

The Great Depression had taught many working-class Baltimoreans to which political party they properly belonged. In 1951 a man from South Baltimore cautioned his neighbors to be skeptical about Republican attacks on President Harry S. Truman and the Democratic "mess in Washington." "It was the GOP that put the country into a hell of a mess with promises of a chicken in every pot," he reminded them.[10] Nevertheless, working whites retained some reservations about the appropriate role of government. Blue-collar recollections of the depression centered chiefly around personal and family issues. The principal lesson Grace DiMartino extracted from the experience was one of personal responsibility—"save."[11] The state may have helped workers get a decent wage or even a job, but the most important resources were individual. "Sure during the depression there was poor people around everyplace," one woman recalled, "but everybody was ambitious."[12]

Postwar white working-class citizenship was shaped by both of these legacies: a conviction that the government should help the "ambitious" deserving and a renewed faith in the power of individual effort. And though both working whites and blacks backed Franklin D. Roosevelt, the New Deal hardly ended racial division in Baltimore. In 1943 it took Theodore McKeldin, a Republican, to assemble a "New Deal" coalition of working white and black votes. But in 1947, while white working-class wards gave "Tommy" 68 percent of their votes, black wards stayed Republican, casting only 44 percent of their ballots for the Little Italy native. East Baltimore had a mayor—but East Baltimore was white.

"Workers' Paradise": Institutions

Tommy D'Alesandro presided over a decade of blue-collar prosperity unparalleled before or since. Although it is clear in retrospect that the city began its slow decline in the 1950s, for white working Baltimoreans the decade was more good than bad. Neighborhood racial transition and school desegregation had only begun to affect them, and they enjoyed an unparal-

Highlandtown, in the heart of Southeast Baltimore. The intersection
of Eastern Avenue and Oldham Street in the 1940s. (Courtesy of the
Baltimore News-American Photograph Collection, Special Collections,
University of Maryland, College Park, Libraries)

leled rise in their standard of living.[13] National social and economic trends
still seemed to favor blue-collar Baltimore during this period, and residents
built strong communities in the good years.

Throughout the period, the average Baltimore family had one income
and was of the working class. The lights came on in blue-collar neighborhoods at about 6:30 in the morning as industrial workers, mostly male, rose
for another day at the factory.[14] In South Baltimore, shipyards hummed.
The Baltimore and Ohio Railroad and American Sugar employed workers
from Locust Point, while the National Enamel and Stamping Company and
the Linen Thread Company served as the economic foundations of South
Baltimore proper.[15] In Canton, Crown Cork and Seal and Revere Copper and
Brass were substantial employers. Western Electric remained the largest
industry within the city limits, while to the east in Baltimore County, Sparrows Point continued to expand, providing jobs across Baltimore but especially in Southeast Baltimore. To the north in Hampden, a few of the old

textile mills remained, and Noxell, a cosmetics plant, gave work to many local residents.[16]

Manufacturing remained the city's largest employer up to 1960, and Baltimore industry continually set production records as new firms opened and existing companies grew. In 1948, 39 new industries entered the area and there were 131 plant expansions.[17] In 1951 nearly all of the money spent on industrial construction went to expand existing facilities.[18] Although industrial employment inside the city limits declined 7.6 percent from 1947 to 1958, industrial employment in the metropolitan area as a whole—which included Sparrows Point, Glenn Martin, and Westinghouse among other large employers—rose, reapproaching wartime levels by the mid-1950s.[19]

The average Baltimorean's real take-home pay climbed steadily throughout the 1950s, outpacing inflation by 7 percent.[20] Members of powerful industrial unions like the United Autoworkers began receiving supplemental unemployment benefits and cost-of-living adjustments that made them the most financially secure of all the city's industrial workers.[21] Albert Arnold, a trimmer at Fisher Body, credited his union with the dramatic improvement in wages and workplace conditions he experienced during the period, although he maintained that he had earned those gains by striking when necessary.[22] As unions grew more prosperous, they extended their reach even if they narrowed their goals. CIO unions sponsored sports teams that participated in a citywide labor league, funded community improvement programs, and built large, modern meeting halls.[23] In 1962 one UAW local arranged a three-week European tour for members, prompting a *Baltimore News-Post* columnist to declare that "The Workers' Paradise Is Here."[24] This was more likely the middle-class writer's idea of paradise. The real "workers' paradise" was not a European jaunt and certainly not the shop floor. As Andrew Levison has noted in his important study of postwar working-class life, to blue collarites, "the working hours feel like stolen time, time taken away from the nonwork hours when one can really live."[25] And it was in the home and the neighborhood where that was possible.

Although boosters had long called Baltimore "a city of homeowners," in 1947 the average working-class family still rented (a six-room row house) rather than owned.[26] By the early 1950s, though, Baltimore's rates of home ownership reached 57.9 percent—among the highest in the nation according to the U.S. Bureau of Labor Statistics.[27] Not until the end of the decade did apartment rental rates again begin to outstrip home buying.[28]

In Baltimore as elsewhere, home ownership was encouraged by programs emanating from Washington. Baltimore veterans were quick to take advantage of the VA home loan guarantees after the war: by 1949 nearly 26,000 had taken out loans and a tenth of them had already paid them off in full.[29] As VA applications peaked in early 1954, the Baltimore office extolled the program's "tremendously stimulating effect toward home security."[30] Where home ownership rates were highest, however, it was due more to initiatives from within the community than to policies made in Washington.

Lacking guarantees from the Veterans Administration or the Federal Housing Administration, banks did not make loans to working-class people, recalled a South Baltimore man. But if building and loan officials "knew you and you had a good reputation [as] a steady worker, they took a chance on you."[31] The heyday of Baltimore's ethnic building and loans came before the depression. Nevertheless, the 1956 City Directory still listed thirteen ethnic building and loans—five of them Polish.[32] It was no coincidence, then, that by 1960 owner occupancy rates in heavily Polish neighborhoods in South-east Baltimore and Locust Point had reached 75 and 80 percent, the high-est in the city.[33] The Czech neighborhoods in Southeast Baltimore north of Highlandtown also had high owner occupancy rates at 75 percent.[34] In Hampden, home ownership among mostly native-stock Protestants aver-aged lower, although in one neighborhood rates hit 71 percent.[35]

Under normal circumstances, "for sale" signs were a rarity in blue-collar Baltimore; when working-class renters were ready to buy, they usually looked in the neighborhoods where they had grown up.[36] Houses changed hands quickly, were advertised by word of mouth, and usually went to rela-tives or friends. As a result, members of extended families came to live in close proximity to one another.[37] By the late 1970s, for example, one High-landtown family had five generations living on a single block.[38] Blue-collar families tended to stay together—one late 1970s study found that on a few Locust Point streets, more than 83 percent of families had lived at the same address for over fifty years.[39] There were exceptions. In Little Italy and Fells Point, for instance, owner occupancy rates in 1960 were below the citywide average at only 26 and 46 percent respectively.[40] Among working whites, those living closer to the harbor were more likely to rent.

If plentiful industrial employment and generally high home ownership rates made for strong postwar white working-class communities, three in-stitutions were key to maintaining them: churches, community organiza-tions, and political clubs. Churches were centers of community life, and in blue-collar Baltimore "the church" most often meant the Roman Catholic Church.

Although it was the seat of the first American Catholic diocese, Baltimore in the 1950s was neither as ethnic nor as Catholic as many north-eastern industrial cities. In 1950 about 11 percent of Philadelphia's and 18 percent of Boston's residents were foreign-born. In Baltimore the figure was 5.4 percent.[41] At the same time, 53 percent of metropolitan Boston's and 41 percent of metropolitan Philadelphia's whites were Catholic. In the Baltimore metropolitan area, 34 percent of whites were Catholic.[42] But other churches did not command the allegiance of working-class people that the Catholic Church did—its churches, schools, and social halls loomed large in urban neighborhoods. With the exception of Protestant Hampden, the white working-class neighborhoods that stayed the most cohesive over time were Catholic ones, magnifying the effects of the church. Still, in 1950 Catholics made up 18 percent of the urban population, and by 1960 the proportion had slipped to 16 percent.[43] The Roman Catholic Archdiocese of Baltimore grew most substantially in working-class suburbs like Glen Burnie, but in white working-class East and South Baltimore the Catholic population increased as well.[44]

In Southeast Baltimore especially, industrial workers generously supported their churches financially and otherwise. In the early 1960s Sacred Heart of Jesus, a German church with increasing numbers of Polish parishioners, was the hub of Highlandtown social life, boasting what the diocese called "extremely active" social clubs and a "large, magnificent and excellent school facility." But it was just one of many parishes in Southeast Baltimore that invoked staunch loyalties.[45] The 1950s was the peak period of construction for Baltimore's suburban parochial schools: two went up for every church that was built. In the city, enrollments declined slightly, holding steady only in Southeast Baltimore.[46] Although their resources were slimmer, Baltimore's urban Catholics were more generous, giving proportionally more of their income to the church than did suburbanites in the postwar years.[47]

A smaller but significant percentage of Baltimore's blue collarites worked not only through the church but also through neighborhood associations to improve their communities. Neighborhood associations had a long history in Baltimore; the first were organized in the 1880s. By 1900 there were over 30 groups across the city, mostly concerned with community enhancement and preservation, although in the 1910s a few started to focus on enforcing racial exclusion as well.[48] Nationwide, neighborhood improvement associations were rare in working-class communities, but Baltimore did not follow this pattern.[49] By 1956 the city was home to some 163 neighborhood organizations, including the South Baltimore Improvement Association, the Can-

A sacred procession in Little Italy. (Courtesy of the Special Collections Department, Maryland Historical Society, Baltimore)

ton Area Council, and the Fells Point Improvement Association.[50] In these areas, however, there were practically no black residents during the 1940s and 1950s, so community groups rarely emphasized racial exclusion to any great extent. Instead, they pursued small goals, lobbying the city for street lighting, paving, and fencing.[51]

Community groups had their broadest impact on working-class lives when they banded together with labor unions and political clubs to form community councils. In the late 1940s and 1950s three of these—the Southwest, the Southeast, and the Eastern Community Councils—served working-class Baltimore. These groups, often led by area small businesses, organized sports programs, recreation centers, and youth social clubs. Much of their emphasis was on fighting juvenile delinquency, then considered a scourge of urban youth.[52]

Next to the church, however, the most powerful institutions in working-class Baltimore were the political clubs. In the mid-1950s there were about thirty of these in the city.[53] As the urban machine continued its decline, power devolved to local and district organizations, the strongest of which were rooted in blue-collar political clubs.[54] The more influential of these clubs included the Sixth District Stonewall Democratic Club (home of the South Baltimore Della-Wyatt organization) and the first district Highland Clipper Club (run by Southeast Baltimore "bosses" George Hofferbert and Thomas D'Alesandro). The Hofferbert-D'Alesandro organization was so effective that it held onto the First District's city council seat for twenty-four years—from 1947 to 1971.[55]

Working-class party politics was a mostly male pursuit, but two of Baltimore's most influential female politicians were from working-class neighborhoods. Alice Canoles started her political career in the 1920s, ringing doorbells to get out the Southeast Baltimore vote. By the postwar years she was leader of the Democratic Women's Club and a power broker in Ward 26.[56] August Klecka ran the Slavic Building and Loan Association and represented Czech voters in the old Gorman-Rasin machine. After he died in 1946 his wife Lillian became Ward 7's most influential figure, even making an unsuccessful run for Congress in 1950.[57]

Election times were, of course, periods of peak activity at the clubs. Shortly before the 1950 primary, Maryland Democratic governor Franklin Lane appeared at seven blue-collar clubs in one night. At the Polish American Hall in Curtis Bay, southwest of Brooklyn, Lane had to navigate the bar and enter a "dingy hall" to relieve a hoarse Mayor D'Alesandro exhorting the members of the Curtis Democratic Club, mostly men in "sweaters and jackets and working clothes," according to the *Sun*. Later that night in Southeast Baltimore, in yet another rear hall behind a bar, D'Alesandro resorted to singing in an attempt to hold the members of the Lithuanian Democratic Club until Lane's arrival.[58]

In less exciting times the clubs sponsored social events like bull and oyster roasts to cement their constituents' loyalties.[59] The day-to-day work of patronage distribution and political deal making was done in regular but informal sessions held at bars or restaurants and attended by a few key politicians and ward bosses. Such deal making often shaded imperceptibly into more insidious activities. The public influence that Joseph Obrycki parlayed into a career as a politician in the heavily Polish Ward 2 derived more from his numbers racket than his bar business.[60] Herbert Gans has argued that "the image of the working-class politician as a beloved neighborhood figure is largely fiction," and working people were indeed skeptical about the club system.[61] "Politics was a big fat party all the time with a whole lot of bull, promising you this and promising you that," one South Baltimore resident claimed.[62]

But others, like Melvyn Buhrman, who ran a South Baltimore bar, were more forgiving. From his perspective a local politician could be counted on to try to get jobs or services for his constituents.[63] And whether politicians were beloved or not, their proximity to the neighborhood made politics more a personal than an institutional transaction. Locals liked to boast of their intimacy with city politicians, and the *Sun* was probably exaggerating just a little when it said in May 1947 that the victorious mayor "knew everyone."[64] It was with some justification, then, that working whites attributed social and economic well-being to community-based initiatives rather than government programs or more broadly based "civic" efforts. The flip side of this doctrine of self-sufficiency was a tradition of voluntarism often publicized by the papers.

argument

In 1947 the *Baltimore Evening Sun* put a personal face on the city's postwar housing shortage in a series on the Mericas, a West Virginia family of nine. It spent seven months in a windowless three-room apartment above a garage and paid fifty dollars a month for the privilege. After the stories appeared, Baltimoreans showered the family with gifts. Donations even paid for a modest house in the Brooklyn Homes development.[65] Two years later, the *South Baltimore Enterprise* ran a story on a woman with a heart condition whose husband had been laid off. The paper pronounced her deserving of help for "her four growing youngsters" and received donations of clothing. This, the paper implied, was the proper way to combat poverty.[66] In 1955 the *Brooklyn News* declared "We Take Care of Our Own" and observed that local civic groups had distributed two hundred baskets of coal, food, and gifts locally over the Christmas season.[67] Similar examples of the importance of voluntarism were well and proudly documented by Baltimore's weeklies throughout the late 1940s and 1950s.

Membership

Home ownership, the church, political clubs, and to some extent union membership provided an institutional basis for white working-class citizenship. Membership, though, was defined not only by participation in these institutions, but also by broader cultural boundaries. By the postwar period, ethnicity was becoming less central than it had once been. National origins remained important to working people's self-images, but second- and third-generation Eastern and Southern Europeans did not set themselves exceptionally far apart from older immigrant-stock or native-stock Baltimoreans, and the concept of "working people" did not have specific ethnic requirements.

Baltimore's nineteenth-century Irish and German enclaves had largely dispersed by the new decade as the old neighborhoods gave way to blacks and new immigrant groups. Thereafter old immigrants were a significant presence in nearly every white working-class neighborhood, but dominant in few. Germans did leave an indelible mark on the city. A few German social and political clubs hung on until the 1920s, and much of Highland-town remained predominantly German into the 1960s.[68] The Irish, on the other hand, left fewer traces. St. Patrick's Day observances were discontinued in 1910, and the last distinctly Irish neighborhood had disappeared by the 1950s.[69] Many of the city's prominent early twentieth-century politicians were Irish, but as a group they left little institutional legacy—with the important exception of the Catholic Church.[70] The Irish and Germans did account for most of Hampden's foreign-stock population, but their overall numbers remained very small there as well.[71]

The largest group of foreign-born and foreign-stock Baltimoreans throughout the twentieth century consisted of Russian Jews. Hemmed in by restrictive covenants, Jews were concentrated primarily in Southeast Baltimore's Ward 6 before World War II. These covenants were ruled unconstitutional by the Supreme Court in 1947, enabling Jews to move out of the central city in a northeasterly direction as they moved steadily up the social scale, leaving their middle-class neighborhoods open to black settlement.[72] Four ethnic groups predominated in white working-class Baltimore during the 1950s. Poles comprised the largest ethnic group in Fell's Point, Canton, Locust Point, and parts of Highlandtown. The Italians—centered around Little Italy, but increasingly present in Highlandtown—were the next largest group. A cohesive Czech community flourished in Southeast Baltimore's Ward 7, and a smaller Lithuanian neighborhood in South Baltimore was strong early in the decade.[73]

Of the seven identifiable ethnic social and political clubs that remained in Baltimore during the 1950s, two were Italian, one was Polish, and one was Lithuanian.[74] Nevertheless, the waning importance of ethnicity is indicated by the total number of these clubs, which fell by 50 percent between 1928 and 1956. In Highlandtown, according to a man who grew up there in the 1950s, residents were aware of others' ethnic differences, "but it didn't determine whether they were good or bad people . . . with of course the exception of the blacks."[75]

In the 1940s and 1950s working-class youths usually organized gangs around allegiance to streets and neighborhoods, although some interethnic rivalry remained.[76] One resident recalled that in the late 1940s an Italian

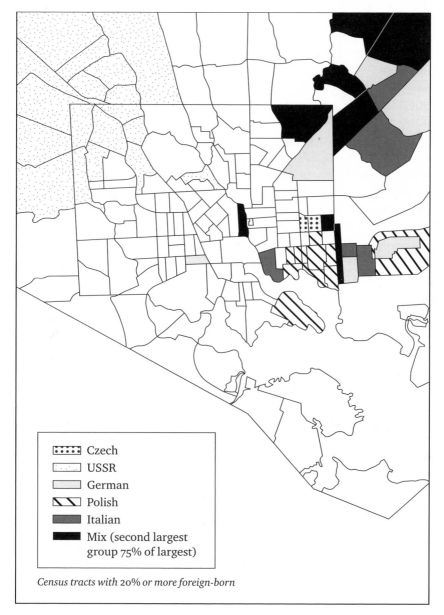

Census tracts with 20% or more foreign-born

MAP 3. Ethnic population, 1960 (*Source:* U.S. Bureau of the Census,
*1960 Census of Population and Housing: Final Report PHC(1)-13, Census Tracts,
Baltimore, Maryland* [Washington, D.C.: GPO, 1962].)

girl dancing with a Polish boy in Patterson Park would have been "enough to start a real riot."[77] Similarly, the Polish and Irish parents of Joey Radomski and Agnes McNeal were deeply disappointed over their children's "mixed marriage."[78] There were no interethnic riots, however, and ethnic intermarriage became frequent in the postwar years. By the 1970s the *East Baltimore Guide* could claim that through the years, intermarriages in the area had led to "a gigantic number of Polish-Italian" families.[79]

Religion, especially the Protestant-Catholic divide, mattered more, partly because it reinforced broader cultural differences between native-stock and ethnic working people, and partly because of the strong gravitational pull that parish institutions had in blue-collar neighborhoods. A Highlandtown resident who went to Sacred Heart school in the 1950s remembered little ethnic hostility. On the other hand, he said, the teachers at Sacred Heart discouraged the children from playing with their public school counterparts. "As long as you hung around somebody who was Catholic," he recalled, the nuns approved.[80] Baltimore confirms Robert Wuthnow's observation that Protestant-Catholic animosity was pronounced in the decade after 1945, although it had dropped off considerably by the 1960s.[81]

Compounding this were memories of the wartime migrants. "They came up here to make that big defense money," South Baltimorean Joe Manning remembered bitterly as late as the 1970s. They "cut a lot of Baltimore people out of those jobs."[82] The persistence of this resentment is in part explained by the fact that even as wartime migrants became integrated into the community, others continued to arrive. Baltimore city planners estimated that about 210,000 southern whites moved to the city in the 1950s, offsetting the roughly 350,000 white Baltimoreans who departed.[83] By the end of the decade, dense pockets of impoverished southern whites had developed in North-Central Baltimore. Manning, like many older Baltimoreans, did not distinguish between the wartime migrants and the newer arrivals. "They," in his formulation, just "moved in on" different streets.[84] Public officials and citizens' groups pronounced "the new urbanite" a major problem but seemed reassured that most of these newcomers did not "mix with city folks."[85]

In the meantime, though, plenty of southerners were weaving themselves into the fabric of working-class Baltimore. During World War II Paul Burnett lived with his family in one of South Baltimore's "Kentucky Colony" apartments and worked for the Baltimore and Ohio Railroad. Ten years later he was a driver for the Diamond Cab Company on the north side of town.[86] Harry Isner, the shipyard worker who in 1941 told a congressional committee of his intention to stay in Baltimore if he could "get some money ahead," did just that. After relocating in Brooklyn, he finally moved southwest just over the city line into Baltimore County and started the Harold W. Isner Home Improvement Corporation in the early 1960s.[87]

Like the Isners, Carol Burke's family made the transition from migrant to suburbanite in one generation. Her parents came from West Virginia to work at the shipyards and moved into Brooklyn Homes in 1942. When the project was converted to low-income housing in 1956, the members of her family moved a few miles southwest to the working-class suburb of Brooklyn Park, where they were among friends from the old neighborhood.[88] The migrants as a group had little direct influence on Baltimore politics, although at least a few of them enjoyed its social aspects. The Linden Democratic Club thrived in an area populated by recent migrants until a police raid turned up poker chips, dice, and a soft drink machine full of ice-cold beer.[89]

Some southerners brought a strong religious tradition with them, helping to dilute the Catholic culture of blue-collar Baltimore. Southern Baptist churches multiplied during these years, and Pentecostal revivals became popular in South Baltimore.[90] Lighter aspects of southern culture also seeped into working-class Baltimore. In the early 1950s the entertainment section of the *Brooklyn News* was headed by the image of a lanky fiddler and a checked-shirted guitarist perched on a barrel.[91] Locals could frequent the Hillbilly Niteclub, or Ed's Musical Bar, which featured acts like the Tennessee Sweethearts.[92] It is revealing that the Brooklyn club, once named "The Walnut Grove" and later "The Coconut Grove," finally became "The Hillbilly Niteclub."[93] The "hillbilly" epithet, venomous during the war, was beginning to lose some of its sting. One Hampden man used the term to describe migrants who lived nearby over the objections of his southern-born wife. "She's a hillbilly, but she's a good one," he said.[94]

What divisions there were between whites were bridged by race. Almost without exception, white working-class Baltimoreans saw black wage earners and their families in racial terms rather than as working people. Blue-collar whites used "work"—especially willingness to work—as an important distinction between the two groups. Most blacks, said a Southwest Baltimore man who claimed to speak from experience on the job, "don't want to work really." Contrasting them to whites, he added, "I and maybe every other average white family workingman doesn't know what to do but work in order to live."[95]

The most concrete—and most consequential—boundaries that blue collarites maintained between themselves and black Baltimoreans were residential. People in Southeast Baltimore pointed with something like pride to a tiny black enclave in the midst of the city's largest all-white area. On the nine hundred block of Baylis Street in Canton, about ten black families had lived, the *Evening Sun* reported in 1971, "for as long as anyone could remember."[96] Apparently no one thought to ask the families themselves what their history was.[97] One resident called the Baylis Street blacks "almost invisible people."[98] What was important to locals was that they kept their homes "spotless," never socialized with whites, and never tried to expand from their tightly circumscribed area. Hampden residents pointed to a nearly identical instance, a single block where blacks—"always nice people"—lived. "They never came out," said a Hampden man, and "never gave nobody no trouble."[99]

The very proximity of blacks underscored and strengthened a white, blue-collar self-image. In the late 1940s and early 1950s, and longer for those whose neighborhoods were less threatened, this was a confident rather than a defensive strain of whiteness. In blue-collar Baltimore as a whole, as in Hampden and Canton, these seemingly impregnable racial boundaries attested to the strength of working-class institutions and the security of the neighborhood. The centrality of this constricted view of racial harmony reveals an important truth about working whites' social vision. Obligations were deeply felt, but working whites' sense of responsibility stopped when it came to outsiders—those not considered "working people."

Obligations and Limitations

Blue-collar obligations toward the community were underscored by changing residential patterns during the postwar period. Residents of even the most cohesive of Baltimore's working-class communities saw children, friends, and neighbors forsake the old neighborhood for homes in the suburbs. In the fall of 1954, two hundred residential subdivisions were being built in Baltimore County and fifty families were moving into new homes every day.[100] By 1956, 86 percent of the Baltimore metropolitan area's housing was being built in the suburbs, and by 1960, 48 percent of the population was suburban.[101] Working-class Baltimoreans tended to take two paths out of the city. South Baltimoreans went farther south into suburbs like Brooklyn Park and Glen Burnie in Anne Arundel County. People

TABLE 2. Population Change, 1940–1980

Year	Population	% Change	% Metro Population	City Rank
1940	859,100	+6.7	79	7
1950	949,708	+10.5	71	6
1960	939,024	−1.1	52	6
1970	905,787	−3.5	44	7
1980	786,775	−13.1	36	10

Sources: U.S. Bureau of the Census, *1940 Census of Population and Housing: Statistics for Census Tracts, Baltimore, Maryland* (Washington, D.C.: GPO, 1942), *Census Tract Statistics, Baltimore, Maryland, and Adjacent Area: Selected Population and Housing Characteristics, 1950* (Washington, D.C.: GPO, 1952), and *1960 Census of Population and Housing: Final Report PHC(1)-13, Census Tracts, Baltimore, Maryland* (Washington, D.C.: GPO, 1962); George H. Callcott, *Maryland and America, 1940–1980* (Baltimore: Johns Hopkins University Press, 1985), 82.

from Southeast Baltimore headed north along two corridors—Belair and Harford Roads—into the area that came to be called, simply, "out the road." Some of those who moved out the road settled within the city limits in communities like Hamilton, and others went into Baltimore County.

Historians and social scientists make much of the postwar suburban flight, including, in the words of Kenneth T. Jackson, "the weakened 'sense of community' which prevails in most metropolitan areas" created by "drive-in culture."[102] But an important countereffect has been little noticed: the exodus left a much deeper appreciation of neighborhood among those who stayed. Most invariably emphasized the convenience of living in the city, where church, stores, neighbors, and family were within walking distance.[103] City dwellers viewed the "suburbs" (as even communities out the road but within the Baltimore city limits came to be called) as sterile and unfriendly—not neighborhoods.[104] Those new suburbanites who regularly revisited the old neighborhood only reinforced this view.[105]

Once the exodus began, those who remained felt betrayed. "I get angry with the young people," said a Polish woman who lived across from Patterson Park. "They break away from everything. We should keep together." Unfortunately, recalled Canton resident Barbara Mikulski, "it became a status thing to get enough money to move 'out the road' to those three inches of grass."[106] The lawn became a point of symbolic contention between urban whites, who professed to prefer pavement over grass, and suburbanites, who seemed to get excessive gratification by having a yard. One city dweller made his opinion clear by defiantly paving his small front lawn entirely with green concrete.[107]

Although most Baltimoreans shopped within the city limits at mid-decade, new suburban stores tried hard to shake local loyalties to urban shopping districts. When the Ritchie Highway Shopping Center in Brooklyn Park opened in November 1955, Governor Theodore McKeldin presided over festivities replete with Dixieland and Hillbilly bands.[108] Older merchants tried to have it both ways, luring their urban customers to the suburbs by playing on customer loyalty. When Robinson's Department Store moved from Brooklyn to Glen Burnie, its proprietor assured South Baltimoreans that he was the "same Mr. Robinson" they had known for over twenty years.[109]

Suburban flight helped strengthen the resolve of urban whites to preserve and protect their neighborhoods, and, as Robinson well knew, the exodus emphasized that working-class citizenship held certain responsibilities to local institutions—stores, churches, and clubs—that had to be upheld. Myrtle DeVaughn, never entertained the idea of leaving. "I just felt an obligation to stay," she said.[110] For Catholics, the strongest sense of obligation was toward the parish. It was the church that most often brought new suburbanites back to the city, and working-class Baltimoreans were usually quicker to identify themselves by their parishes than by official neighborhood names. According to one priest, phrases like "I'm from St. Stanislaus" or "I'm from Sacred Heart" were commonly heard in Southeast Baltimore.[111] In Southeast Baltimore, St. Brigid's was the home parish to blue collarites of a variety of ethnic backgrounds and thrived on the high wages of steel and automobile workers. But in the mid-1960s the archdiocese lamented that St. Brigid's "has been little concerned with civic and social questions beyond its boundaries."[112] In Baltimore, as elsewhere, working-class whites built strong, cohesive—but exclusionary—communities behind what John McGreevy has dubbed "Parish Boundaries."[113]

Like the parish, other working-class institutions were essentially inward-looking. The site of Johnny Jones Tavern, a Highlandtown institution for generations, was not even identified. "We don't need no sign," the proprietor said in the early 1970s. "We all grew up in this neighborhood, been together since we were kids. Our parents hung around with each other. Every man at that bar," Johnny Jones explained, "is an old friend."[114] This bar may have been a commercial establishment, but it was more a private than a public institution.

All white working-class Baltimoreans observed one very important boundary: the row house threshold. It was an unspoken rule that the neighborhood was for neighbors, but except on special occasions, the house was for family.[115] This rule sheds light on the tradition of "stoop sitting." It was a way to socialize while keeping definite boundaries of public versus private intact. This worked well in warm weather, when neighbors found ample opportunity to talk. Otherwise, one woman said, when she saw her neighbor washing the front step—sparkling front steps were a sign of respectability in row-house Baltimore—she would go out and do the same. "That's the way we see one another in wintertime."[116]

In South and East Baltimore's row-house neighborhoods, few front yards intervened between the living room and the street; instead, painted window screens and displays presented a public face that blocked visual access.[117] In keeping the home off-limits to all but family and the closest friends, working-class whites showed no reluctance to impose boundaries. The house-to-house visiting of the middle-class suburbanite was out of the question in blue-collar Baltimore.[118]

Working-Class "Affluence"

In 1954 the *Enterprise* lauded the material benefits of the postwar boom. "Today every 6th person in the South and West Side has an auto; every 8th person has a television set, 3 persons to every radio. Two out of every three families have a telephone."[119] In this formulation, working-class affluence amounted to transportation (the car), communication (the phone), and above all entertainment. For the first time, Baltimore's working people had considerable time to be entertained and enough money to pay for it. But white working-class affluence was distinctly different from the more middle-class version that came to predominate in postwar American culture. Blue collarites engaged in different leisure activities, read different papers, and even experienced the coming of television in slightly different ways than did middle-class suburbanites.

The *Enterprise* article went on to note that "before World War I the Southside worker put in a 60-hour week. Today he averages from 35–40 hours." For Baltimore's full-time blue-collar workers (most of them men), the postwar increase in leisure time seems to have been as important as improvements in working conditions. In 1947 the average Baltimore wage earner bowled in a company league on Wednesday night (duckpins, a distinctly Baltimorean pursuit), shopped, and ate out with his wife on Thursdays. On Sunday, they took in a movie.[120] This, however, was before the

Scrubbing the white marble steps, a Baltimore tradition and social event.
(Photograph by A. Aubrey Bodine, Special Collections Department,
Maryland Historical Society, Baltimore)

working-class standard of living increased considerably. Expenses for the average Baltimorean rose 13 percent in the 1950s, but incomes grew 19 percent, and major purchases made with the balance transformed blue-collar leisure life.[121]

In the late 1940s a local firm began marketing Formstone, a combination of dyed concrete and crushed rock that could be applied over a brick front and sculpted to look like stone block. Around 1950 the innovation caught on among blue-collar homeowners, and before long some twenty-five imitators were changing the face of working-class Baltimore. "It looked like shantytown when it was red brick," one local recalled. "The man came and Formstoned it . . . made it look like Hollywood."[122] Blue-collar Baltimoreans—sometimes whole blocks chipped in—made substantial investments in Formstone: covering a typical working-class row house cost $325 (more than 10 percent of the average blue-collar annual wage) in the mid-1950s. There was good reason besides the aesthetic. Most East and South Baltimore row houses had been built with an inferior brick that required frequent painting. Formstone, on the other hand, to the distress of gentrifiers in later decades, was remarkably durable. And because not everyone could make the investment, as the face of the city changed in the decades after World War II, the presence of Formstone was often a good indicator of the health of a neighborhood. Middle-class detractors routinely scoffed at this blue-collar fondness for synthetic stone, dismissing it as a pernicious fad foisted on unwitting ethnics. But if their efforts to boost property values inspired snickers from middle-class esthetes, few working-class Baltimoreans cared.[123]

Capital improvements did not stop at the exterior. Another sign of working-class affluence was the "club cellar," something akin to the middle-class family room or den. The best of these had pine-paneled walls, linoleum tile floors, and a bar. On special occasions they became meeting places or entertainment centers for whole neighborhoods. More commonly, the club cellar was a place for the family to watch television, an innovation that, more than any other, transformed everyday blue-collar life.[124]

Baltimore's first TV station, Channel 2, owned by the *Sun* papers, began broadcasting in October 1947. Channel 11, owned by the Hearst Corporation, went on the air in March 1948, and Channel 13 started up in November. These three stations dominated Baltimore broadcasting for the next twenty-three years.[125] For a brief time—one study called it the "tavern phase"—television brought people together because bar owners invested in the still-expensive form of entertainment to guarantee a booming business, particularly when sporting events were on. In early 1948 Johnson's Tavern reminded locals that its set was "one of the best on the Southside." Whether viewed in the bar or at home, a Baltimore Colts game quickly came to mean "it will be television tonight."[126]

At Christmas 1949 in South Baltimore, a TV set could be had for a $25.00 down payment (still about 60 percent of the average blue-collar weekly wage) and $2.50 weekly.[127] By 1951, 70 percent of Baltimore's working-class families had sets. Antennas rose "as proudly, albeit incongruously, from tenement roofs as from the roofs of new row housing," the *Sun* reported.[128] In blue-collar Baltimore, where evening stoop sitting had been a valued social tradition, television truncated social life as people went into their houses to watch the same programs separately rather than talk outside. One Highlandtown woman's sister-in-law, on seeing her new set, guessed— accurately, as it turned out—"we won't socialize any more. We're going to watch the box."[129]

Television was the newest but hardly the only media voice to reach white working-class Baltimore. Right after World War II the city had five radio stations, all of them AM. By 1955 there were six more, including three FM stations. Most carried a predictable mix of music, sports, serials, and variety shows, although in 1952 WITH radio host Buddy Deane started dropping music by Fats Domino and other black artists in between pop and orchestral numbers.[130] Baltimore's famous morning and evening *Sun* were unpopular with working people. They were loyal readers of the local Hearst paper, particularly the ten-star edition which carried the latest sports news.[131] The *News-Post,* like other Hearst publications, hawked sensationalism and scandal and took a plain folk populist stance. It combined equal parts of shrill anticommunism and jingoistic patriotism. For forty years the paper sponsored Southeast Baltimore's annual "I Am an American Day Parade."[132]

In postwar working-class urban locales, the community press, almost always functioning primarily as a "shoppers guide," was a major link between working people and local institutions. Baltimore had fewer community papers per capita than did most industrial cities in the 1950s, possibly because more people shopped downtown than in many other places. The most influential, the *South Baltimore Enterprise,* claimed a readership of 250,000 at mid-decade. The *East Baltimore Guide* reached about 40,000 readers during the same period. Both of these papers voiced the concerns of the small businesses that advertised in them and reflected their anxiety over the power of large institutions, both local and federal. Both papers attracted a faithful working-class readership while appealing to honest small proprietors and industrious wage workers alike; both stood up for the concerns of their constituents when more mainstream publications did not.[133]

The favorite pastime of working-class Baltimoreans was gambling. Men were generally more faithful to the track than to other spectator sports, and it was not by chance that Baltimore's first TV broadcast was live coverage of the horse races at Pimlico Downs.[134] Bingo, well advertised in the community papers, was equally popular with women.[135] In 1956, the year the team signed Johnny Unitas as quarterback, working-class Baltimoreans began turning out to support the Colts in ever-increasing numbers. Lithuanians were proud that the trucker's son from Pennsylvania coal country shared their ethnic heritage. His appeal to working people lay partly in his background, partly in his "enduring and silent" demeanor, and partly in his humility—he was one of them. So much so in fact, that during his rookie year Unitas worked at Sparrows Point. By 1957, when he was named the National Football League's most valuable player, Unitas had moved up to become a salesman for a corrugated box company. But the erstwhile steelworker did not disappoint his blue-collar fans. Late the next year, when he led the Colts to victory over the Giants in New York after eight minutes and fifteen seconds of sudden death overtime, it touched off street celebrations back in Baltimore. Unitas was invited on the *Ed Sullivan Show,* but, characteristically, he demurred.[136]

Because of the baseball team's initially dismal performance, Baltimoreans displayed little enthusiasm for the Orioles after they came to town in 1954.[137] Nevertheless, the Orioles, like the Colts, helped tear down the walls separating middle class and white working-class Baltimore. Perhaps the barriers were never lower than in the fall of 1966, when, in what one journalist called "the single greatest high in Baltimore's post–World War II experience," the Orioles won the World Series.[138] But in sports, as in other fields, white and black remained on opposite sides of a social divide. Even before the Orioles arrived, the local NAACP protested the American League's grant of the franchise to Jim Crow Baltimore. The team fielded black players from the beginning, but few African Americans attended the games. Through the 1950s the ball club encouraged this, afraid that blacks might keep suburbanites and urban blue collarites from packing the stands.[139] The crowds at the football stadium were equally white. When black player Buddy Young started with the Colts in 1953, he tried to spur black attendance by having tickets sold at a gas station in Northwest Baltimore.[140]

Class and the Meaning of Work

In the 1950s some intellectuals predicted the rise of the "affluent" worker and declared the working class an obsolete notion, but postwar prosperity seemed to confuse observers and participants alike about the meaning of class.[141] In blue-collar Baltimore, observers looking for working-class people who considered themselves affluent or shared much in common with middle-class professionals would have been disappointed. But they would also have found few whose self-images were shaped primarily by the job.

In 1960, 30 percent of Baltimore's workforce was employed in manufacturing, but in white working-class neighborhoods the percentages ran higher. In South Baltimore, 35 percent of workers were in manufacturing; in Hampden, 39 percent. In Canton and Highlandtown, where the number of jobs exceeded the size of the labor force, 48 percent of workers were employed in manufacturing.[142] There was relatively little occupational diversity here; few urban professionals lived anywhere near blue-collar workers. Those who "belonged" either worked in a factory, were members of a family supported by a factory worker, or, like tavern owners and small business people, served factory workers. "I can never recall in the 1950s as a kid seeing somebody coming home from work with a tie and a suit on and a brief case," Highlandtown native George O'Connor recalled. "You had your choice whether you wanted to build cars or work on steel . . . but you were gonna do that."[143]

Industrial wage work was an important qualification for white working-class citizenship, but, as O'Connor suggested, it was considered less an opportunity than a birthright: it was something you were "gonna" do. Postwar economic growth did bring increased opportunities, but working whites recognized only limited ones. One steelworker remembered that when he was growing up in the fifties, only shipyard workers and steelworkers "had cars or movie money."[144] He saw landing a job at Bethlehem Steel as a step up in—but not out of—the working class.

Blue collarites most often used the church to pinpoint themselves within the community, but the workplace was a close second. And though professionals might describe the type of work they did, for blue collarites it sufficed to say where they worked. That working-class whites saw industrial work as a key component of their identity is not surprising in a period in which manufacturing work was plentiful and dependable. But this in itself was not enough. Blacks, who were certainly not considered members of the community, also worked in industry, though in smaller numbers.[145]

Although industrial unions were responsible for the high wages that were transforming working-class life, blue-collar Baltimoreans seemed to prize gains made in the quality of the workplace over wage increases. Josephine Purdy, who worked at National Enamel and Stamping in South Baltimore, believed that working people valued unions more for their ability "to improve conditions" than for "the amount of money they can get you."[146] At Crown Cork and Seal, workers struck for several months in 1953 to get union recognition. Before that, machine operator Daniel Griffin recalled, the company had provided "oyster roasts, bull roasts . . . and a week's pay for Christmas. But that don't help your family." For Griffin, wage increases helped, but more important was job security.[147]

Although they recognized that unions rather than employers had made workplaces tolerable and jobs secure, blue collarites still did not understand their allegiance as "working" people to be chiefly to the union, and many remained mistrustful of organized labor. The 1946 strike wave and the inflation that followed heightened skepticism about unions. The *South Baltimore Enterprise* reflected this attitude when it noted in 1946 that "we have always been a champion of labor, but at the same time we've been fair with capital, for both must work hand in glove for best results." This weekly, which claimed to represent a "workmen's community" or a "working-class community," nevertheless identified with citizens not described in terms of workplace.[148] "There is a lot of grumbling on the streets today by John Q. Citizen," the paper wrote, "who feels that the government should step in and quickly put an end to the strikes."[149] This is not entirely surprising. In general, community papers tended to avoid mentioning unions, which exemplified the large institutions that threatened the local power.[150] And, as could be expected, shoppers' newspapers saw their readers more as consumers than producers. But their positions were consistent, their readership was broad and loyal, and their message cannot be easily dismissed.

The strongest anti-union sentiment in working-class Baltimore could be found in Hampden, where the textile industry had long cultivated a tradition of paternalism.[151] One Hampden woman bitterly remembered crossing picket lines as her fellow workers tried to unionize the Berne Hat Company, where she was employed as a hand sewer in the 1940s and 1950s. When the company went out of business, she blamed the union.[152] Even some whose working years predated the New Deal retained strong anti-union sentiments. Ben Womer, a longtime Sparrows Point employee, saw little difference between the company and the union. "When the company had control they done as they damn pleased, and then when the CIO come in they pretty well controlled things. So the working man," said Womer, "he had things—well I don't know."[153] A retired ironworker similarly did not distinguish between businesses and labor. "Labor unions," he wrote Senator Millard Tydings in reference to the Taft-Hartley Act, "should be regulated and answerable at law the same as any other business."[154]

Strikes in the early days of industrial unionism could shape attitudes for a lifetime. Mildred Slechta, who clearly understood that "the union looks out for the employee's benefits, whereas management looks out for the management side," could not overcome her lifelong antipathy toward labor. "I might have been foolish," she said, "but I was so anti-union. I had seen in my own family what unions had done. . . . All I could think of were strikes." Her mother had been involved in the wartime Western Electric strike, and "it was a lean Christmas for us," she recalled.[155]

Working-class women like Mrs. Slechta, most of whom were responsible for making ends meet, had especially negative feelings about organized labor. One Steelworkers Union activist recalled that when strikes approached, most of the men were "ready to go out," but wives were more often concerned about lost income. "Some of the women understood, some of them supported their husbands," he said, "but I'd say the greatest majority was always thinking about what was being lost."[156] "It always seems to balance out to me," said Jeanette Browning, whose husband worked at American Can. "If you're on strike you never make that up, never. But if you get a raise, the majority of the merchandise and the food goes up."[157] John Ragin, who had worked at Glenn Martin before becoming a baker, shared this view. He blamed both management and labor for inflation. "If management paid the employee a fair share," Ragin reasoned, "he wouldn't have to support all these unions who take hundreds of millions a year." Fundamentally, his antipathy toward unions was deeply personal. He chose not to join the bakers' union because, he said, "you have to give part of your soul."[158]

Despite some blue-collar ambivalence about unions, resentment against "labor bosses" was consistent. Even staunch union advocates could condemn labor leaders.[159] "If unions are necessary," said *The Clipper,* a shoppers' newspaper, "it isn't because any union official thinks so. It's because the people you see every day think so." The paper went on to list working people—"the postman, the butcher, the truck driver, the teacher, the grocery clerk . . ."—and to wholeheartedly endorse their unions.[160] By recognizing specific occupations, this paper was able to champion working people and the work they did without conferring any legitimacy on their organizations or their leaders, a significant distinction.

Ambivalence turned to antipathy when it came to public sector unions.

By 1953 the issue of municipal unionism had been hotly contested in Baltimore for over a decade. Before World War II, public sector unionism was rare and, in most cases, even the feeblest attempts to disrupt city services were vigilantly suppressed.[161] The Teamsters chartered Baltimore's first city union in 1941, and although city leaders doubted whether the step was legal, wartime labor shortages gave them little choice.[162] The union helped boost the wages of city laborers—most of them sanitation workers—from $0.45 an hour in 1941 to more than $1.22 an hour by late 1952. At the end of December 1956, however, the municipal workers voted to strike for a 50-cent hourly increase. "These fellows have read about the steel and coal settlements," a union representative wrote, "and a loaf of bread costs them as much as it does anyone else."[163]

The municipal workers may have felt their union and their right to strike to be as legitimate as those in the private sector, but city leaders did not agree. "What the union really threatens," said Mayor D'Alesandro, "is a strike against the public." D'Alesandro deftly separated questions about the legitimacy of unions from the issue of a public strike. More explicitly than The Clipper had done five years earlier, he differentiated between city employees "of loyalty and responsibility" and "irresponsible" union leaders who committed their members to "reckless action" for their own benefit.[164]

The union went on strike, and the mayor withdrew recognition; as garbage began to pile up around the city, residents flooded the mayor's office with letters. Some working people expressed solidarity with the garbage men, but most did not.[165] One striker's wife essentially accepted the mayor's characterization of the union leaders but went on to suggest that the city was "playing the employees for a sucker."[166] A Hampden woman placed the blame squarely on the union. "While there may have been merit on the sides of both city and strikers there was none on the side of the union," she wrote.[167] Municipal unions did not have the legitimacy of those in the private sector because, as opponents invariably pointed out, strikes threatened the city as a whole. Equally important, it was the "taxpayer" who footed the bill.[168]

In the 1940s and 1950s the identity of "taxpayer" came to rival that of "producer" among blue collarites for the first time. Federal income taxes first became a working-class concern during World War II.[169] Working people were even more concerned about ever-rising city and state taxes. One of the issues that had helped defeat Governor Lane in his 1950 reelection bid was his imposition of a state sales tax. Before the election, Sixth District politician Joseph Wyatt warned Lane that the sales tax was "a sore spot in

South Baltimore."[170] Earlier in the year residents of South Baltimore had launched a petition drive to stop the Board of Estimates from reassessing property there.[171] Councilman Joseph Mach, a shipyard worker turned bar owner who represented Czechs in Baltimore's Second District in the 1950s and 1960s, established his political career by fighting reassessment.[172]

Increases in taxes on industry appeared to have a sinister secondary effect on blue collarites. After the city repealed a tax exemption for manufacturers in 1957, industrial employment began to slip noticeably for the first time.[173] Particularly hard-hit was the shipbuilding industry, which lost market share to shipyards overseas.[174] In the county, the Martin Company (formerly Glenn Martin), dependent on a dwindling share of defense contracts, also went through periodic layoffs before giving up aircraft production to focus on aerospace technology in the early 1960s.[175] In 1957 South Baltimore's Linen Thread Company joined National Enamel and Stamping, which had left two years earlier, in moving south.[176] South Baltimoreans who chose not to follow Linen Thread to Alabama expressed confusion. "I have no idea what I'm going to do," said a forty-seven-year-old employee, "I've only had two jobs in my life."[177]

Through the 1960s, though, few white working-class Baltimoreans were forced to ask these kinds of questions. The continued expansion of large employers like Bethlehem Steel and Western Electric, the diversity of the city's manufacturing base, and the fact that about 20 percent of Baltimore jobs were supported by defense spending kept employment relatively stable.[178] Wage work, the common denominator, remained plentiful. At the same time, distinctions between white work and black work continued to be well defined. In most of the city's industries, although proportions of blacks employed had risen since World War II, African Americans remained overrepresented in the dirtiest, least desirable jobs.[179] In 1960, 68 percent of all unskilled workers residing in Baltimore were black, while 92 percent of skilled residents were white.[180]

Industrial workers, however, seldom described themselves as "working-class." Blue-collar whites' use of the term "class" is problematic but informative. "Working-class" was sometimes used in self-description when money was involved. An *Enterprise* columnist wrote that "the southside is a working class society with an average take home pay of $40 per week."[181] Descriptions that hinged on income easily sidestepped the notion of class, though. The *East Baltimore Guide* offered the following characterization: "East Baltimore is comprised mostly of working people, men and women who make their 'bread and butter' right here in our own community."[182]

Working whites used aspiration as much as income to distinguish themselves from others. "People who want bigger homes and all that sort of
thing, they don't want to live in Highlandtown," said one man. "That's a
different class. Not ours."[183]

Uses of the terms "working" and "middle" depended on context and
utility. During the wartime debate over the Herring Run housing project,
Lutheran minister Luke Schmucker, previously critical of white migrant
workers, elevated them to the status of "middle class defense workers"
when contrasting them with black migrants.[184] One second-generation
Polish woman from Highlandtown used the terms together but linked them
to consumptive ability. She described her community as containing "working people and some middle class." Working people, she explained, could
"never go out and travel and buy cars and all." For her, ability to con-
sume remained secondary to ambition as an important middle-class trait,
although in Highlandtown "everybody was ambitious." But in a notable
contrast to the way a neighbor described "people who want bigger homes,"
her definition of ambition had a collective connotation. She seemed to suggest that Highlandtown's middle class had risen as a group—not individu-
ally. "I would say there were working people who became middle class as
the years went by. After so many years as times have improved and all."[185]
Others may have believed that postwar affluence had boosted their status.
For several years beginning in 1948, the *South Baltimore Enterprise* ran a
homegrown cartoon strip called "Southside Antics." The hero of the strip,
who invariably got in trouble—usually at home, sometimes in the neighborhood, but seldom at work—was called "Mr. Middle."[186]

Clearly, as David Halle has suggested in his important study of workers
in the 1970s, blue collarites tended to see themselves differently at home
and at work. Ira Katznelson has gone further to describe a "split consciousness of work and community" among working people. The greater mistrust
of unions among women, who were more firmly ensconced in the neighborhood than men, bears this out. So does the increasing interchangeability
of the terms "middle class" and "working class" in the years when home
ownership and taxpayer status both gained ground. But blue-collar whites
most often described themselves as "working" people, although they understood the term in a cultural rather than an economic sense. "Working" applied to both the job and the neighborhood; therefore, white working-class
consciousness can be understood as bridging both work and community.[187]
In the postwar years, working whites saw politics as affecting the community much more than the workplace. And in contrast to the shop floor,

where the fruit of their labor still belonged to the boss, the neighborhood was, at least to a degree, *"workers'* paradise."

The 1950s were confident times, and the same optimism that boosted the middle-class suburban dream also gave rise to blue-collar Babbitry of a sort. But white working-class Baltimoreans and their counterparts elsewhere undoubtedly took the rhetoric of a workers' paradise and "making your own heaven" with a grain of salt. Although the years from 1945 to 1965 hardly marked a blue-collar "golden age," they were relatively good years. And just as the more educated and the less rooted put their hopes in ideas, working people invest a great deal in the institutions of daily life: the neighborhood became a repository of their hopes and dreams. For a time, policymakers, purveyors of culture, and whims of fate seemed to harken to white working-class concerns. But the moment was fleeting, and, as Gerald Suttles has observed, when the white working-class community came under threat, it was "defended according to what it might become rather than for what it is or has been."[188]

As social and economic change relentlessly transformed the urban landscape, efforts at community building from within and the emphasis on obligations that went with it steadily gave way to community preservation— a struggle that forced whites into defensive appeals to their rights. As blue collarites searched for ways to enunciate their concerns and to reshape public policy, they turned to an existing race-based language of protest that affirmed community institutions, accentuated neighborhood boundaries, and encompassed the crosscutting identities of religion, ethnicity, and sex in one breath. The political implications of that decision would be enormous.

CHAPTER 4

The Right to Live in the Manner We Choose

In late February 1945 the Fulton Improvement Association, representing working- and middle-class home owners on the city's near west side, ran a classified advertisement in the *Baltimore Sun*. It was a warning "to real estate dealers, speculators, property owners and their agents, building and loan associations—and all others concerned." We are "strongly organized," the notice stated, "and determined to resist by all legal, moral and persuasive means" any efforts to "force us to move from our homes."[1] This was the opening salvo in a long battle between happily rooted whites and blacks who were finally breaking out of inner-city ghettos. This dispute over territory symbolized a larger emerging conflict between the rights of blacks to live and work on equal terms with whites and the rights of whites to preserve the racial exclusivity that was a foundation of blue-collar life. "The Right to Live in the Manner We Choose are the very things for which our boys are fighting," the notice concluded.

This "right" to enforce existing community boundaries, and therefore white exclusivity, was the premise of white working-class protest for two decades after World War II. These were the early years of what has been called the "rights revolution," when Americans of all kinds began staking absolute claims to entitlements based on social, cultural, and, less often, economic identities. The civil rights movement did the most to launch this new era of what Mary Ann Glendon has called "rights talk," but the urban blue collarites who were expected to compensate for racial inequities in their neighborhoods and schools were remarkably quick to counter with their own rights-based claims, claims that ultimately breached the public consciousness under the rubric of "white backlash."[2] The conception of rights held by white working-class people during these years drew in equal part from southern segregationism and the traditional white working-class

83

racism that underlay countless instances of conflict in northern industrial cities in the first half of the twentieth century: incidents ranging from adolescent skirmishes to full-scale race riots.[3]

But even then, in clashes over housing there was more going on than sheer race hatred. Sometimes designated "neighborhood rights," "home owners rights," or in the case of the Fulton Avenue residents "The Right to Live in the Manner We Choose," these claims were almost always defended, and often enunciated, as "white rights."[4] Local politicians, community leaders, and even, as in the case at Fulton Avenue, local clergy offered their wholehearted support to these efforts. Yet, because blue-collar Baltimoreans argued—often explicitly—in racial terms, liberal political leaders justly intent on safeguarding the emerging civil rights revolution could easily dismiss their arguments on the grounds of racism.

In the 1950s social relationships between Baltimore's blacks and whites were transformed. At the beginning of the decade, the structure of Jim Crow remained largely intact. By 1960 most of what were understood to be "public" spaces were integrated: the majority of hotels and restaurants were open to blacks. The desegregation of schools and neighborhoods, institutions that working-class whites considered to be community-based and in a sense more private than public, was more difficult. As Paul Kleppner has pointed out in his study of Chicago, on some matters working-class whites were willing—if reluctantly—to compromise. But "on housing and schools, they would fight to the bitter end."[5]

Among the traumas that shaped white working-class politics and culture in the 1950s, school desegregation was most acute, a thrust from on high that seemed to overturn a key white working-class institution overnight. But the defining issue of the decade and most persistent headache was the problem of housing for blacks. The gradual—and in some cases abrupt—transition of whole sections of the city from white to black also symbolized a larger process: the transformation of Baltimore from a city accepting of a racially exclusive white working-class community to a city whose political, social, and cultural climate seemed overtly hostile.

The anger, fear, and frustration touched off by residential transition in the 1950s is not reducible to a single cause. Neither racism nor economic self-interest is an adequate explanation. Intermixed with the bald claims to racial prerogatives were justifiable concerns over property values. There were good reasons why the house was an all-powerful symbol for the white working class and why it was so passionately defended. It was a working-class family's most valuable possession, usually held more tenuously than the property of the middle class. Working people had usually made deep sacrifices and foreclosed a host of other opportunities to make the investment. Its loss represented the squandering of all those other possibilities, as well as the forfeiture of an investment.[6] Blue-collar home owners, therefore, were reaching toward a critique that defined the problem in cultural terms—as a broadly based threat to a way of life. Well into the 1960s, Baltimoreans of all kinds—politicians, property owners, and working whites—sought to give voice to this host of new concerns through a language of white rights—one that would ultimately prove inaccurate and insufficient.

Fulton Avenue Breakthrough

Until 1945, Fulton Avenue was the western boundary of black settlement in Baltimore. Blacks lived along the east side of the street, and whites occupied the row houses along the west side. Both groups "understood" that this line would not be challenged. Black settlement was further contained to the north by Druid Hill Park and to the south by Baltimore Street. The upheavals of World War II forced a rupture in the Fulton Avenue line. In late 1944 and early 1945 African Americans began moving across the street, prompting the Fulton Improvement Association to take its stand with a notice in the *Sun*. Nevertheless, by March 1945 about fifty homes had changed hands and "for sale" signs were posted all along the west side of Fulton Avenue.[7]

The members of the Fulton Improvement Association drew much psychological and material sustenance from organized religion. They held their first meetings at St. Martin's Catholic Church and proudly claimed the support of two Baptist churches, one Methodist church, and one United Brethren church as well. "Churches Lead Hate Crusade" proclaimed the headline in the *Baltimore Afro-American.* Despite this characterization, the Fulton Improvement Association adamantly denied racist motivations. The group's published "warning" scrupulously avoided any mention of race, reserving its venom for realtors and "all others concerned." Maurice Sturm, the leader of the group, claimed that the advertisement was "not directed against colored citizens." Instead, he claimed, his group objected to "the tactics which these real estate dealers are using to give the impression that we are going to have colored neighbors."[8]

The ministers involved adopted a pragmatic view: since whites always fled from areas of black settlement, keeping their parishes intact meant keeping their neighborhoods white. Father Louis O'Donovan of St. Martin's said that "we just don't want our people crowded out." Another minister pointed to precedent: "The whites will move out. They have done this in other neighborhoods and they will do it here." The ministers, like Sturm, denied that their dispute was with black citizens. One even claimed that blacks were "being used by these real estate dealers for sinister purposes." While leaders took the rhetorical high road, a few residents used time-tested methods of harassment on new black home owners, breaking windows and provoking the "constant supervision of police."[9] Others threatened the Jewish realtors making the Fulton Avenue sales.[10]

As their list of allies attests, the white activists of Fulton Avenue were hardly extremists and their mission should not be dismissed as the quixotic. Only thirty years earlier, an uncannily similar effort was remarkably effective, establishing a bulwark of legal segregation that survived until World War I. In Jim Crow Baltimore the principle of white exclusivity went largely unquestioned, but in the post–New Deal legal and political atmosphere it could no longer be enforced. City leaders expressed sympathy for white residents but could offer no solution. Only the *Afro-American* charged the Fulton Avenue whites with racism. The president of the Baltimore Real Estate Board asserted that "it would be futile to argue that there should be no prejudice against the movement of colored people into areas occupied by white people."[11] Thomas Waxter, head of a mayoral commission on housing, found that although blacks were not at fault, "white residents cannot be blamed" for their opposition, either. The real culprits, Waxter said, were realtors, though "nothing legally can be done about it."[12]

It was this reality—that white exclusivity could not be legally protected—that most angered working whites. It seemed perverse that city leaders could not safeguard what they considered to be a cornerstone of urban life. In a letter to Mayor Theodore McKeldin, one city employee wondered why, since Jews were "unofficially" excluded from certain parts of the city, blacks could not be as well. "It couldn't be that you are thinking about election next year," he intimated, reminding the Republican mayor that Democrats like himself had put him in office.[13] Another woman asked McKeldin to "please try and do something" to stop realtors from representing her area as a "colored neighborhood, *because it isn't so.*"[14]

Despite some initial resistance, it took only a few sales to convince Fulton Avenue whites to abandon the neighborhood, leaving a buffer zone of empty houses. One resident recalled that "whites would evacuate a block or two blocks, and black people would move in. The evacuation would take place first."[15] By July 1945 there were hundreds of properties available to blacks in the formerly white area. With neighborhood efforts failing, the

Fulton Improvement Association tried to put pressure on city hall.[16] On 26 July Maurice Sturm, 3 city councilmen, and 350 residents met with the mayor. "All the white people want is to be left alone. We don't want to move into the Negro area and we don't want them to move into ours," said Councilman John Luber, who lived near Fulton Avenue. Publicly, McKeldin displayed sympathy with white concerns but claimed that there was nothing he could do.[17] Privately, however, the mayor urged the white protesters to "outgrow their prejudice."[18] "We expected some sort of action and we got nothing," said Luber after the meeting.[19]

What civil rights leaders referred to as the "Fulton Avenue Breakthrough" set the pattern for more than a decade of residential turnover. The mechanism that Fulton Avenue residents called "block-breaking"—realtors' use of racial fear to convince whites to sell cheaply—had been established, and on Fulton Avenue, as elsewhere, whites were unable to even consider the possibility of residential integration.

Perceptions of politics and politicians were inalterably shaped by experiences like this. Although they welcomed anyone offering to champion white against black interests, on Fulton Avenue, as elsewhere, realtors —usually Jewish—were also seen as key perpetrators. Blacks, therefore, could be depicted to some extent as victims, lending credence to whites' arguments that the issue was one of economic power more than racial exclusion. This made matters all the more striking when white protests fell on deaf ears. Few could believe that their politicians were really unable to restrain the realtors. Instead, working- and middle-class whites began to think that they were listening to other voices.

Neighborhood transition proceeded on a relatively small scale through the 1940s and into the mid-1950s. Nevertheless, 1950, in Edward Orser's estimation, "marked a watershed in the racial geography of the west side." Up to that time, housing west of the Fulton Avenue line was rarely listed according to race. Afterward, advertisements for "colored homes" became commonplace: a formerly white section of the city was now understood to be black.[20] White frustration, meanwhile, grew more acute. In 1951 one resident, speaking for "many people in the same boat I am," wrote Mayor D'Alesandro: "If you don't do something about these negroes breaking block after block in West Baltimore, I'm afraid we will have to take things into our own hands."[21] As this letter indicates, although realtors were vilified, blacks remained an easy target, especially among those inclined to "take things into our own hands." As during the war, it was easy—too easy—to blame southern migrants for racial trouble.

On Friday, 11 October 1947, two black families began moving into apart-

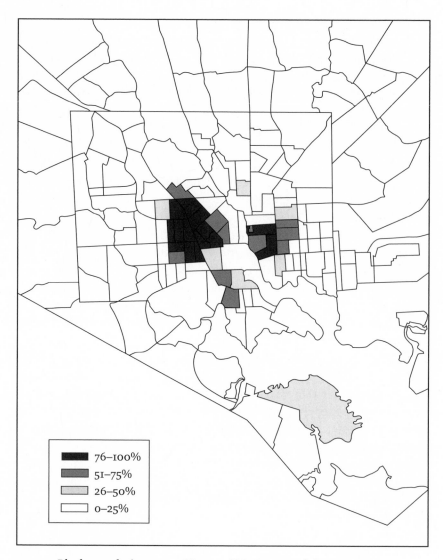

MAP 4. Black population, 1940 (*Source:* U.S. Bureau of the Census,
*1940 Census of Population and Housing: Statistics for Census Tracts,
Baltimore, Maryland* [Washington, D.C.: GPO, 1942].)

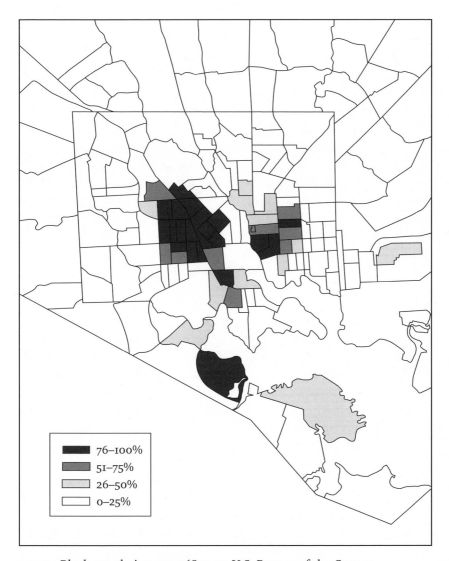

MAP 5. Black population, 1950 (*Source:* U.S. Bureau of the Census,
*1950 Census of Population and Housing: Statistics for Census Tracts,
Baltimore, Maryland* [Washington, D.C.: GPO, 1952].)

ments on Fayette Street, located in an all-white neighborhood near the southern boundary of the expanding area of black settlement. As twenty-seven-year-old Carnell Simmons hauled furniture inside, southern whites who lived in the area stood by uneasily. Others perched in windowsills above. The *Afro-American* caricatured the residents as characters from the Erskine Caldwell novel *Tobacco Road*. According to the Baltimore police, these residents "had caused quite some trouble among themselves during recent years," and the *Afro-American* reporter considered the "strains of hillbilly music" emanating from local taverns an ominous sign.[22]

At around nine o'clock that night the new residents heard a shot and the sound of shattering glass. When another window was broken two hours later, Simmons and his family gathered in one room. At three in the morning they discovered that a fire had been set in the vestibule of the house and saw a white man standing beyond it. Simmons's wife pushed her way out the door and beyond the intruder. But when another resident tried repeatedly to get through, the white man pushed him back, slamming the front door. Simmons fired three times through the door and sent a bullet through the forehead of William Mayo, a forty-nine-year-old seaman from Quincy, Massachusetts. When police arrived, they arrested all the occupants of the house and charged Simmons with Mayo's murder.[23] Simmons was a World War II veteran, and he claimed, in words made famous in Detroit's Ossian Sweet case twenty-two years earlier, that "a man's home is his castle." He was released on bail in a few days. Within two weeks a Baltimore judge agreed that Simmons had only "exercised the rights of a man to protect his home."[24]

In the late 1940s white and black Baltimoreans maintained two irreconcilable versions of the rights that wartime sacrifice had conferred on them: the right to exclude and the right to be included. In other industrial cities this conflict appeared for a time to be irrepressible. In Chicago, mobs of working-class whites mobilized repeatedly to oppose black housing initiatives in so-called white neighborhoods, creating seven major housing disturbances and dozens of smaller ones in the years from 1946 to 1957.[25] In Detroit, there were more than two hundred separate incidents during roughly the same period.[26]

Baltimore escaped this level of conflict because through most of this period black incursions took place in middle-class Jewish neighborhoods. The most significant instance in which blacks displaced working whites occurred in a neighborhood of relatively recent blue-collar settlement. Moreover, the balance of power was less lopsided in Baltimore—a powerful black leadership drew support from a black community much larger than that of other industrial cities. Just as the Fulton Avenue residents hoped to preserve their neighborhood for their sons returning from war, so the *Afro-American* based Simmons's right to protect his new home on his distinguished service in the Pacific theater. Few whites would have approved of Mayo's means, but most would have agreed with his ends. In 1947, however, and to a growing degree throughout the 1950s, civil rights leaders had the law on their side.

Among those present at the dismissal of the Simmons case were the NAACP's Lillie Jackson and Joseph Neal, a United Steelworkers Union and Urban League official. Wartime experience convinced civil rights leaders like these that their best hope for change was through politics. The resulting efforts doubled Baltimore's black voter registration from 1940 to 1952. When liberal Republican Theodore McKeldin became governor in 1950, he continued to support civil rights and worked with the NAACP and Urban League to push for expanded opportunities for blacks.[27] Early in the decade some key southern segregationist traditions crumbled after only limited resistance from white rights advocates. Restaurants at Baltimore's railroad and bus stations were opened to blacks. Lunch counters at three large department stores were integrated, as were two of Baltimore's largest theaters. Some public parks and golf courses were integrated, and large departments stores had dropped racial bars from all but certain womens' wear departments.[28] Nevertheless, half of the city's hospitals remained off-limits to blacks, and those that were not discriminated. Segregation still remained at most parks and beaches.[29]

Despite these gains, black Baltimore suffered economic and social hardships aplenty early in the decade. In 1950, after a postwar dip, Baltimore's population hit 950,000. The black proportion increased modestly at first to 24 percent in 1950—up 4 percent in ten years. Then it rose another 3 percent during the next five years.[30] From 1950 to 1955, 32,000 additional blacks crowded into the city, and as the population rose, average income levels fell.[31] Not surprisingly, black poverty rates shot up: by 1955 fully three-fourths of black housing was located in recognized "blight" areas.[32] Among the hardest-hit black institutions were the schools. For years, the Baltimore City School Board had operated dual systems. By the early 1950s the black schools were predictably crowded and deteriorating. To relieve overcrowding the board implemented shift classes, and in 1950, 84 percent of students who attended them were black.[33]

The transition of west side neighborhoods from white to black brought some initial sustained protest and a few scattered acts of violence. But a predictable pattern of isolated protest followed by flight ensued. What finally roused whites into sustained opposition was an effort to improve schooling initiated nationally by Thurgood Marshall, a veteran of the Baltimore NAACP, who in 1954 represented the NAACP Legal Defense Fund before the Supreme Court.

"We Want Our Rights"

" 'The newspapers is all liars,' declaimed the tall mountain woman in red. 'Ain't there nobody gonna give decent white folks a break?' " In 1954 James Rorty covered the integration of Baltimore's schools for the journal *Commentary*. In early October, at a racetrack rally in Glen Burnie, about five miles south of Baltimore, Rorty found both southern and ethnic blue-collar workers united to keep the schools and the neighborhoods they shared white.[34] The mountain woman's words, however, expressed discontent about more than desegregation. By the time of the rally the "best elements" of the city had turned against the residents of South Baltimore.[35] Like the mountain woman in red, many white working-class Baltimoreans were beginning to see elite institutions like the newspapers as acting counter to their interests. But although a broader understanding of their rights was developing, working whites continued to use racial arguments rooted in the late-nineteenth-century South.

Baltimore's *Sun* had become a firm civil rights supporter by the 1950s. Nevertheless, when the Supreme Court found separate but equal schools unconstitutional in the *Brown v. Board of Education* decision on 17 May 1954, it gave the initiative only "cautious approval."[36] But Superintendent of Schools John H. Fischer was determined to make Baltimore the first major city in the nation to act in the wake of the decision. Fischer had earlier abolished districting, allowing Baltimore children to attend any school they desired, although distinctions between white and black schools remained. In the wake of the *Brown* decision, Fischer removed this last bar and allowed blacks to enter white schools; in the fall of 1954 a few of them did.[37] Where large numbers of students were black, the transition was relatively peaceful. It was in South Baltimore, where black percentages were small and the color line was closely watched, that the strongest protest arose.[38]

In the fall of 1954, residents of Pigtown began meeting to discuss integration. The Southwest Baltimore neighborhood, located just south of the 1947 Fayette Street incident, had a history of turbulent race relations. Only five years earlier a white teenager had fatally stabbed a black teenager in Pigtown's Carroll Park during a gang fight.[39] Now, twelve black kindergartners had entered the local elementary school, which had a total enrollment of 558.[40]

Pigtown residents had long bristled under the condescension of outsiders. In 1898 uptown opponents had labeled local politician Frank Wachter a "Pigtown bumpkin." Wachter turned the slur into a rallying cry, and Southwest Baltimore elected him to Congress, where he enthusiastically lashed out against upper-class "silk stocking advocates."[41] Fifty years later Pigtown residents had no such champion, and when they pressed their case against integration with Superintendent Fischer, they were rebuffed.[42]

On Thursday, 30 September 1954, about thirty women started picketing the school. Wilma Longmire, a Tennessee native, had two sons in the elementary school and a daughter in junior high. She was "set off" by her daughter's having showered with a black girl at school. "We just started picketing and didn't care what would happen to us. It was that strong," she recalled.[43] The protesters' signs declared that "segregation is our heritage" and "we want equal but segregated schools."[44] A few announced that "we want our rights."[45]

On Friday morning, picketing continued in Pigtown and spread to other elementary schools, but the focus of city attention shifted to South Baltimore's Southern High School, where 39 black students—2 percent of the student body—had enrolled. Southern was not the first Baltimore high school to be integrated. In 1952 the school board had admitted 15 advanced black high school students to Baltimore Polytechnic with few repercussions.[46] But Southern, unlike Poly, was considered a neighborhood school, and to locals that made a big difference.[47] That morning, about 500 Southern High students formed a picket line, adults joined in, and the crowd swelled to around 2,000.[48] Fistfights broke out, the crowd nearly overturned a squad car, and police made 6 arrests.[49]

Over the weekend, Baltimore's civic, religious, and social welfare groups, described by one journalist as "the best elements in the whole community," convened and issued statements to the *Sun*.[50] Church leaders called it "good Americanism" to conform to the Supreme Court decision and dubbed the protests "fodder for the propaganda machine of communism." A Johns Hopkins psychiatrist pronounced the picketers not "sincerely interested in the welfare of children, including their own."[51] The *Sun* poked fun at the misspelling and crude lettering that characterized many of the protesters' placards. More insulting to the participants were hints that the protesters

Women and children protest at the elementary school in Pigtown,
1 October 1954. (Courtesy of the *Baltimore News-American* Photograph
Collection, Special Collections, University of Maryland, College Park,
Libraries)

were mere pawns of outside agents. In the *Enterprise,* which fiercely defended the protesters, a South Baltimore construction worker rejected the
idea. The people were "biding their time until some organized objection
could be raised," he countered.[52]

Southern High School principal John Schwatka made a televised plea:
"Look into your hearts, you southerners . . . prevent another day of fear in
our community."[53] Nevertheless, the protest did last another day. Charles
Luthardt, a carpenter with two sons at the high school, harangued the
crowd around Southern; he was arrested and put on probation. Meanwhile, picketing continued at eleven other schools across the city. Among
these was Gwynns Falls Junior High, situated in the white- and blue-collar
Edmondson Village neighborhood just across a valley from the far western
edge of recent black settlement.[54] There, as at Pigtown, the picketers were
predominantly female. One student remembered local women as "fearful."
"The biggest fear they had was their children would pick up some of the
traits they saw in the black community," she said.[55]

The next day, after the police department announced a "get tough" policy, pickets scattered.[56] The school protests were quashed, but at Ritchie Raceway in Glen Burnie that night, the seven hundred people who had gathered to hear Luthardt and Bryant Bowles of the National Association for the Advancement of White People were not contrite.[57] Some protesters admitted having "no stomach" for the extremism expressed by Bowles and Luthardt. But nor did they agree with civic leaders that they were un-American, aiding communists, or uninterested in the welfare of their children.[58]

Despite the condescension of city leaders, the South Baltimore protesters were not merely irrationally lashing out: they had concrete reasons for fearing integration. As in Pigtown, the neighborhoods surrounding the eight other South Baltimore elementary schools picketed that week were blue collar. The majority of residents were home owners and were much less likely to move than those in other areas of the city. Most important, seven of the nine schools were situated in, or adjacent to, "blighted" areas—the common term in the 1950s for areas that were mostly black and badly deteriorating.[59] The threat to their neighborhoods was real, and it involved more than just integration.

The street protests were a last resort rather than a sudden impulse; one citizens group had already lodged a court challenge, and a South Baltimore councilman pressed the matter at city hall.[60] But they marched out of hope rather than out of desperation. On 30 September the Milford, Delaware, School Board canceled its integration plan following organized protests led by Bowles.[61] Baltimoreans considered it reasonable to try to duplicate his feat.

School integration gave rise to a number of white supremacist, anti-integration organizations. The largest of these, the Maryland Petition Committee, was strongest in the counties to the north and south of the city, although it had a few adherents in Baltimore, most notably the vehemently racist attorney George Washington Williams. Williams was also a member of the Baltimore Association for States Rights, which flourished for a few years at mid-decade. Nick Puslaskie, a blue-collar worker and the lone male participant in the first morning of picketing in Pigtown, became a charter member of the Baltimore Association for States Rights. The association's first director was Wilma Longmire, the Tennessee-born mother of three. Other charter members included a maintenance man and a truck driver.[62] Both groups were dormant by 1958, but in the 1960s the Maryland Petition Committee reemerged as the state's most powerful anti-integrationist organization, attracting both moderate and extreme white supremacists.

Both groups linked traditional states rights arguments with fervent anti-communist rhetoric.[63]

Baltimore's most ubiquitous and militant white supremacist for the next two decades emerged from the Southern High School protests. Forty-six-year-old Charles Luthardt, a former cab driver and a member of the all-white Baltimore local of the United Brotherhood of Carpenters, opened a short-lived Maryland chapter of the National Association for the Advancement of White People in a Locust Point row house in November 1954.[64] By 1962 he had reemerged with a group called the Fighting American Nationalists, which combined anti-Semitism, white supremacy, and anticommunist doctrines.[65] Luthardt alone among Baltimore's white rights activists harbored personal political ambitions. He ran in the 1960 and 1966 Democratic gubernatorial primaries, garnering 0.9 percent of the Baltimore vote on his first attempt and taking 1.7 percent on the second try.[66] In Baltimore, extremists like Luthardt were usually on the scene when racial conflict arose, although rarely did they carry much influence among other whites. Furman Templeton of the Baltimore Urban League claimed on one occasion that rabid racists like George Washington Williams actually did "a great deal to help our cause."[67] Arnold Hirsch has noted a similar effect in Chicago, where the most virulently racist group was "notable only for its weakness."[68]

Templeton's assessment confirms that the time when direct action could stem black advances was passing. Up to the 1940s, although city ordinances enforced racial exclusion, blue collarites relied primarily on harassment and intimidation to keep their neighborhoods white. School integration was not even thought possible. By 1954, however, with Baltimore's establishment firmly behind civil rights and desegregation the law of the land, new methods of keeping blue-collar neighborhoods white were in order. The white working people of South Baltimore—all "southerners" to Principal Schwatka—displayed to James Rorty "a frustrated and confused class-consciousness" that night at the raceway.[69] Although resentment of blacks and anger at certain whites—Jewish realtors and indifferent politicians—remained intertwined, the growth of black rights consciousness was leading whites toward a stronger conception of working-class rights, although one still enunciated in terms of whiteness. In response, a few politicians took up white supremacist politics, which was experiencing a rebirth in the South, and adapted it to the industrial city. At the polls, a month after the school protests ended, blue-collar Baltimoreans voted as a class, but with no confusion.

Old-Time Racial Politics

"You Can Vote, Your Children Can't."[70] This and similar statements adorned South Baltimore placards in late September and early October 1954. George Della must have been paying attention. That fall marked what one journalist called Maryland's "first election in modern times to have racial segregation as an open issue."[71] In early October H. C. "Curley" Byrd, an Eastern Shoreman and Democratic candidate for governor, endorsed the doctrine of "separate but equal" in his race against incumbent Theodore McKeldin.[72] On 22 October state senator Della, whose family had been in Baltimore politics since the 1880s, urged his South Baltimore constituents to vote Democrat so that "we may come back and have white supremacy again in our schools."[73] These attempts to tear the Democratic Party away from its nominal pro-civil rights moorings put labor in a difficult position. The state CIO demanded a private meeting with Byrd, announced its dismay, and then stood by the Democrat. Della's position was all too clear, and the CIO withdrew its support.[74]

McKeldin won by sweeping the black wards and Baltimore's Jewish and upper-middle-class Protestant districts.[75] But blue-collar Baltimore embraced Byrd's segregationist message. Wards 1, 23, and 24 gave Byrd 70 percent of their vote, and McKeldin lost all thirteen South and East Baltimore wards where, four years earlier, he had won eleven. South Baltimore's precincts gave Byrd margins of more than 70 percent. Even along Eutaw Street, McKeldin's boyhood home, Byrd took 62 percent of the vote.[76] In the more middle-class precincts surrounding Gwynns Falls Junior High, Byrd's margins still hit 60 percent.[77] Middle-class voters elsewhere did not support Byrd. In Hamilton, an area not threatened by racial change, voters gave McKeldin a 62 percent margin.[78]

Byrd was no southern conservative in the pre–New Deal mold. He attacked the Taft-Hartley Act and declared organized labor "as good for the employer as the employee."[79] Despite the CIO's desire to uphold the ideal of interracial labor solidarity, it had little choice but to back "the lesser of two evils."[80] Byrd's popularity demonstrated that blue-collar voters welcomed a chance to fight for what can be called a "white right to exclude" in the political arena. Della was also reelected, and CIO leaders wrung their hands over "the South Baltimore element."[81]

Although the 1954 campaigns were heavily infused with southern segregationist sentiment, the old rhetoric of white rights was being transformed as white supremacy soaked up the newly emerging criticisms of liberal institutions that threatened blue-collar life. Nevertheless, the individual targets of blue-collar protest did not yet amount to a unified whole. The *South Baltimore Enterprise* had lashed out at the closest agent of the Second Reconstruction, the "carpetbagging school board."[82] A construction worker who testified to the homegrown nature of the protests targeted the NAACP. The "mountain woman" at the race track blamed the newspapers. A few criticized the Supreme Court and leaders in Washington, but no description beyond "states rights" effectively portrayed desegregation and what came with it as part of a unified assault on working people's "mainstream" values. It was therefore easy for politicians, civic leaders, and unaffected middle-class citizens to dismiss working-class complaints on the grounds of racism. Yet, for blue collarites, race alone was an insufficient explanation for what was happening to their neighborhoods.

Blockbusting

By the mid-1950s a visitor to Northwest Baltimore could find entire blocks lined with "for sale" signs down both sides of the street. In neighborhoods on Baltimore's west and northwest sides, and to a lesser extent in the east, the "block-breaking" techniques devised by realtors were being refined to an art and the pattern established on Fulton Avenue was reemerging on a much larger scale.[83] Scattered resistance and white evacuation accompanied anger at realtors. Blue-collar resentment against black settlers was increasingly tempered by an understanding that blacks, too, were victims. Blockbusters harnessed blue-collar Baltimore's investment in whiteness to the real estate market and so created a mechanism by which fortunes were made.

In the late 1940s, even as racial transition hit the area around Fulton Avenue, white Baltimoreans elsewhere were confident that their neighborhoods would remain as they were. Whites in threatened areas reassured themselves by drawing imaginary boundaries between black and white. It was a "grocery store tradition," one West Baltimore resident recalled, that blacks would never move south of Baltimore Street.[84] In Edmondson Village, residents spent the first half of the 1950s convincing themselves that the line of black settlement west of Fulton Avenue would not cross the Gwynns Falls valley. They reassured themselves that "it will never come across that bridge, never," recalled Vera Johnson. "And that's how we lived; we convinced ourselves of all that."[85]

But there, as elsewhere, the deluge came shortly after the integration of the schools, leaving more than a few white Baltimoreans with the impression that school desegregation had been the cause and residential turnover the effect. One woman who lived in the recently integrated area near Gwynns Falls Junior High claimed that "it was the new integration law. You just didn't go to school with black people; you just didn't live with them."[86]

In the 1940s Fulton Avenue residents called what had happened to their neighborhoods "block-breaking."[87] During the next ten years the practice had become familiar nationwide as real estate speculators in industrial cities from Boston to Chicago engaged in the practice, and by 1955, when a spate of Baltimore newspaper articles documented it, the name "blockbusting" had appeared, although its novelty was indicated by the use of quotation marks.[88] By 1956, the word was no longer new, and the Maryland Commission on Interracial Problems and Relations called it "the most troublesome area of friction between races." Complaints were piling up at the commission's offices from home owners and improvement associations who castigated realtors for "putting in undesirable tenants with a view to frightening the residents into selling their properties at panic prices." Committees were formed, conferences were held, and it was finally determined that the solution was for "whites to stay put."[89] Blockbusting was perfectly legal, state authorities found, and therefore they determined that their "only avenue of approach was to educate white citizens."[90]

White citizens, however, thought that the bureaucrats were the ones who needed to be educated. "If you never lived in a neighborhood where the ruthless block busters are working then you have no idea what it is like," a resident of the middle- and working-class Govans neighborhood in North Baltimore wrote the city housing authority.[91] The writer recounted a year-long campaign by agents of the Manning-Shaw real estate agency who canvassed the neighborhood by telephone and in person. "They get a colored family in a block and then they tell the people they had better sell for you know the situation around here," the correspondent wrote, "when all the time they are making the situation." One of the ways Manning-Shaw "made the situation" was to place bright orange "sold" signs on properties as soon as they were listed, thus keeping the pressure on holdouts at a peak.[92]

Then, using racial fears as leverage, realtors extracted huge profits. Usually, they placed the first black family on a white block by offering the white seller a price well above market level and the black buyer a price well below. This accomplished, they went down the block making offers. The first few sellers could expect high prices, but after the exodus began, prices plummeted. Whites who waited too long suffered severe losses. Once the dynamics of blockbusting became familiar, whites were all the more apt to flee quickly. In threatened neighborhoods, even those who wanted to be loyal to their neighbors put their own interests first. "I'm not going to be the first one to sell to a black, but I'm sure not going to be the last," was a common attitude.[93]

Blockbusting did provide badly needed housing to Baltimore's blacks, but at a very high cost. Once formerly white properties were obtained at prices well below market value (sometimes 50 percent below), they were sold to blacks at prices far exceeding market value (often 50 percent above).[94] Black families were saddled with excessive mortgages and homes they could not keep up. Some subdivided their houses and rented out apartments to meet steep mortgage payments. In the Fulton Avenue area, for example, 28 percent of newly acquired properties were made into apartments after the sale.[95]

Realtors boosted their profits by using land installment contracts. These required little or no money down but added on large interest payments. In 1955 the Maryland Commission on Interracial Problems and Relations found that over 50 percent of black purchasers were using this method, and that in many cases ownership could be considered "highly tentative" at best. Some black families lost their entire investment when they were unable to meet the installments, often due on a weekly basis.[96]

White residents recognized blockbusting for the exploitation that it was and were baffled by the failure of city officials to do anything about it. Even more disturbing was the tendency of officials to brush off the problem. Politicians, bureaucrats, and civil rights leaders alike recognized that there was more to whites' complaints than sheer racism, but through most of the decade, official responses ignored the fact. In a 1958 public relations campaign, for instance, the Baltimore Urban League maintained that whites were wrong to argue that black settlement meant lower property values. Instead, the league pointed out, realtors and private property owners who charged blacks too much, and the city itself which often reduced services to black areas, were to blame. This curious argument, still being made by scholars of residential change, accurate though it may have been in absolving blacks of personal responsibility, overlooked the simple fact that regardless of who was to blame, the effect was the same: neighborhoods did deteriorate when blacks moved in, and whites were correct in pointing this out.[97]

Another favorite tactic was to argue that in some places—especially upper-middle-class professional areas hardly representative of Baltimore as a whole—neighborhoods did not deteriorate. This was the tack taken by the 1959 *Saturday Evening Post* article "When a Negro Moves Next Door," which lauded the success of integration in upscale Ashburton. Even the head of the Baltimore Citizens Planning and Housing Association, which was committed to peaceful integration, admitted that the article "painted too optimistic a picture."[98] Similarly, Baltimore Neighborhoods Incorporated, an organization of professionals dedicated to easing racial transition, conducted a survey of home owners in the early 1960s and slanted its findings to convey a sense of racial harmony. One member refused to accept the gloss, arguing with his colleagues that what they really found was "a situation where in the opinion of the respondents, almost half the white families in a neighborhood where a negro family moved in would move out precipitously."[99]

Some genuine, if ineffective, attempts were made to deal with the problem. In 1959 the Manning-Shaw agency had its license suspended for all of three months. The next year, Baltimore Neighborhoods Incorporated drafted and pushed through the city council an antiblockbusting ordinance that remained largely unenforceable.[100]

Despite the efforts of city leaders to put a good face on blockbusting, reality got in the way. By 1960 most of West and Northwest Baltimore had changed from white to black. About half of the middle- and working-class Edmondson Village area had turned over, while to the north the affluent Jewish neighborhoods of Park Heights, Ashburton, and Windsor Hills were undergoing transition. Although for a time, neighborhoods like Ashburton were proudly integrated, after a few years they became all-black as well.[101] By 1960, some neighborhoods in Northeast Baltimore were also undergoing blockbusting, and on the northern fringes of ethnic East Baltimore white residents "ran like it was the plague," said one black newcomer. Baltimore Street was the northern boundary of white ethnic settlement for two decades.[102]

The overall pattern of neighborhood turnover is revealing. The neighborhoods that gave way most easily to black settlement were upscale Jewish areas. In fact, there is almost no evidence of protest by residents of these areas. As in Chicago, Detroit, and Boston, Jews were much less likely to resist because they had a lower rates of home ownership, they tended to be more sympathetic toward civil rights, and, as Gerald Gamm has demonstrated in his work on Boston, their religious institutions were far more mobile than those of parish-centered Catholic areas.[103]

Another area that quickly turned over was the relatively new Edmondson Village, where most homes had been built in the 1920s. Although ties to the neighborhood may not have been as strong as in South and Southeast Baltimore, Edmondson residents were nevertheless reluctant to leave what in some ways resembled ethnic working-class Baltimore. About half white collar and half blue collar in 1950, Edmondson Village was a mix of Protestants and Catholics, and the social life of the community, even for Protestants, very much centered around St. Bernardine's parish. St. Bernardine's parish priest, one resident recalled, "swore that blacks would never move in."[104] Like a mostly Italian East Baltimore neighborhood that turned over in the 1950s, Edmondson Village was contiguous with previous areas of black settlement, and that made all the difference. Only in the Govans area, where the Manning-Shaw agency was so industrious, did a mostly black neighborhood form in the midst of whites.

Viewed in the national context, what is perhaps most remarkable about Baltimore is the absence of sustained violent conflict like that discussed by Arnold Hirsch and Thomas Sugrue in their studies of Chicago and Detroit. The answer to this seems to be in the nature of the affected areas. In these cities, what Gerald Suttles has dubbed "defended neighborhoods" were inhabited primarily by ethnic working-class Catholics whose neighborhoods of long standing were directly threatened by black encroachment.[105] With the exception of the relatively small Italian neighborhood in East Baltimore, these conditions never applied. Instead, it was in Southwest Baltimore, where the large majority of residents were Protestant, that the turnover came. One might speculate that if neighborhoods like Highlandtown, Canton, or Locust Point had been threatened with black housing projects, violent resistance on a par with Chicago and Detroit may well have developed.[106]

Blue-collar whites did not resort to politically oriented protest against blockbusting, a diffuse process, rather than a sharply focused episode like the housing project incidents that usually elicited violent demonstrations elsewhere. Abstract as it was, blockbusting cast a shadow across urban white consciousness: a dim realization that events in the city—indeed, even events in their own neighborhoods—were beyond locals' control. It did not, however, despite the wishes of pro-integrationist leaders, lead working whites to revise their commitment to keeping the working-class community white. Few ever considered integration a real possibility. One woman said that "people just felt that they weren't going to live with blacks."[107] There was always the implication that black arrival meant white departure. Residents "can't move to make room for negroes," wrote one white.[108] In "making a place for the colored," wrote another, "where will the whites go?"[109]

There was certainly much unabashed racism among angry whites, some of whom saw blacks as a "rough unclean class of people."[110] But the fear and anger created by blockbusting went well beyond issues of race. Many people, like a middle-class Ashburton man, were quick to attribute white discontent to concern about property values. "Racial hatreds," he said, were of little consequence when the value of a person's home, "perhaps his life's work seems at stake."[111] This was very significant, but to working whites, for whom the neighborhood was a valuable resource, blockbusting meant much more. "Its not an economic pressure," said an Edmondson Village man, "it's a personal feeling."[112] The Urban League's Furman Templeton seemed to understand this. "It isn't the deep prejudices," he said, "it's the discouragement that strikes a neighborhood as soon as a negro family moves in . . . when the signs go up."[113] Blockbusting underscored how vulnerable whites' most important institutions were when conceptions of "the neighborhood" made no allowance for a black presence.

As a result, a deep anxiety permeated white working-class Baltimore; this was only sharpened by city leaders' seeming disinclination to do anything about the problem. In 1956 a Govans resident said of her neighbors that blockbusting "is on their minds day and night." "It seems to be the main subject of conversation in this community. Those blockbusters have cast a gloom over this section of our city."[114] Apprehension and despair underscored expressions of helplessness. One Edmondson Avenue woman saw blockbusting as an inexorable force. "It kept crawling and crawling," she said.[115] Above all, among Baltimore's whites was a growing sense that they had been victimized by outside forces—forces that were not easily personified by black faces. Urban whites were "forced to live in a situation they did not help to create," said one woman.[116] "They saw a very secure world changing very drastically and they couldn't accept it. In some respect it was forced down their throats," said another.[117]

Blockbusting made urban whites increasingly sensitive to injustices perpetrated by an establishment that favored blacks at the expense of whites. But it would take much more to deepen whites' understanding of their problem. When it came to housing, shady realtors and powerless politicians remained more abstract targets than black neighbors. As late as the 1970s, a Highlandtown man still held that "the greatest fear among the homeowners in this area is that a black family is gonna move in next door."[118]

Steel and Civil Rights

Through the 1950s most white working-class Baltimoreans—Highlandtown residents included—were not directly affected by blockbusting. They were far more likely to work near blacks than live near them. In the 1950s most Baltimore AFL unions preserved racial barriers: the Carpenters and Long-shoremen's Unions both maintained Jim Crow locals. The CIO locals, on the other hand, were proudly integrated. In 1949 the city's largest CIO unions—the United Steelworkers, the United Autoworkers, and the Ship-yard Workers—had black memberships of 33, 25, and 20 percent respectively.[119]

The integrated nature of the CIO, a condition that stemmed as much from the imperatives of organizing broadly in the industrial workplace as it did from the honorable goals of its leadership, opened the way for a host of problems. Most of them were due to the fact that the white workers and local leaders were much less committed to racial equality than the International. The disparity between the ideal of racial progressivism and the reality of shop floor resistance was a constant challenge during these years, and, as Bruce Nelson has pointed out, the union at all levels too often "served as the guardian of white job expectations."[120]

In the 1950s there were no African Americans on the elected executive board of UAW Local 738, which represented workers at the Martin Company. Late in the decade, in an attempt to remedy the situation, black workers began forming their own caucus to challenge the four mostly white caucuses. John Alden, the local's president, accused black caucus leaders of "trying to trade on race and exploit racial conditions." Though he would have welcomed a black on the executive board, said Alden, there did not "seem to be any smart enough." As it was, the black caucus directed "union energy" away from more "important issues of bargaining policy and employment conditions."[121]

In GM's UAW Local 678, officers claimed that there was no racial political conflict. There the problem was one of opportunity. Although in 1961 about a fifth of the plant's 2,500 workers were black, the union reported "no negroes in any skilled job." Of about 500 blacks in the plant, 400 were laborers. Not only were blacks and whites at GM segregated by "dirty and clean jobs," but blacks, by company policy, had no chance of advancement. They were all, according to the union, "in non-promotable jobs."[122]

Even in the CIO unions, then, appearances could be deceiving. In the early 1950s blacks made up one-third of the workforce at Bethlehem Steel but were overwhelmingly concentrated in the dirtiest, least desirable jobs at the blast furnaces, coke ovens, and open hearths. Ed Gorman, who started at Sparrows Point in 1951, took his physical examination with a black man: "The black guy right away went to the open hearth and I went to the tin side," he recalled.[123] Nevertheless, as they had during World War II, Baltimore's employers could blame the white workers themselves for upholding segregation. In 1951, when Bethlehem tried to implement an apprenticeship program for black bricklayers, whites threatened a walkout.[124] To black workers, both company and union seemed equally at fault. "Every time you'd ask some union guy about it he'd say that's the system," recalled one black worker. "If you ask the company guy about it he'd say its none of your business."[125]

By the late 1950s, the problems created by these hiring policies were being played out in union politics. The United Steelworkers Union had long been among Baltimore's most activist CIO unions. John Klauzenberg, a left-wing progressive with a history of civil rights sympathy, was Local 2610's longtime president.[126] Joseph Neal, one of the first black organizers at Sparrows Point, was a United Steelworkers Union District Eight staff representative and a leader of the Baltimore Urban League. Despite the efforts of activists like Neal and Klauzenberg, white steelworkers sought to maintain the prerogatives of race by keeping blacks relegated to unskilled positions throughout the 1950s. Whenever blacks moved into new positions in the plant, short-lived walkouts followed. Although the union held firm in most cases, when Klauzenberg tried to get a black worker into an apprenticeship program for electricians in 1956, "the whites in the department ganged up and the proceedings broke down."[127]

Still, the extent of the union's responsibility for segregating Sparrows Point is debatable because it was accomplished through hiring patterns that the union could not control. Compounding the problem for black workers was the fact that in the areas in which they were hired, seniority lines were short. At the steel plant, possibilities for advancement depended on "unit seniority." White units tended to have long lines of seniority allowing workers to move into better, higher-paying jobs over time. Black units tended to have very short lines of seniority. The ultimate expressions of this were the "black gangs" of unskilled laborers—essentially dead-end jobs. The company also segregated toilets, locker rooms, and showers by race.[128]

In 1956, some of these most rigid forms of segregation began to give way. The company officially desegregated its facilities, although workers continued to observe segregation informally. The union also pushed for, and got, a supplementary agreement to the contract that did away with the black gangs and gave limited transfer options to black workers, enabling them to move from dead-end units to units with more possibilities for promotion. There remained a catch, however: any worker transferring from one unit to another would be obliged to start at the bottom of the next unit. For black workers, many of whom had years of experience and had gained relatively high wages, this meant taking a drastic pay cut in return for a chance, rather than a guarantee, of later promotion. Not surprisingly, this option did little to solve the basic problem.[129] Even the limited gains blacks made in 1956 were apparently too much for some white employees. In that year, in United Steelworkers Local 2610, one unionist exploited this race-based resentment in an attempt to divide and conquer.

Ruke, Rule, and Ruin

Sparrows Point was home to two United Steelworkers Union locals, both among the largest in the nation. Local 2610 represented workers in the "basic steel" side of the plant, where unskilled, dirty jobs predominated. Local 2609 stood for those in the "finishing side," where basic steel was processed into finished forms like I-beams, pipes, and plates—operations where skilled work was more abundant. The concentration of blacks in unskilled work was reflected in the makeup of these two locals. By 1961, Local 2609 had a total membership of 8,500 workers and was 25 to 35 percent black.[130] Local 2610 had a membership of 12,000 and was 60 percent black. Because black workers had a larger potential power base in Local 2610, racial conflict had always been more pronounced there. But in 1961, in what was a monumental understatement, Local 2610 president John Klauzenberg told the U.S. Commission on Civil Rights that there were no "race rivalries in this union except at election time."[131]

Klauzenberg had headed up Local 2610 almost since its inception in the late 1930s. In 1956 he was defeated by a relative newcomer named John Ruke.[132] In a local that was then 65 percent white, Ruke used the issue of race to obtain the office. In a clumsy effort to consolidate his gains, he exploited it even more baldly.[133]

Ruke, like Baltimore's local politicians, had run a race-based campaign in 1954. When he lost by a narrow margin, he demanded a recount and lodged charges against fellow unionists.[134] In the June 1956 campaign, Steelworkers Union staff representatives, consigning much of the white vote to Ruke, tried to discredit a third candidate as "anti-negro" and en-

Shift change on the finishing side at Sparrows Point in the 1950s. (Courtesy of the *Baltimore News-American* Photograph Collection, Special Collections, University of Maryland, College Park, Libraries)

couraged blacks to support Klauzenberg.[135] Voter turnout was the largest ever for a union election. In a contest waged along racial lines, however, Ruke had the edge, and with the opposition split evenly between the two other candidates, Ruke won the presidency.[136]

In March 1957 Ruke began filing charges against black officers in Local 2610. Opponents at first sidestepped the issue of race and built a case against him on less contentious grounds, but Ruke countered on 9 April by removing a black vice president from office. The next evening, when blacks rallied in protest, Ruke brought in city policemen to maintain a perimeter outside the union hall. In an astoundingly callous act, considering the agency's anti-union reputation, Ruke contracted Pinkerton detectives to maintain "order" inside the hall.[137] Black union members were used to the outright discrimination practiced by the company, but never before had the union itself been so flagrant an enemy. At a May meeting, a former grievance committeeman told his fellow black workers, "we as a negro race have got to fight the white people and fight them hard, not only down at Sparrows Point, but right here in the union hall."[138] On 31 May the United Steelworkers relieved Ruke of his duties and appointed an administrator to run 2610.[139]

As they had in the 1940s, anticommunism and racism sustained one another in 1950s Baltimore. The conflict in Local 2610 coincided with the House Un-American Activities Committee's Baltimore hearings in 1957. The tide of anxiety over domestic communism had long since ebbed in the city, so most locals seem to have considered the hearings, broadcast on television, as more of a curiosity than anything else.[140] Nevertheless, blue collarites showed little tolerance, let alone sympathy for, contemporaries called before the HUAC. "It is really shocking to find many people with warped or twisted minds from our East Baltimore section," wrote one man to the *East Baltimore Guide*. A few locals sought reprisals, lobbing bricks through the front windows of a Southeast Baltimore woman who had taken the Fifth Amendment sixteen times. At Sparrows Point, employees in the electrical repair shop refused to work with a man who had invoked the Fifth twenty-eight times.[141]

The government's star witness in the 1957 hearings was Bethlehem Steel employee Clifford Miller, a West Virginia native who had joined the Communist Party once on his own initiative, quit, and rejoined at the behest of the Federal Bureau of Investigation. Miller, a member of Local 2610, identified five of his fellow union members as having been Communist Party members.[142] Bethlehem immediately suspended the workers, and Ruke tried to expel them from the union, but before he could do so the Steelworkers Union district director took over the case and lodged grievances over the discharges.[143] Miller used his newfound celebrity to defend Ruke, charging that the "God-fearing anti-communist" had been punished because he was not a "rubber stamp" for an insufficiently vigilant International.[144]

Ruke, as Local 2610 members admitted to the International, had deliberately "drawn the color line," and his followers continued to defend their perceived rights as whites over the International's opposition. After Ruke's suspension, one of his partisans circulated a card entitled "SLEEP WHITE BROTHER." "Dancing and laughter prevailed on Penn. Ave. today. The

MINORITY trounced the MAJORITY," it said. In claiming that theirs was the will of the majority and that their opponents were a noisy minority, the white unionists had found a potentially powerful argument. With the administratorship in place, Ruke's sympathizers, calling themselves the "Committee for Freedom," depicted themselves doubly victimized, not only by the black minority, but also by the "tyrannical" International. "Let's Get Back Our Rights," the committee exhorted.[145]

Baltimore's CIO unions had always had problems defending racial equality, but the local union leadership had usually been out in front of the membership in enforcing equal rights. Ruke's move was audacious by any standard and likely an attempt to capitalize on the white discontent that was growing stronger in the community and on the job in the 1950s. But as the South Baltimore protesters had learned, the time when direct action could turn back black advances was ending and new means had to be found. Moreover, the language of white rights, let alone of "white supremacy," was a dead end. Appeals to other kinds of rights were becoming increasingly more accurate.

Critics of the United Steelworkers Union charged it with complicity in racial segregation by agreeing to separate seniority lines. But except for Ruke's brief tenure, Baltimore Local 2610 seems to have done as well as could be expected considering the sentiment of so many workers. When the administratorship was lifted, Klauzenberg, the veteran liberal, was back in the president's office. Starting in 1958, the United Steelworkers Union, in conjunction with the Baltimore Urban League, embarked on a two-year social work project called "To Strengthen the Minority Family." Klauzenberg and District Eight staff representative Joseph Neal were both on the committee administering the project.[146] Such efforts had, at most, only brief impact. In the 1960s, as increasing black activism and mounting white discontent pushed both groups away from the center, the influence of civil rights "moderates" like these declined precipitously, and Sparrows Point remained plagued by resentment forged in race-based conflict.

To the Lunch Counter

From World War II to 1960 white working-class political consciousness, most often enunciated in terms of white rights, developed in tandem with the growing rights consciousness of blacks. Although in the protests and campaigns of 1954 Baltimore's working whites seem to have displayed an unprecedented degree of white racism, this was not necessarily the case.

Previously, the blue-collar commitment to white schools and white neighborhoods had never been seriously challenged. But in the years after World
War II, as challenges mounted with perplexing frequency, working whites
turned to a familiar and all-encompassing argument to express their concerns.

School integration was a symbolic defeat, but the most lasting scars
were left by neighborhood racial transition. White working-class citizenship, developed by ethnic and native-stock whites since the beginning of
the century, was constructed on a framework of white institutions and confined within sharply demarcated neighborhood boundaries. In the postwar years, as blue collarites invested their rising incomes and expanding leisure time in the community, white neighborhoods were a growing
source of pride. When the essential vulnerability of these neighborhoods
was so vividly demonstrated in the mid-1950s, white working-class confidence began to give way to defensiveness. Even as the centrifugal forces
of affluence, education, and suburbia conspired to pull the working-class
community apart, the external pressures unleashed by postwar economic,
political, racial, and geographic change worked to create a new, less con-
genial communal solidarity within their "defended neighborhoods."[147]

But whites were increasingly hedged in not only by black neighbors but
also by the very language through which they made their case. The inability
of city leaders to address the real problems of blockbusting, the liberal dismissal of protest over school desegregation, and the Steelworkers' handling
of the Local 2610 controversy all demonstrated clearly that claims based
on whiteness were claims that could not be respected. Almost as soon as
blue collarites took up the white supremacist argument, its usefulness was
at an end.

More valuable were emerging claims to other rights based on merit
rather than skin color. Though blue-collar Baltimoreans had enunciated
such claims since 1945, they were always drowned out by race claims that
shouted rather than spoke. Because they were ineffective and inaccurate,
the words used by protesting parents and indignant white steelworkers
evolved as circumstances challenged blue collarites to think about and express their problems in new ways. What emerged was a populist argument
also based on rights, but rights of common or working people rather than
white people.

The civil rights movement and the manner in which it was defended may
also have helped lead working whites toward a new vocabulary of political protest. In the 1940s and 1950s, whites resentful of black gains made at

their expense fought for white rights. It was crucial that black leaders were espousing not black rights, but "civil" rights—rights that commanded universal respect. By the 1960s working whites were moving toward a similar position in gaining a deeper understanding and a better articulation of the causes of their discontent.

Blue-collar claims were sharpened as much by developments within the civil rights movement as within the white working class. By the early 1960s, growing militancy within the movement was dividing Baltimore's civil rights leadership. Juanita Jackson Mitchell, the daughter of Lillie Jackson, took over the Baltimore NAACP and embarked on a more confrontational course, characterizing some of the city's oldest white civil rights supporters as "Mr. Charlies" and accusing the Urban League of undercutting the "uncompromising militancy of the NAACP."[148] But it was another group, the Congress of Racial Equality (CORE) that would henceforth set the tenor for the civil rights movement in Baltimore, spurring both blacks and whites to redefine their respective rights-based claims in the process.

Although CORE had led a few sit-ins at downtown Baltimore restaurants during the mid-1950s, the local civil rights movement began a new and more decisively confrontational phase in March 1960. Just a month after the Greensboro, North Carolina, sit-ins, black students from Baltimore's Morgan State College, joined by whites from Johns Hopkins University, staged a sit-in that successfully desegregated lunch counters at the city's Northwood Shopping Center.[149] From that point on, nonviolent direct action grew in frequency and scope. The black freedom movement had come to Baltimore, and it changed how whites—both sympathetic and antagonistic—viewed their city and the nation. As the more militant movement turned away from civil rights and toward black rights, it put working whites' counterclaims on firmer ground. They would speak for "working" people, not just whites, in the future.

CHAPTER 5

Spiro Agnew Country

In early 1957 an obscure thirty-eight-year-old lawyer was elected president of the Loch Raven Community Council in Baltimore County. Spiro Agnew, the son of a Greek restauranteur, had grown up in Northwest Baltimore and served overseas in World War II. In 1946 he moved his new family to the suburbs and switched from the Democratic to the Republican Party.[1] Agnew was the quintessential suburbanite. Although he was born over a florist's shop in downtown Baltimore, his family left the inner city before he was a year old. His world revolved more around upward mobility than around family, neighborhood, and work. And mobile he was; just over a decade after winning his first elective office, Agnew stepped into the second highest office in the nation. When he ran for Baltimore County executive and governor of Maryland, Agnew was the Republican suburbanite's candidate. But by the late 1960s, after years of growing frustration, Baltimore's blue-collar Democrats thought they had found a champion in Agnew.

By 1970 journalists, academics, and the middle class public believed that working whites had recently become more aggressively racist and more politically conservative. There was really more continuity than change in white working-class politics, however. Urban white working people retained a strong sense of commitment toward neighborhood, religious, and ethnic institutions, and they remained convinced that theirs were "mainstream" institutions. By 1970 that seemed no longer to be the case. What had changed fundamentally in the 1960s was the context within which working whites honored those personal and community commitments made long ago.

Blue-collar discontent became more visible in the 1960s because it was then that blue collarites began to realize that the greatest threats to their parochial world were national, not local in origin. In the 1940s and 1950s

112

local action had been the first recourse in combating challenges to the blue-collar working-class community. But in the 1960s the ability of "liberal" politicians, theoreticians, and Supreme Court justices to disrupt the daily life of the white working class became clear. It was still possible to resist the incursions of "outsiders" coming into blue-collar communities and telling people how to live, but the fight was increasingly futile: the outsiders seemed to possess the legitimacy that only the powerful could bestow. The old wells of white working-class political power had seemingly dried up, and the search for new ones could only take place in the public realm. As the rights revolution swung into full gear, and other groups pressed noisily for their due, working whites realized, not unreasonably, that to stay quiescent was to remain powerless.

At the same time, the message now reaching the nation's ears was qualitatively different from that enunciated in the neighborhoods and cities of 1950s America. It was in the 1960s that particularized grievances with the actions and aspirations of blacks were overshadowed by a more generalized resentment of the abdication of responsible political leadership by those in power. In the clamor for rights—an easy way to make gains, blue collarites believed—too many had renounced their obligations and the hard work that went with them. It had been a cornerstone of white working-class political culture that it was the proper role of government not to provide for the people, but to enable citizens to discharge their responsibilities to the community. By the late 1960s it seemed abundantly clear that liberal political leaders were not only failing to demand responsible behavior from all Americans, they were encouraging lawlessness and irresponsibility by some.

This realization was an important one. It impelled working whites to reevaluate the words and ideas through which they sought to recapture what had been lost. In peeling away the dead integument of white supremacy, they set free an old but enduring language of populism. In its revitalized form this populist appeal encapsulated blue-collar concerns and validated them in ways older appeals could not. By the end of the decade, white working-class discontent had become focused on the threat posed to "working" people—regardless of race—by the irresponsible actions of powerful elites. Blue collarites had largely abandoned race talk and were enunciating their concerns in populist language that had long been in the mainstream of American political discourse. They condemned the threat posed to the industrious and responsible many by a privileged and untrustworthy few. And what the anticommunist episode indicated, the events of the sixties seemed to confirm: the elites to be feared and fought lay in the halls of government, not the boardrooms of corporate America.

This is not to say that overt white racism and the deep working-class commitment to whiteness disappeared. Race-based resentment was often not far from the surface and some whites retained forthrightly "white supremacist" views, but the complex relationship between race, class, politics, and language was reconfigured. As the quality of urban life declined under mounting crime, as black activists grew increasingly militant in their actions and their language, and as "mainstream" politicians grew increasingly tolerant of these changes and even seemed to promote them, working whites became convinced that their problem was not racial but cultural. By the end of the sixties they were fighting not over turf, but over culture; not over black and white, but over right and wrong. And when urban working-class Democrats came to these conclusions, the suburban Republican was already there.

Turf Wars

The decade's first major instances of racial conflict harkened back to the 1950s in that they were primarily localized fights heavily infused with race-based resentment. The successful 1960 lunch counter protests led by students from Morgan State College served as a benchmark for Baltimore's civil rights community. But to some extent these were easy victories: the lunch counters were public commercial establishments most often frequented by middle-class whites, and there was little sustained resistance to their integration. But then, buoyed by success, black activists began to look elsewhere. One place they looked was South Baltimore.[2]

Baltimore's municipal swimming pools had been desegregated in 1956. Some observers expected racial conflict, but little materialized. Most blacks swam at the Druid Hill pool, near the newly black neighborhoods in the northwest. A few ventured to other pools, but there were no significant disputes in the 1950s. One reason for this was that whites stayed home. Public pool attendance dropped precipitously in 1956 and stayed low throughout the 1950s.[3] More important, at the pools, as elsewhere, de facto segregation reigned—black swimmers stayed out of recognized white neighborhoods.[4] The NAACP decided to put this unofficial segregation to the test at Riverside Park in the heart of South Baltimore.

In mid-August 1962 children and teens from the black neighborhoods northwest of South Baltimore started swimming at Riverside Pool under

South Baltimore residents look on as police escort black swimmers and protesters away from Riverside Pool. (Courtesy of the *Baltimore News-American* Photograph Collection, Special Collections, University of Maryland, College Park, Libraries)

the watchful eye of the NAACP. On Labor Day, after three weeks of simmering resentment, local whites acted. When the swimmers arrived, they were greeted with what one remembered as "the usual profanity and jeering" from about two hundred onlookers. Then the crowd grew—an hour later it numbered a thousand. Charles Luthardt and thirteen members of his racist Fighting American Nationalists picketed. Angry locals circled the pool and shouted and cheered white swimmers who tore into a black effigy. The police made eight arrests and had to escort the black swimmers away from the scene. "I had looked in the face of an angry, ugly, hate-maddened mob," recalled one in attendance.[5] Two days later, members of the NAACP youth council returned to Riverside Park, provoking more limited skirmishes that resulted in seven additional arrests.[6]

A year later the NAACP touched off some less violent turf wars when it pushed for changes in Baltimore's beleaguered school system. By the early 1960s many Baltimore schools, voluntarily desegregated in 1954, had been effectively resegregated by ongoing neighborhood transition. In 1958, just over half of Baltimore's public schools were segregated, and white reliance on parochial and private schools ensured that crowding remained much more a problem for black schools than white ones.[7]

In September 1963 liberal school board members, under pressure from the NAACP, implemented a plan to remedy de facto segregation requiring the busing of students.[8] When classes began, parents at affected schools rallied. In most white neighborhoods where black students were bused in for the first time, parents stood by curiously. But in Hamilton, one hundred white parents organized in protest. The leader of the protesting parents, an accountant, said that "we believe integration should not be forced on us by the whim of Negro pressure groups."[9] Just inside the city limits in Northwest Baltimore, Hamilton was home to many former Southeast Baltimoreans. Between 1940 and 1960 the area had become increasingly ethnic as Germans, Italians, and Poles fled "out the road," but Hamilton residents were better educated than blue-collar urbanites and they were predominantly clerical workers. These urban suburbanites claimed that they did not want their "clean, law-abiding, tax-paying residential section" turned into a "battlefield" by "ambitious Negro politicians" and other subversives.[10]

Back in Highlandtown, two hundred angry parents confronted school board representatives. Some voiced their resentments in traditional racial exclusionist terms. Said one parent: "A lot of people don't want the colored here. They don't belong here." Others displayed more anger with white liberals than with blacks. "That's all I hear is School Board, School Board, School Board. Who is the School Board?" asked one woman. "You'll never get to see them," replied another.[11]

At Riverside Pool and in the 1963 school desegregation protests, white Baltimoreans still acted locally to protect local institutions. Nevertheless, in the latter instance especially, the focus of their anger was broadening, and even whites in outlying areas of the city were beginning to become as concerned with racial change as those in the older neighborhoods.

Lawmakers, Philosophers, and Clergymen

Although the Supreme Court's *Brown v. Board of Education* decision, politicians' seeming helplessness in the face of blockbusting, and the school board's bowing to black pressure groups in 1963 helped erode working whites' confidence in government, most still believed that it could be a force for good. In the mid-1950s a South Baltimore barber who headed the local Parent-Teacher Association complained that urban renewal programs had passed his area by. He wanted improvements for South Baltimore residents who had "no desire to join the movement northward [to the Baltimore County suburbs]."[12] The city's declining shipbuilding industry was of constant concern. In 1962, when Bethlehem slashed its Key Highway Shipyard workforce from 2,600 to 300, angry workers turned against the mayor, and a South Baltimore councilman introduced a resolution asking for federal action.[13] Likewise, the politicians behind "big government" were treasured if they protected the interests of the white working class. U.S. congressman Edward Garmatz kept a lock on his seat for decades by consistently pushing appropriations for the shipbuilding industry.[14]

Working whites developed a distaste for big government only when it seemed to undermine their security. When civil rights groups decried police brutality and secured badly needed reform legislation, blue-collar Baltimoreans saw only lax law enforcement—just another example of skewed government priorities. By the early 1960s blue-collar Baltimoreans had become increasingly uneasy about crime. Many believed that the problem was unprecedented and wrote of "a present upsurge" or "current crime dilemma."[15] The *East Baltimore Guide* watched crime rates rise along with a perception that police officers were increasingly reluctant to use force. The paper blamed "lawmakers" who "put the rights of the criminal above the rights of the law abiding citizen."[16] When a few blacks arrested at Riverside Park in 1962 leveled brutality charges against the police, the *South Baltimore Enterprise* countered by questioning politicians and "philosophers" who sought to protect "barbarians" at the expense of society.[17]

On Labor Day 1962, as whites lashed out in South Baltimore, the Baltimore chapter of the Congress of Racial Equality picketed "All-Nations Day" at the all-white Gwynn Oak Amusement Park for the ninth year in a row. Gwynn Oak lay just over the city line from West Baltimore neighborhoods that were changing from white to black in the early 1960s, and integrating the park had been CORE's chief goal since the previous decade.[18]

The Baltimore chapter of CORE had been founded by a white Johns Hopkins psychologist in 1953.[19] By the early 1960s the chapter was in decline and so predominantly white that, in the words of one member, "we had to integrate the picket line."[20] In 1963 the National Commission on Religion and Race, an interfaith group of clergy and lay activists, joined the Baltimore CORE in a Fourth of July protest at the park.[21] Among the 283 over-whelmingly white participants from New York, Philadelphia, Washington, and Baltimore were nationally prominent clerics representing the Protes-tant, Catholic, and Jewish faiths. These included Eugene Carson Blake, the highest official of the United Presbyterian Church, Bishop Daniel Corrigan of the National Council of the Episcopal Church, and Rabbi Morris Lieber-man of Baltimore. Among the nine Catholic priests present was Monsignor Austin J. Healy of the Roman Catholic Archdiocese of Baltimore.[22]

The park's proprietors, encouraged by angry white onlookers and Lut-hardt's counterpicketing Fighting American Nationalists, refused admis-sion to the integrated group. When the protesters attempted to enter anyway, 275 were arrested and charged with trespassing and disorderly conduct.[23] Working whites wrote the *Baltimore Sun* in protest, and "cru-sading priests and ministers" who went "beyond their own bailiwicks to tell other people how to live" joined lawmakers and philosophers in the pantheon of outsiders disrupting working-class life.[24] Spiro Agnew, then Baltimore County executive, said that the protesters had "lost sight of their responsibilities."[25]

Gwynn Oak had been a problem for the Catholic Church before. In 1962 the Knights of Columbus insisted on holding their Labor Day outing at the park despite protests by civil rights groups. In response, Archbishop Law-rence Shehan barred parochial schools in the diocese from using Gwynn Oak.[26] Now, with Baltimore Catholic clergy taking part in direct action protest for the first time, blue-collar whites were furious.[27] "Open defi-ance of the law," one Catholic wrote regarding the nine Baltimore priests, "cannot be condoned, no matter who the violators are." Another Catholic woman decided that she and her family did "not need any rabble-rousing priests anymore." The priests involved received letters from their parish-ioners that were, in the words of a correspondent to the Jesuit journal *America,* "universally abusive and hostile."[28]

By 1963 the Catholic Church was deeply divided.[29] Its parishioners con-tinued to value the racial exclusivity enforced by parish boundaries, but church leadership was increasingly liberal, pro-integrationist, and intent on obliterating those boundaries. "The state of confusion among Catholics is now thoroughly out in the open," wrote *America*'s Baltimore correspon-dent. "Catholic life here can never be quite the same again."[30] But there was more to the controversy than a desire to preserve the white parish.

A fundamental principle of American religious life had long been that the best way to change society was to reform the soul of the individual.

But dogged white resistance to civil rights had convinced liberal religious leaders to seek social change first and worry about souls later. This decision, more than anything else, cut a deep divide between the progressive and the orthodox within religious groups that persists to this day. As Robert Wuthnow has pointed out, the controversy over Gwynn Oak was "as much over proper methods of engaging the public conscience as it was over racial equality."[31] Some common ground did remain: church leadership and laity alike were united on the issue of school prayer, which moved from the Baltimore school system to the national spotlight in the early 1960s.

In October 1960 North Baltimore resident Madalyn Murray kept her son home from school. An avowed atheist, she charged that by sanctioning school prayer the Baltimore City School Board had violated her son's constitutional rights.[32] No politician, professor, or activist minister galled blue-collar Baltimoreans more than Murray, who smugly asserted that "row houses breed row minds."[33] Her case, bundled with others, made it to the Supreme Court as *Abington School District v. Schempp,* and on 17 June 1963 the Court ruled that school-sanctioned prayer violated the U.S. Constitution.[34]

At a time when nearly 70 percent of Americans belonged to a church or synagogue, the decision struck working-class Americans like a bolt from the blue. Only nine years earlier President Dwight Eisenhower had signed legislation adding "one nation under God" to the pledge of allegiance, declaring that "our government makes no sense unless it is founded on a deeply felt religious faith."[35] Baltimoreans felt that their own religious freedom had been abrogated by an undemocratic Supreme Court. The wife of a Martin Company crane operator claimed to treasure America's "strong spiritual base." "After 200 years," she said, "the Supreme Court apparently feels the right *not* to worship is more important."[36] A Middle River mechanic wrote, "Where are our rights as Americans if we can't even vote for an issue as important as this one?"[37] A local U.S. congressman pledged early hearings on the decision that Archbishop Shehan called a "regrettable step" by the Court.[38]

On 29 April 1964, at the congressional hearings on school prayer, Bishop Fulton J. Sheen, then the country's most influential Catholic, shared the limelight with George Wallace, the nation's most influential segregationist. Alabama's governor had just won 34 percent of the vote in Wisconsin's Democratic presidential primary and would soon be campaigning in Maryland.[39]

Southern Politics Comes North

"It is fantastic," George Wallace told the House Judiciary Committee, that the American people must "beseech the Congress for restoration of our cherished right to permit our children to participate in a simple invocation." The rights of the people were being trampled, he declared, by subscribers to a "judicial philosophy," itself "the bitter fruit of liberal dogma," that had already destroyed "the democratic institution of local schools controlled by local elected officials."[40] In his testimony that day and throughout his 1964 campaign that gave birth to the term "white backlash," the Alabaman linked latent racial fears with manifest indignation about liberal elites whose misguided policies were integrating schools, tolerating lawlessness, and destroying America's religious foundations.

In September 1963 Wallace attended a conference on urban problems in Baltimore.[41] Afterward he publicly considered entering Maryland's 1964 Democratic presidential primary despite the opposition of the state leaders. "No respectable politician will identify with the Southern Governor's candidacy," warned the state attorney general.[42] In March 1964 Wallace filed, and the "respectable politicians" responded on cue. Lyndon Johnson needed a "favorite son" candidate to keep the Democratic vote from Wallace, and since Governor Millard Tawes had recently backed an unpopular tax boost, Senator Daniel Brewster agreed to do the job. But state Democrats waited to file. "We don't want to dignify Wallace by answering him right away," they condescended.[43]

Condescension quickly deteriorated into bitter invective. On 20 March the Archdiocese of Baltimore dubbed Wallace a "law-defying racist" and held him personally responsible for the recent bombing deaths at the black Sixteenth Street Baptist Church in Birmingham. The *Catholic Review* said that no "patriotic American, much less an informed, conscientious Catholic," could back Wallace.[44] An Episcopal bishop compared Wallace followers to Nazis.[45] As they had in 1954, the political establishment, the media, and the "best elements" of the city strove to marginalize the voices of working-class whites. But in the wake of the Supreme Court's continued activism, blue-collar workers saw a larger threat than they had ten years earlier: a seemingly omnipotent federal government. A Baltimore County electrician's wife urged people to "keep themselves informed of what is actually happening to our democratic way . . . before Wallace . . . is put out of circulation."[46]

George Wallace opens his Maryland presidential primary campaign at the Lord Baltimore Hotel in April 1964. (Courtesy of the *Baltimore News-American* Photograph Collection, Special Collections, University of Maryland, College Park, Libraries)

The *Sun* portrayed the southerner's campaign as an unwarranted intrusion, something "alien to the historic spirit of Maryland." The *South Baltimore Enterprise* countered that the spirit in question bore a "stronger resemblance to Governor Wallace than to Senator Brewster. That is, unless all history stopped on May 17, 1954 and then was written anew." The paper situated itself and its working-class readership in a Democratic tradition rooted in the segregationist South rather than in the New Deal. But instead of harkening back to the Lost Cause and dwelling on race, the *Enterprise* used rhetoric that would resonate through the politics of the next thirty years: "If you want the Federal Government to tell you how to live, vote for Brewster. If you want to tell yourself and your children how to live, vote for Wallace."[47]

On May fifth Wallace won 30 percent of the vote in the Indiana primary. Three days later he kicked off his Maryland campaign. In ten personal appearances, he hammered home a few basic points as he delivered variants of one speech.[48] Wallace scrupulously kept race baiting out of his speeches, but the issue was never far from the surface. He still struck states' rights chords, declaring that "the people of Maryland can run their state" better than Washington can, but Wallace drew from deeper rhetorical reserves than the tired tirades of the Old South.[49] In populist tones he condemned the burgeoning liberal establishment and counterposed the many across America to the few in Washington. The president and the Supreme Court, he charged, had high-handedly overridden "elected representatives who reflect the decisions of the people." Although he condemned the excesses of the executive and judicial branches, Wallace astutely retained those shreds of the New Deal fabric that still served. He professed his wholehearted support of the industrial labor unions that owed their existence to New Deal activism.[50] Wallace was not antigovernment. Instead, as Michael Kazin has observed, "he explicitly favored a government that aided the common folk—as long as it stayed out of their schools, their unions, and their family lives."[51]

Most important, Wallace seemed to accord white working people the dignity and respect that other Democratic leaders had withdrawn. "People have the wisdom, the sense of justice and the decency to govern their own local affairs," he said. They alone know best how to "raise their families and develop their children." He affirmed that his supporters were the true custodians of traditional American values and institutions. "We have a duty," he asserted, to "exercise the heritage bequeathed to us by those who stood firm against adversity, fought their way across this country, and established a strong, virile United States." As Jody Carlson succinctly put it, Wallace made "no appeals to marginal men."[52]

Wallace's refusal to make personal attacks contrasted sharply with his opponents' ridicule of the candidate and his supporters. *Baltimore Evening Sun* columnist Bradford Jacobs took up the invective, sharpened it with disdain for things southern, and hurled it at the governor's Maryland defenders. The "Wallace claque" he wrote, "whoop and holler and stamp on the floor at the sight of him. . . . They squeal with redneck delight whenever, in his kindly way, he slips the liberals the knife."[53] The religion of the South was a ready metaphor for those who ridiculed Wallace's "states' rights evangelism."[54]

The *Sun* distanced Maryland from the Deep South, labeling Wallace a "trespasser" intruding into "one of the great moral issues of our time, without possessing the depth of character to recognize that it is a moral issue."[55] Working-class Baltimore reversed the "morality" argument, finding Wallace's detractors disingenuous. The *Enterprise* pronounced the *Sun*'s charge "a cheap instrument of guilt psychology" wielded by a "local establishment whose morality is a pocket book morality." South Baltimore, the paper countered, had seen its share of real trespassers, "armed with every engine of civil disobedience." But to Wallace's enemies, the paper concluded, "way out there in their private swimming pools and clubs, segregated by sheer wealth, it won't mean much."[56]

Vincent Tallarico, a tire salesman, described a new chilling political atmosphere consonant with the Murray decision and condemned those who used patriotism to stigmatize Wallace supporters: "I am concerned when the name of Governor George Wallace is mentioned and the reply is 'I'm voting for him, but please don't quote me'. . . . I am concerned that one woman can change the beliefs of our American way of life in proclaiming that there is no Supreme Being. . . . I have experienced something like many of you, which I thought never existed in America. The *Americanism* method of instilling 'FEAR' in the minds of the American voter."[57]

As election day approached, fear began creeping into the minds of state Democratic leaders. Wallace, it appeared, just might win. The *Sun* acknowledged that his "opponents, having underrated his sophistication, are outflanked and left to seem alarmists." Instead, the southerner appeared the more "reasonable man."[58]

The state AFL-CIO Committee on Political Education did everything it could for Brewster but had to fight leaders and rank and filers who defiantly backed Wallace.[59] Among them was John Devlin, a Bethlehem Steel employee and a member of United Steelworkers Local 2610. Speaking as head of a coalition of political clubs in East Baltimore's First Legislative District, home to thousands of steelworkers, Devlin praised Wallace's "fight against Federal interference" in state concerns.[60] In early May United Steelworkers president David McDonald, dismayed by the Wallace vote in Indiana steel towns, wired his Baltimore district director to "make every possible effort" for Brewster.[61] Brewster needed the help. His foray into Baltimore's steel country produced, even by the *Sun*'s estimate, a "skimpy" crowd. Wallace, on the other hand, asked packed rallies of blue-collar workers to consider that if federal officials began telling corporations who to employ, "what does that do for your seniority rights? It destroys them." Wallace understood that working whites had few prerogatives on the job—with the as-yet undisputed exception of seniority rights.[62]

Maryland Democrats finally sent for McDonald himself. The night before the election, McDonald, Governor Tawes, and Massachusetts senator Edward Kennedy stumped East and South Baltimore in street-corner rallies fueled by abundant free beer.[63] But the problem was finding people to drink it. At one East Baltimore Polish American club, Brewster encountered only a handful of sullen officers and several unopened kegs.[64] Across the harbor and over the city line, Wallace closed his campaign at the Glen Burnie armory. Only half of the three thousand people who showed up could get in to see him, he was interrupted over sixty times by applause, and he left the stage to cries of "we love you George."[65]

The next morning, according to a local editor, blue-collar workers in Glen Burnie "went to the polls with big grins on their faces and voted with relish."[66] It is unlikely that many South and East Baltimore union members woke up that day with hangovers from Brewster beer. If they did, once in the voting booth they were sufficiently alert to pull the lever for Wallace. In his best showing yet, the governor took 43 percent of the Maryland vote as the pattern evident in the 1954 governor's race reappeared. Brewster carried the city only because of the black community's impressive voter mobilization. At 50 percent it was more than double the usual figure.[67]

Although not as united in favor of Wallace as blacks were in opposition, white support was broad. Middle-class conservatives in Baltimore County and on the Eastern Shore backed Wallace. In middle-class Hamilton, where a year before parents had protested school desegregation, the southerner got 55 percent of the vote. But his strongest backers were blue collarites.[68] In East and South Baltimore blue-collar wards 1, 23, and 24 combined, Wallace got 64 percent of the vote. In South Baltimore, the margins for Wallace ran in the high 60 percent range. In the Second Precinct of Ward 21, where the 1954 school desegregation protests had begun, Wallace got 71 percent of the vote. In Ward 24's Fourth Precinct—the site of Southern High School— Wallace took 67 percent. On average, the margins in East Baltimore ran in the low sixties. Farther east, in predominantly ethnic and more heavily unionized Highlandtown, they only reached the high fifties.[69]

"Never in the history of the state did colored voters deal more summarily with a candidate popular in other areas," boasted the *Baltimore Afro-American*'s political analyst.[70] He missed a more foreboding implication, though: never had Maryland's electorate fractured so cleanly along racial lines. Martin Luther King was more circumspect. The Maryland returns, he observed, proved to white America that "segregation is a national and not a sectional problem."[71]

Like King, Wallace biographer Dan T. Carter believes that Wallace's appeal was shaped primarily by racial fears. This "alchemist of the new social conservatism" tapped the reservoir of race, admixing only so much anti-communism, cultural nostalgia, and right-wing economics as necessary for effect.[72] Thomas and Mary Edsall similarly see "race-coded strategies" as accounting for Wallace's—and later Richard Nixon's—white working-class appeal.[73]

But these readings give Wallace too much credit and underestimate the power of his message. Wallace did not singlehandedly transform the dross of segregation into populist political gold: his supporters shaped his message as much as he gave voice to their resentments. More important, hidden race resentment is a weak reed on which to support so formidable a phenomenon as the new social conservatism. The three presidential campaigns of George Wallace were sustained by more than twenty years of white working-class experience. Some of those experiences did revolve around race, but increasingly they did not. It is suggestive to note that Wallace began as a southern populist and became a champion of segregation out of political expediency. It was the same for blue-collar urbanites who cut their political teeth during the days of the New Deal, the last time that they could remember when powerful politicians championed working people. The power of the new social conservatism, then, came not from the alchemist's wizardry but from the long-term vitality of the populist impulse in American history. It also benefited, and still does today, from the fact that liberals—civil rights leaders and historians among them—have so consistently underestimated it.

Escalation and Polarization, 1966

If the 1964 primary suggested that local concerns were now national ones, the events of 1966 confirmed it beyond dispute. Before that year, many of blue-collar Baltimore's problems still seemed local and solvable. Working whites continued to believe that black activists might be restrained in their attempts to reshape the racial boundaries of the city, overturning blue-collar institutions in the process. The blue-collar districts still had a dependable and effective barrier to change: the city council. By the end of 1966, however, black activists and white politicians had escalated the conflict, transforming concrete concerns over neighborhoods into symbolic concerns over culture.

The population of the city changed from 35 percent to 42 percent black in the early 1960s as areas of black settlement kept expanding.[74] By the end of 1966, nearly all of the twenty thousand whites who had lived in the Edmondson Avenue area in 1955 were gone. Most had heeded the invitations of suburban friends to "come on out here with the white people."[75] Two years later some areas along the city's western boundaries were 50 to 75 percent black.[76]

In the early 1960s, blacks who lived in Baltimore's eastern ghetto began moving to the north and east; although the white neighborhoods in the south and southeast were little affected, residents grew concerned.[77] In ethnic Southeast Baltimore, the idea of open housing defied logic and long-standing tradition. Many residents, said one man, were determined to "sell to whoever they want" since "most of their houses came from their parents and friends of their parents." In the early to mid-1960s, as neighborhood turnover intensified to the north, residents of Highlandtown put "we won't sell" signs in their windows.[78] Under pressure from without, working whites drew more closely together than ever before. In Canton, when word got out that a black family had moved into an apartment nearby, Polish, Italian, and Irish residents confronted the landlord together.[79]

By mid-decade, fair housing legislation had become the most divisive issue in local politics, but blue-collar Baltimoreans felt that they were faithfully defended by their city councilmen. In 1963 and again in 1965 a black councilman had introduced open housing legislation. Both times the initiatives were defeated. Then city council president Thomas D'Alesandro III (the son of the former mayor) introduced another open housing bill.[80] By early 1966 the fate of this bill was also in doubt, so Cardinal (formerly Archbishop) Lawrence Shehan made an unprecedented appearance before the city council. At a heavily attended hearing held at the War Memorial building, Shehan asked the council to bow to the "moral argument" implicit in the issue. About a third of the two thousand people in attendance booed the cardinal. They gave a warmer reception to a fundamentalist minister, a self-proclaimed "humble parish pastor," who called the issue a matter of "individual freedom." A woman from the small but vocal Baltimore Catholic Anti-Communist League accused Shehan of trying to lead a "double career as priest and politician."[81]

If ethnic and religious divisions were being bridged in common cause, labor's solidarity was badly weakened. Catholic UAW official Albert Mattes called the treatment given to Shehan a "horrible disgrace."[82] In this instance, as in others, there was a great deal of distance between union leadership and the rank and file. Less than two years earlier, a UAW member who had won a Baltimore County Council seat with union support, vetoed a public accommodations bill to the consternation of the Baltimore AFL-CIO.[83] When it came to social legislation, Baltimore's city council members, much more than labor leaders, acted as guardians of white working-class interests. Throughout the 1960s city council members representing the First and Sixth Districts could be counted on to vote against civil rights and antipoverty initiatives.[84] In rare cases when they did not, their constituents quickly brought them back into line.[85] In 1966 these council members behaved predictably, defeating the housing bill by a 13 to 8 vote.[86]

Reverend Joseph Connolly, one of those who had been arrested at Gwynn Oak, publicly noted that of the thirteen Catholics on the city council, only one voted for the bill. He laid the blame squarely on "neighborhood priests whose white parishioners still harbor racism."[87] One Baltimorean disagreed, claiming that Cardinal Shehan was booed "not by segregationists but by citizens."[88] Surely race was involved, but by rejecting all other arguments against open housing, the liberal clergy further discredited itself in the eyes of working-class Baltimoreans who were convinced that experience was a better guide than the dictates of activist ministers.

CORE had much to thank the liberal clergy for; the successful integration of Gwynn Oak Park in 1963 had revitalized the Baltimore chapter. Three years later the CORE national office began planning a pilot project to mobilize the poor and create a black political power base in an important city. One staffer sent the national office an assessment of conditions in Baltimore. He found Baltimore promising, citing the city's weak police department, the three-time defeat of open occupancy, the Gwynn Oak achievement, the predictable opposition of Luthardt's Fighting Ameri-

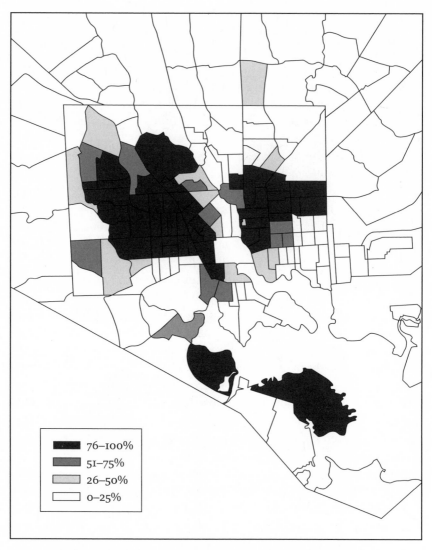

MAP 6. Black population, 1960 (*Source:* U.S. Bureau of the Census, *1960 Census of Population and Housing: Census Tracts, Baltimore, Maryland, Standard Metropolitan Statistical Area* [Washington, D.C.: GPO, 1962].)

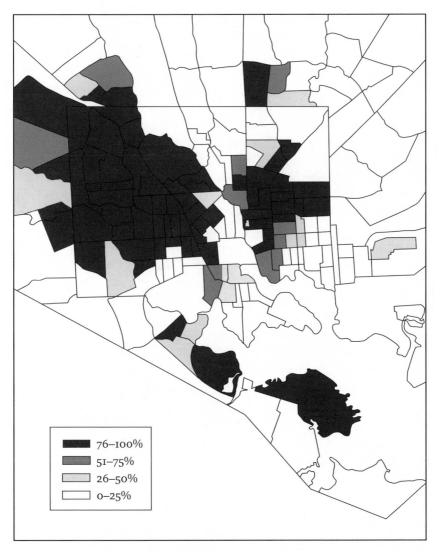

MAP 7. Black population, 1970 (*Source:* U.S. Bureau of the Census, *1970 Census of Population and Housing: Census Tracts, Baltimore, Maryland, Standard Metropolitan Statistical Area* [Washington, D.C.: GPO, 1972].)

can Nationalists, and the fact that George Wallace had "used Maryland as his proving ground outside the South."[89]

CORE's national office decided to use Maryland as a proving ground as well. On 14 April the congress announced that Baltimore would be its "Target City" for 1966.[90] Although Target City director Lincoln Lynch asserted that any violence that occurred would be at the instigation of whites, CORE was not above doing some verbal instigating of its own. Lynch declared the operation "a war" and said that CORE "did not propose to make public [its] battle plans before the proper time."[91]

Baltimoreans were stunned. "What are people to do?" one woman wrote Mayor Theodore McKeldin. "When I say people I mean decent citizens (colored and white) that go to work every day. . . . It is bad enough the way things are now in Baltimore . . . now we can look forward to riots, picketing, and the possibility of everything we have worked for being destroyed."[92] A Hampden man, suspecting that the group "could be Communist inspired," asked the mayor to simply prohibit CORE from coming to Baltimore.[93] Locals' suspicion of outsiders was in part justified. The Baltimore chapter of CORE split over the Target City project. Baltimore members wanted to continue an existing open housing campaign rather than focus on "street people." Consequently, CORE had to rely heavily on volunteers from outside Baltimore to conduct their Target City campaign.[94]

The local campaign did gain CORE some quick favorable publicity. Its picketing of an all-white luxury apartment complex downtown had attracted counterpickets from the tiny Maryland Ku Klux Klan, led by Vernon Naimaster. Naimaster was a former bus driver from Essex, a working-class suburb where many Martin and Bethlehem Steel employees lived. Naimaster was the kind of white racist whom CORE leaders appreciated. His opposition, they believed, could only gain them more sympathy. By 1 May the confrontations had escalated, with Klan marchers appearing in full regalia and for the first time joined by Luthardt's Fighting American Nationalists.[95]

Throughout May CORE stayed in the headlines with its apartment house protests, but it never got a confrontation on the scale that it desired.[96] Mayor McKeldin skillfully undercut it by setting up task forces to study urban problems. General George Gelston of the Maryland National Guard, who had handled major racial disturbances in the Eastern Shore city of Cambridge before being made police commissioner, was equally adept at defusing controversy before it turned to confrontation.[97] But what CORE did achieve was disturbing enough to working-class whites.

Curiously, in the black inner city a few white working-class bars still thrived. These taverns catered to white factory workers during the day and to displaced white residents returning to the old neighborhood in the evening. Many had been under the same proprietorship for years. The bars, said one CORE veteran, "had become white islands." Whites could sit down and be served, but blacks could only get carryout in their own neighborhoods. CORE organizers hoped that by picketing the bars they could mobilize low-income blacks around the issue, and in at least one instance they were right. In late May a crowd of 2,500 to 3,000 blacks gathered around counter-picketing Klansmen at Ritter's Bar. Two city policemen were hit by rocks hurled from the crowd as they escorted the Klansmen away.[98] The well-publicized police injuries elicited angry responses from even the city's liberals. McKeldin said that in this instance CORE's approach "doesn't give a good impression." Baltimore's leading liberal attorney, who had once represented Madalyn Murray, publicly repudiated CORE after the incident.[99]

In the spring and summer of 1966 Target City organizers held a series of street rallies in the Baltimore ghettoes. From CORE's perspective, these rallies, which attracted crowds of fifty to four hundred, were effective because they were "obviously a continual threat to public order." Through May and June CORE events regularly attracted a contingent of Klansmen, Luthardt's Fighting American Nationalists, and, in lesser numbers, members of the Catholic Anti-Communist League. At one event CORE members teased Robert Robusto, the head of the Catholic league, for being the sole representative of his group. Robusto admitted that his organization did not have too many "strong hearted people." Nevertheless, he claimed, "I'm as extreme as anybody else!"[100]

The most substantial white counterinitiative came from the Baltimore branch of the National States Rights Party. The NSRP was a virulently racist, anti-Semitic group led locally by a nineteen-year-old Joseph Carroll from suburban Lutherville. Richard Norton, another young local leader, was from Northeast Baltimore.[101] Carroll and Norton thought that they had found a more receptive environment in Southeast Baltimore than in the suburbs. They operated their Vinland bookstore in a prominent Highlandtown storefront throughout the late 1960s and held their own series of rallies in Southeast Baltimore's Patterson Park in the summer of 1966.[102]

Carroll secured the proper permits and persuaded the NSRP's Reverend Connie Lynch, a self-proclaimed inciter of race riots, to speak in Baltimore. On Wednesday, 25 July 1966, Lynch appeared on a stage adorned with the symbol of the NSRP, a Confederate flag with a Nazi SS lightning bolt superimposed on it. Wearing a string tie and a vest tailored from a Confederate flag, Lynch denounced CORE, communists, Jews, the NAACP, the Supreme Court, President Johnson, and the FBI. He castigated gun-control legislation and proclaimed his dedication to the preservation of the "pure races."[103]

About five hundred people, mostly teenagers, attended the first rally. Even CORE described the youth in attendance as "more curious than anything else."[104] More such "white man's rallies" were scheduled through the weekend, and despite the inflammatory rhetoric from the rostrum and condemnations by Mayor McKeldin, city officials claimed that they had no choice but to let the rallies continue so long as they remained peaceful. On Thursday night, Lynch greeted a crowd of eight hundred "in the name of Jesus Christ" and announced his intention to defend "God, the white race, and constitutional government."[105]

On Friday evening the crowd swelled to one thousand, and Lynch got what he was after. Some who had gathered, chanting "kill the niggers," broke away from the rally, assaulted a white left-wing radical who had been heckling from the edge of the throng, and made a series of forays into the ghetto area north of the park, attacking a black man who was quickly rescued by police.[106] That night, a twenty-minute battle broke out in a black East Baltimore neighborhood as black and white youths assaulted each other with bottles, rocks, and metal pipes.[107]

On Saturday, Carroll, Lynch, and Norton were arrested, and NSRP was barred from holding the rally scheduled for South Baltimore's Riverside Park that evening. Although the possibility of violence was, according to the *Sun,* "the sole topic of conversation" in South Baltimore, evening brought only Robert Robusto passing out NSRP leaflets and denouncing the Catholic priests who had been walking the neighborhoods all day trying to calm the locals. "Those people have created the situation," Robusto said, by preaching "all this racial justice and live with your brother stuff."[108]

Neither Robusto nor Connie Lynch spoke for more than a tiny group of white working-class Baltimoreans. That afternoon in South Baltimore, locals may have been talking about the rallies, but they carried on as usual. One barber, more interested in baseball scores than race riots, rebuffed an inquiring *Sun* reporter, saying: "I don't know about you. Myself I want to live." An American Legion carnival, bingo tournaments, and baseball games all went on as usual.[109] A Highlandtown man who remembered the NSRP rallies well felt that in general people "just sort of ignored them." He had never known anyone to enter the NSRP's Vinland bookstore.[110]

Young people look on as arrests are made at Patterson Park following the NSRP Rally on Friday, 27 July 1966. (Courtesy of the *Baltimore News-American* Photograph Collection, Special Collections, University of Maryland, College Park, Libraries)

Blue-collar Baltimore did learn a lesson from the NSRP rallies, but it was substantially different from that drawn by the mainstream press and politicians. C. D. Crowley, the editor of the *East Baltimore Guide,* reported on the large number of calls and letters his paper had received. Most locals had been offended by the language used and annoyed by the volume of the public address system, he noted. Some also "decried the entire idea of stark racism." The people of East Baltimore had no taste for the ugly extremism displayed at the rallies, and most went on with their daily activities. The larger lesson to be drawn, wrote Crowley, was that "respect for the law has reached a new low." But how could young people like those at the NSRP rallies be taught to respect the law, he asked, "when they see instance after instance of group leaders, including clergymen, breaking the law with impunity?" "Why should they worry about the law when they read that big shots have announced that they have no obligation to obey a law that didn't agree with their way of thinking?"[111]

Crowley's synopsis of white working-class grievances is notable for its lack of race talk. The efforts of "big shots"—lawmakers, philosophers, clergymen, and CORE—coupled with increasing crime and urban disorder were having an important effect. Whites were beginning to see issues of black and white as secondary symptoms, not primary causes. They could not agree with the "stark racism" displayed at Patterson Park—instead, the rhetoric of race was being displaced by the rhetoric of law and order. That the former was giving way to the latter for concrete reasons indicates that the popular appeals to "law and order" that saturated urban American politics by the late 1960s were not merely racism in disguise—they were qualitatively different. The 1966 gubernatorial election, between Democratic candidate George Mahoney and rising Baltimore County executive Spiro Agnew, marked an important transition point. Mahoney's campaign bridged the gap between the starker racism of George Wallace and the law-and-order platform espoused by a later incarnation of Spiro Agnew.

"The Only Man That Can Save This Neighborhood"

In the late 1960s George Mahoney was finishing a long career as a spoiler. It was an axiom of Maryland politics that Republicans could win only when the Democrats were divided, and no one could divide Democrats like the paving contractor from Baltimore County. In 1950 Mahoney's challenge to incumbent Franklin Lane had helped usher McKeldin into the governor's office. Four years later Mahoney repeated the feat, cutting deeply into "Curley" Byrd's support. Mahoney had run and lost in four other races since 1950, but he was no mere "perennial" candidate. Despite his penchant for running one-issue campaigns, he always attracted an impressive following, though never quite large enough.[112] Mahoney, according to one historian, always "stood for whatever he thought people wanted but could never figure out what it was."[113]

In 1966 Mahoney thought that he had finally figured it out. "All you need is one good face off between those State's Righters and CORE," one Maryland political observer wrote in 1966, "and watch what happens on election day."[114] Mahoney was willing to find out. In so doing he picked up the very expression that had helped keep black Southwest Baltimore homesteader Carnell Simmons out of jail almost twenty years earlier. "One of the basic precepts of our Founding Fathers was that a man's home is his castle," he announced in a speech that became the basis for his entire campaign.[115] To Mahoney's strongest supporters, the issue was as much the working-class community as the home. At a mid-August firemen's carnival parade held in the working-class suburb of Landsdowne, a spectator called out after Mahoney: "That guy is the only man that can save this neighborhood."[116]

One of Mahoney's primary challengers was Carleton Sickles, who ran with the blessing of the liberal wing of the Maryland Democratic Party headed by Senator Joseph Tydings, the stepson of Millard Tydings. Among the other primary entrants was Thomas Finan, who represented the pro-business, conservative wing of the party.[117] Mahoney stepped in with a campaign built around the phrase, "Your home is your castle, protect it!" and polarized the party, forcing all the other candidates—Sickles excepted—to come out against open occupancy as well.

Mahoney's popularity with working whites put the state AFL-CIO, which had been backing Sickles in the Maryland House of Delegates for years, in a bind. The *Sun* noted that trade unionists from East Baltimore and the industrial suburbs who could otherwise have been counted on to vote for Sickles found it "hard to accept the prospect of living in a racially mixed neighborhood."[118] The UAW's Albert Mattes lobbied for Sickles in East Baltimore but to no avail. A Canton man resented Mattes's insinuation that anyone who did not support open housing was a racist. "It seems in my opinion Mr. Mattes is one in reverse," he wrote.[119] Another East Baltimorean attacked the local UAW's campaign, which endorsed the Sickles ticket and opposed "local political bosses." Baltimoreans, he said, preferred "political bosses whom we can vote out of office at our discretion" over "labor bosses in Detroit who our votes cannot touch."[120]

John Devlin, the steelworker who had organized for Wallace in 1964, ran for the Maryland House of Delegates in the primary, touting his credentials as a "Democrat, Veteran, and Union Member" and echoing the "a man's home is his castle" theme.[121] Even Edward Garmatz, the card-carrying union electrician and veteran congressman from Baltimore, felt the need to proclaim loudly and often (though only in white working-class districts) that he was against open housing.[122]

It is doubtful that many East Baltimore union members were contrite when, after the primary, Jerry Wurf of the American Federation of State, County, and Municipal Employees complained to the Maryland AFL-CIO that "30 percent of the voters voted for bigotry."[123] In a field of eight candidates, that 30 percent was enough for a victory. In Baltimore City, despite a large and well-organized black voting bloc, Mahoney won by four thousand votes.[124] In East Baltimore's Ward 1, Mahoney got 68 percent of the vote compared with the labor candidate's 13 percent. "Members of organized labor have deserted their union in the field of political action," lamented Mattes.[125] Although one UAW local announced that it would back a third-party candidate in the general election, the state AFL-CIO Committee on Political Education decided to put Republican Spiro Agnew at the top of its "workingman's" ballots.[126] Baltimore's AFL-CIO, in a ringing testament to its own political irrelevance, wrote off the city's most heavily blue-collar districts. "We left them alone," admitted the AFL-CIO chairman.[127]

Mahoney's win may have left the state Democratic Party in disarray, but in Baltimore's white working-class wards the nomination was business as usual. Both important machines, the Hofferbert-D'Alesandro machine (named for the ex-mayor, still active in the group) in East Baltimore's First District and the Hodges-Leone machine (which had recently supplanted the Della-Wyatt organization) in South Baltimore's Sixth District had backed Mahoney in the primaries.[128]

One of the dominant themes in white working-class discourse during this period was the importance of "democracy," usually understood in its simplest form: the will of the majority rightfully trumps that of the minority. In Baltimore, blue-collar politics clearly displayed what David Halle has identified as "the point of view of an extreme democrat."[129] This perspective helped foster the emergence of blue-collar rights talk in the 1950s and 1960s. As early as October 1954, one Baltimore mother carried a sign that mixed the concept of rights with the ultimate expression of democracy—the vote. "We want our Rights," her placard read, "We voted for the School Loan—Why This?"[130] In the wake of the 1963 decision on school prayer a Dundalk woman asked Mayor McKeldin to stand up for "our children's rights [and] our citizen's rights." "What rights do the schools have anymore? The federal government is definitely taking over," she concluded.[131]

Working whites accurately perceived that on the federal level, the executive branch and especially the judiciary branch were doing much of the governing. Congress rarely came in for working-class reproach during the postwar years, largely, it could be argued, because it left unpopular steps up to the other two branches of government. The effect of this was a growing suspicion among working-class citizens that democracy was slipping away. Baltimoreans put more faith in what one woman described as "the *Supreme*

People" rather than in the Supreme Court.[132] In 1966 a Highlandtown man complained that "open housing is not a democratic procedure but rather a dictatorial policy."[133] The city council's resistance to civil rights legislation in Baltimore during the 1960s must have reassured working whites that in local politics at least, their voices were being heard.

During the general campaign, Mahoney stuck to his "castle" platform and denied that it had any racial implications. Spiro Agnew, he countered, with his "outright appeals to the negro population," was the one practicing racism. By the end of the campaign, though, he had attached a law-and-order plank to his open housing platform. In Baltimore's blue-collar areas, Mahoney voiced the general belief that the streets were becoming increasingly unsafe. In South Baltimore he promised to lift restraints on law enforcement officers. "Who do they think they are?" said Mahoney, referring to lawbreakers of indeterminate race. "They think they can go along and do anything they want." His implication became clearer as he continued: the police are told to treat "certain people with kid gloves." As governor he promised he would instruct policemen to "hit first, fire first."[134]

Spiro Agnew had never been a civil rights proponent, and his own position on open housing legislation had been one of lukewarm acceptance at best. But in contrast to Mahoney he appeared moderate if not liberal on the issue and began to attract black support.[135] He cultivated it by charging Mahoney with complicity in white hate mongering: "Remember all those cars with Mahoney bumper stickers on them when the National States Rights Party nearly caused a riot in Patterson Park," he said.[136]

On 8 November 1966 Marylanders went to the polls in the largest turnout for a gubernatorial election ever. Mahoney, in the words of the *Sun*, was buried under "an avalanche of negro and suburban white collar votes." But if middle-class whites in the suburbs disregarded Mahoney's message, those closer in did not. Precincts in middle-class Hamilton went for Mahoney by 53 percent. The blue-collar vote was even more substantial, and in the city as a whole polarization between black and white Baltimore voters was at least as stark as in the 1964 primary. Despite the wishes of organized labor and the efforts of the local Catholic leadership (the *Catholic Review* published a devastating attack on Mahoney a week before the election), the same working-class whites who had voted by a 64 percent margin for George Wallace gave Mahoney 71 percent of the vote.[137]

Agnew, whose highest aspiration only nine years earlier had been a seat on the Loch Raven Community Council, was governor-elect of Maryland. The 1966 governor's race, however, had been incorrectly characterized as a conflict between racists and civil rights champions. After the election, one analyst warned that "it would be a great mistake to interpret the Agnew victory as a mandate for open housing."[138] Spiro Agnew would soon prove that he was no "liberal."

Law, Order, and Race, 1968

With the Mahoney campaign, concern over open housing in blue-collar Baltimore crested. By 1966, blockbusting had begun to taper off and racial transition was making fewer headlines. In the Czech neighborhood border-ing East Baltimore's black area, anger at black home buyers had, by 1967, given way to "fatalistic acceptance," according to the *Evening Sun*.[139] Crime had become the much more important issue. Violent crime affecting home and family was of deepest concern to urban whites, but it seemed to shade imperceptibly into other kinds of lawlessness perpetrated by urban blacks and, increasingly, white activists. "A general respect for other people and the law," lamented one East Baltimorean in early 1968, "is as absent in the affluent whites as in the impoverished negroes."[140] Both kinds of lawbreak-ing heightened working-class resentment against politicians who seemed at best unable, and at worst unwilling, to do anything about it, no matter how many tax dollars were at their disposal. "Law and order" had ridden into the political mainstream on the back of the open housing issue, but it was soon standing on its own and commanding the respect of voters and politicians alike. By 1968 the problems faced by Baltimore's working whites were impossible to explain in terms of race but easily encapsulated without recourse to race talk at all.[141]

The nation was engulfed by a crime wave of tidal proportions in the 1960s. During the first six years of the decade crime rose 60 percent while the population increased only 10 percent. From 1966 to 1971 crime shot up another 83 percent. By mid-decade, both crime rates and public apprehen-sion had reached unprecedented levels. Explanations abound. Some cite the maturing of the baby boom generation to young adulthood—the prime age for lawbreaking. In Baltimore, as in other blue-collar cities, gradual deindustrialization no doubt contributed to impoverishment and helped drive up crime rates. But even so, the increase was entirely out of propor-tion to the city's industrial decline. Another contributing factor locally was the boom in heroin use, mostly among inner-city blacks, beginning around 1965.[142] In the 1950s shoplifting had been the preferred means of support-ing a habit, but by the late 1960s it had given way to burglary and violent crime. In Baltimore City from 1965 to 1970, burglaries tripled and robberies quintupled.[143]

For blue-collar whites as for others, an important reference point was the murder rate. In 1961 the Maryland murder rate was at its low point for the sixties at 4 percent below the national average. From 1961 to 1968 the national murder rate rose 45 percent while the Maryland rate shot up 106 percent.[144] In the summer of 1968 the newspapers announced that Baltimore's murder rate was fifth highest among America's major cities. In early 1969, on the basis of a new study, the *Baltimore News-American* (formerly the *News-Post*) proclaimed Baltimore to be "the number one crime city in the nation," its murder rate second only to Houston.[145]

To blue-collar Baltimoreans, the rising crime rates seemed explicitly linked to the failures of liberal government. An editorial in the *East Baltimore Guide* of 16 January 1968 observed that politicians "have yet to provide the man who is concerned with the safety of his family any evidence that they will protect him." Therefore, "every citizen has good reason to worry and seek out do-it-yourself protection." A month later, six out of seven letters to the editor of the *East Baltimore Guide* were on "the crime crisis." One woman lamented that the "cry of citizens about crime is drowned out by the louder voices of our elected officials who cry 'More Taxes!' "[146]

In 1969 *Life* magazine featured a six-week study of the city conducted by the Harris Poll. "Baltimore," *Life* announced, "is a city of silent terror." Three-fourths of Baltimoreans had changed their daily lives out of fear of crime. Evening church services were a thing of the past, and sales of security devices and handguns had soared. "In the daily lives of many citizens," the study found, "the fear of crime takes an even greater toll than crime itself."[147]

To white Baltimoreans, this change seemed directly connected to the racial transformation of the city's neighborhoods. By 1966 a woman in Northeast Baltimore had seen her white neighborhood give way to high-density black housing. She wrote McKeldin that "it is truly a shame to see this old, but well maintained, neighborhood going to slums in such a short period of time."[148] The same year another woman, "born and raised in North East Baltimore," complained about the neighborhoods of recent black settlement north of Patterson Park, making the link explicit. "Until this equal rights came along, North East Baltimore was a clean, safe section to live in," she said.[149]

Working-class whites had long emphasized the responsibility of residents to their neighborhood, and this shaped their reaction to the prospect

of urban decline. Blacks, many believed, simply did not put in the work necessary to keep up what were now their neighborhoods.[150] When McKeldin
appeared on television touring an inner-city slum, one woman noticed that
several "able bodied men" from the area were accompanying him. McKeldin, she wrote, should have insisted that *they must do something* about
conditions," rather than talking about "what the City of Baltimore is going
to do for them." She saw a simple solution in "Brooms, Water Pails, and
Cleaning rags used by *them* not everybody else."[151]

By 1967 Baltimoreans were sure that the government, which should en-
courage the use of soap and water and punish criminals, whether black or
white, was going to do neither. Said one East Baltimore man: "The fault lies
with the government, state and city authorities" who protect and condone
criminals "at the expense of the good citizen."[152] Throughout his political career Theodore McKeldin had shown a high degree of compassion for
blacks, Jews, and female voters. "The minority groups—they elected me,"
he once admitted.[153] But by 1967 it was clear that the mayor, who had
been seen skipping rope with inner-city children while Detroit and Newark
burned, could not win reelection: his attention to the black community had
alienated too many Baltimore whites.[154] That fall Thomas D'Alesandro III
took over the mayor's office. When he kept up McKeldin's attention to the
black community, angry Democrats told him to "stop naming commissions."
One Highlandtown critic believed that the interests of average citizens were
being ignored by "irresponsible officials," including the new mayor.[155]

It appeared that the responsiveness of government to working whites
was inversely proportional to the tax burden.[156] Property taxes, long a sore
spot for blue collarites, had been increasing steadily since 1958.[157] An April
1968 study found that city and state income taxes for Baltimore residents
were, with minor exceptions, the highest among the country's ten largest
cities.[158] "Working people may as well go on relief," despaired one woman.[159]
More important, citizens felt that they were not getting what they paid for.
"We are approaching a tyranny imposed by crime and high taxes—too little
of which monies are used for the good of the honest working people who
pay the bills here," wrote one man.[160]

To many, it seemed all too clear where the tax dollars—particularly at
the federal level—were going. Baltimore's welfare rolls exploded during
the decade. In 1960, 5,218 families with nearly 18,000 children were on welfare. Ten years later there were 26,666 families with 77,000 children on the
rolls—five times as many.[161] The city had one of the nation's first Community Action Programs, a Great Society antipoverty initiative supported by

both federal and city funds. Baltimore's Community Action Program spending started at $4 million in 1965 and peaked at $15 million in 1969.[162] And when tax money for "Great Society projects" was not going to programs for the poor, observed the *East Baltimore Guide,* it was being spent to benefit the "so-called cream of society."[163]

Despair at the Great Society's failures and rising fear of crime took place before a backdrop of urban violence unprecedented in American history. The landmarks are familiar: Watts in 1965, Hough in Cleveland and 36 other major urban riots in 1966. By the end of Summer 1967 there had been another 164 urban riots, the worst in Newark and Detroit. Then on 4 April 1968 Martin Luther King was assassinated. Up until then, Baltimore's leaders had been proud that their city had escaped the spreading racial violence. Even after fires started in Washington, D.C., Mayor D'Alesandro, only a few months in office, hoped that his city would be spared. But on 6 April, late on a Saturday afternoon, a bottle thrown from a crowd of black teenagers on the northeast side of the downtown broke a window at the Fashion Hat Shop, and four days and nights of rioting began.[164]

The 1968 riot confirmed many working whites' worst fears and yet again underscored the importance of neighborhood self-sufficiency. It discredited a Democratic political leader and made a Republican a hero. By 11:00 that Saturday night, city officials declared the riot out of control and Governor Agnew ordered 5,500 National Guard troops into Baltimore. By Sunday night the rioting had spread to the west and the Guard was overwhelmed. Governor Agnew requested federal troops, and the Guard was put under federal command.[165] Agnew had given the Guard strict orders not to shoot looters, a move that did much to minimize casualties, but when word got back to Southeast Baltimore that National Guardsmen and police officers just "stood by" while rioters destroyed property, whites prepared to defend themselves. "As far as they were concerned," recalled one resident, "law and order had to be maintained even if it had to be maintained by the individual."[166]

As the riot progressed, whites in Southeast Baltimore set "definite lines" to be defended. In some instances people were seen gathering with guns and other weapons.[167] Residents of Little Italy, which was close to the rioting and near a black public housing project, felt particularly vulnerable. There, according to two witnesses, whites took to rooftops with weapons for a time.[168] George O'Connor's landlord left a loaded shotgun in the hallway "in case the blacks decided to mount an assault on Highlandtown," he recalled.[169] This tendency toward vigilantism grew naturally out of working whites' belief in self-help and their loss of faith in civil authorities. In January 1969 the *East Baltimore Guide* tacitly acknowledged this when it lashed out at the *Evening Sun* for "covering up" violent crimes by burying accounts in the back pages: "Let us have no precipitous reaction. Let us avoid any thought of vigilante irresponsibility, the *Evening Sun* treatment seems to say."[170]

Working whites made much of their leaders' responses to the event. During the riots, D'Alesandro called on the city's black leadership, both "moderate and militant" in the *Sun*'s words, to help maintain order.[171] Agnew's position against shooting looters was unpopular but quickly forgotten. What whites remembered was the stand he took in the aftermath of the riot that changed his life and national politics as well.

Agnew had been growing increasingly disturbed with "black power" since late 1967. That July, rioting broke out in Cambridge on Maryland's Eastern shore after an incendiary speech was delivered by H. Rap Brown of the Student Nonviolent Coordinating Committee (SNCC), which, despite its name, had renounced nonviolence for radical black militancy and "black power." When Agnew received a copy of Brown's speech a few months later, he was shocked by the rhetoric; he was appalled when Brown's inflammatory words did not have the same effect on Maryland's moderate black leaders.[172] In early 1968, when SNCC leaders set up a Baltimore office and called the city's war on crime "a war on the black man," black moderates condemned them. On 24 March, in an effort to heal this split, the moderates and the militants had a secret meeting. Agnew heard of it and began planning to rebuke civil rights leaders for their collusion with extremists. Although the riot intervened, Agnew stuck to his plan, making his statement far more potent than it otherwise would have been.[173]

On 11 April, with 6 dead, 700 injured, 1,000 businesses destroyed, damage costs reaching $14 million, and ashes still smoldering, Agnew called a meeting with civil rights leaders, many of whom had just come off the streets in attempts to calm the black community. There, city and state officials sat before the black leaders—"like a white jury sitting in judgement on the slave folk," recalled one man present—and Agnew delivered his rebuke.[174]

Agnew's initial remarks seemed tailored for a third party not present—Baltimore's white working-class community. "I did not request your presence to bid for peace with the public dollar," he began. Then he called attention to the white men seated beside him. "Look around you and you may

The speech that made a vice president. Spiro Agnew rebukes Baltimore's black leadership in the wake of the April 1968 riots. (Courtesy of the *Baltimore News-American* Photograph Collection, Special Collections, University of Maryland, College Park, Libraries)

notice that everyone here is a leader—and that each leader present has *worked* his way to the top."[175] As black leaders began walking out, Agnew blamed Baltimore's black moderates for refusing to speak out against extremists and cast the riots as the inevitable result. By the time he was done, only half of the audience remained. The NAACP's Juanita Jackson Mitchell spoke for them, blaming the city for making "burners and looters" of their children. Mayor D'Alesandro issued a public statement deploring Agnew's comments. Liberals and blacks hated the speech, but working-class whites in Baltimore and across the country loved it.[176] The *Baltimore Labor Herald* went so far as to call it "one of the outstanding speeches of the century."[177]

In 1967 working whites who fondly remembered the mayoralty of another Thomas D'Alesandro had elected his son by a record margin. But in the civil rights era, the younger D'Alesandro was forced to choose between black support and a blue-collar constituency.[178] Even before the riot, a growing number of working whites agreed with an East Baltimore seamstress who claimed, "along with so many other loyal Democrats," to have "become disillusioned." She accused D'Alesandro of "bending to the will of various negro factions" in a way that proved he was "not the D'Alesandro his father was."[179] After the riot he paled in comparison to Agnew, who had the courage to denounce what the wife of a Martin Company worker called "not just the white man's racism but black man's racism too."[180]

The 1968 riot marks the point when most remaining vestiges of race talk passed out of the language of working-class discontent. Rising crime helped smother blatantly racist resentments, but equally important was the new-found ability of whites—in the wake of "black power"—to charge blacks with racism as well. Where whites had formerly pressed for exclusionary, race-based rights, now blacks seemed to be doing so. Blue collarites considered black power as illegitimate as Agnew did: the problem seemed to be that other powerful whites did not. Blue-collar discontent moved to a different level: "racism" explained little, "liberalism" explained much. A North Baltimore clerk, who had seen D'Alesandro and some spokesmen for the "white community" on television, complained to the mayor's office that "moneyed men" from exclusive neighborhoods did not represent the "middle class," whose "only right is to pay taxes" that provide "goodies for the loafers and goof-offs who loot and riot. Whose only philosophy is to get what you can without working." In contrast, he said, Agnew "displayed a rare trait in public officials. He had the courage to say what had to be said."[181]

Another person who thought highly of Agnew's speech was Patrick Buchanan, and he sent a copy to his boss Richard Nixon.[182] Nixon had met Agnew a few months earlier and was impressed. "There can be a mystique about a man. You can look him in the eye and know he's got it. This guy has got it," Nixon later said. Prior to 11 April, Agnew's prospects had not been bright. His term as county executive had been made possible only because of a split in the ranks of the Baltimore County Democratic Party. George Mahoney had rescued him from certain defeat for a second term by making him governor the same way. "If he would hold still for a minute," said Maryland Democrat Paul Sarbanes, "we'd nail him." Agnew might have been thinking along these lines on 11 April, when he told his critics: "Don't you know I'm committing political suicide when I sit here and do this?"[183]

But Agnew's luck held. In August Nixon decided that he thought enough of Agnew's mystique to make him his running mate. In Agnew's acceptance speech at the Republican National Convention, a bit of the 1966 social liberal resurfaced when he called for an end to racial discrimination. But the new Agnew won out. "Anarchy, rioting, and even civil disobedience have no constructive purpose in a constitutional republic," declared the candidate.[184] As the 1968 presidential campaign began, Agnew assumed the role of Nixon's blunt-spoken hatchet man and began working to carve votes away from George Wallace, who had complicated the race by entering as an independent. Agnew ran against one would-be Wallace in 1966. Two years later he had become one himself.

In Baltimore, those voters who had backed Wallace in 1964 and Mahoney in 1966 made a revealing choice. Although the third-party bid provided another opportunity to vote for the southerner, Wallace remained a protest candidate. Nixon, on the other hand, was electable. But there was another difference between the candidates. Wallace, no matter what he said, would forever be the "racist's" candidate. Nixon and especially his running mate were expressing a more potent, and indeed more accurate, sentiment. "Law and order" easily encapsulated white-working peoples' fears about the decline of their neighborhoods and their resentments against leaders who had turned their backs on blue-collar culture. The phrase "law and order" appealed not solely to an ephemeral and generalized resentment, but to a host of material grievances. Equally important, the words carried ample gravity of their own—they were much more than gauze for racist resentments too ugly to be voiced. By 1968, not only were blacks breaking laws with seeming impunity, but whites—college students and clergy—were as well. Indeed, the clergymen and women who troubled Baltimoreans most that year were practicing much more than nonviolent resistance.

On 17 May 1968, a beautiful Friday afternoon, three women were working at the local draft board upstairs in the Knights of Columbus building in Catonsville, just west of Baltimore. When the head clerk turned and recognized Baltimore priest Philip Berrigan, she thought, "Oh my Lord something is going to happen."[185] Berrigan, his brother Daniel, a professor at Cornell University, and seven other Catholic priests politely called the women "murderers," filled two wastebaskets full of draft records, and burned them in the parking lot.[186] On 7 October, with the presidential campaign under way, the trial of the "Catonsville Nine" began in Baltimore. A Peace Action Committee, coordinating demonstrations in support of the Berrigans, sent out flyers inviting protesters to "Agnew Country."[187]

On the morning of the seventh, 1,500 antiwar marchers filled the streets of Baltimore, challenged only by a handful of NSRP counterpickets who waved an American flag in front of the post office.[188] In North Baltimore, near Johns Hopkins University, two working-class women watched the paraders convene. They were less concerned with hippies' cries of "smash the state" than with the nuns and priests who followed them singing (in what was an all-white parade) "We Shall Overcome." "I suppose you'll tell us how to live next Sunday from the pulpit," one women called out. "They'll meet their match tonight," another remarked, for George Wallace was making a campaign appearance at the Baltimore Civic Center.[189]

That night, Wallace, who had kicked off his drive into the northern states at Glen Burnie in June, exhorted a crowd of 7,500. His partisans, said the *Sun* in an account reminiscent of its 1964 story, "stomped, shouted, and shook fists" as their man berated hecklers. Wallace attacked the usual targets, including the breakdown of law and order, the Supreme Court, and the misuse of federal tax money.[190] But his greatest applause came when, in a now-familiar routine, the southerner told his hecklers—some black and some white—that he had "two four letter words you don't know: S-O-A-P and W-O-R-K." The crowd, said the *Sun,* "went wild." For the Baltimoreans who supported Wallace, Garry Wills wrote, "work [was] the magic word."[191]

Strained by the Wallace and Agnew candidacies, the ties of party loyalty that had kept Baltimore's working whites allied with the Democrats were weakening. By the fall of 1968, the national press was making much of blue-collar support for Wallace.[192] The AFL-CIO fought Wallace hard, both on the national and state level. The state AFL-CIO Committee on Political Education distributed half a million anti-Wallace pamphlets, including one entitled "Do Maryland Workers Want Alabama Wages?"[193] But the *Labor Herald* unapologetically championed Wallace. Nearly every issue's political column started with observations like "if the election were held today Wallace would win." One columnist claimed to speak for the "average guy" angered by "uneducated blacks" who were using federal money to tell people to "burn everything the Whitey owns" and filthy hippies who were burning draft cards—people who "get paid for not working." As this labor spokesman saw it, these issues had an immediacy that the AFL-CIO's economic arguments lacked.[194]

In the *East Baltimore Guide,* the UAW's Albert Mattes asked his fellow Democrats "to be loyal to their party this crucial year of 1968." "It seems to me," countered East Baltimore mechanic Ray Murawski, "that the Democratic party should have been loyal to the people during their term in office." Murawski claimed that he had "no intention" of voting for Wallace but cautioned Baltimoreans not to be "swayed by false loyalty complexes."[195] C. D. Crowley, the paper's editor, wrote that even though "there is virtue in being faithful to one's party . . . I'm going to vote for Nixon." As for labor's argument that the Democrats made Social Security and Medicare possible, a "disillusioned Democrat" wrote that both would be "totally useless if we are murdered on the streets." A Highlandtown man said simply, "Ted Agnew has stood up for us and we should stand up for him."[196]

Some of the Southeast Baltimoreans who had gone "out the road" appear to have stood up for Agnew as well. In Hamilton, Nixon got 51 percent of the vote and the Nixon and Wallace totals combined hit 64 percent—there was not much left for the Democrats. But party loyalty was stronger among urban blue collarites. Wards 1, 23, and 24 combined gave the Democrats 53 percent of the vote, but only because some unionists appear to have heeded the call for party loyalty. In heavily unionized Southeast Baltimore, Hubert Humphrey garnered 54 percent of the vote, but in South Baltimore's Wards 23 and 24, the Wallace and Nixon votes combined kept Humphrey's share below 50 percent of the total.[197]

Spiro Agnew Country

Although enough blue-collar whites stuck with the Democrats to give Humphrey a thin edge, white working-class defectors helped elect Nixon, a man pledged to listen to the voices of the same "forgotten Americans, the non-shouters, the nondemonstrators," who had been so heartened by Agnew's 11 April 1968 speech.[198] In Baltimore, 1968, the year of the pivotal racial event of the decade, marked the moment when the politics of race began to recede from the political stage.

By the 1960s New Deal liberalism was dead, succeeded by a rights-based liberalism that could no longer protect, or even sanction, the institutions and ideals of the urban white working class. Early in the decade, blue collarites staked their own rights-based claims, but they were "race-based" rather than "civil" rights. At the dawning of the Great Society, the national Democratic Party had no place for these claims, but from the South came a politics of populism that was much more accommodating. In 1964 a majority of Baltimore's white working voters agreed with Pearl Lowery, a carpenter's wife, who said, "if the State of Maryland does not have anyone who will stand up for the rights of whites as well as colored, then we can support someone who will, even though he is from Alabama."[199]

In 1968 a new white working-class champion emerged closer to home. For John Ragin, a baker from Southwest Baltimore of second-generation Hungarian descent, it was the 11 April speech that sold him on Agnew. In 1970 Ragin claimed to be "mostly-Democrat." But "I'll switch if I like," he said, and he had presidential hopes for Agnew: "If he keeps hitting the nail on the head the way he's doing now, I think he'll go someplace." In 1964 George Wallace stood up for white rights. Six years later, as Ragin saw it, Spiro Agnew stood up for the "little man" against the "big money."[200] In a space of six years working whites had begun to see and enunciate their problems differently. George Wallace was a master practitioner of southern politics. Spiro Agnew was from overwhelmingly white Baltimore County, not Alabama. He had little experience with the politics of race and needed none. His message was one of right versus wrong rather than black versus white, and it was to the former rather than the latter that white working-class voters responded in 1968.

Despite the travails of the 1960s, a slim majority of Baltimore's working-class whites stuck with the party of labor in 1968. Still, blue collarites did not mind being from "Spiro Agnew Country." A 1970 Gallup Poll found Agnew to be the third most admired man in America behind Richard Nixon and Billy Graham, but it took working people longer than it did Agnew to switch parties.[201] In July 1972 steelworkers and retirees in a Highlandtown bar told a reporter that Southeast Baltimore was "Spiro Agnew Country." The journalist reminded them that Agnew had lost there in 1968. "Course he did," one of the patrons replied without missing a beat, "he ain't a Democrat!"[202]

In the last few months of 1969, nearly every news magazine reported on "troubled," "forgotten," or "middle" Americans. Whatever they were called, most anecdotes revolved around urban blue collarites. The networks ran shows championing small-town American values, but the one that took hold was *All in the Family* with the comforting message that there was little more than bluster beneath the seemingly menacing exterior of the "troubled American." Although the term had been around since 1964, the sudden and spectacular reemergence of the "white backlash" stereotype late in the decade suggests that the grounds of the political debate had shifted.[203] In the 1960s concerns that had existed for decades were now being fought out in the national political arena, and, more problematically, they were being argued in terms quite legitimate in American political discourse. By 1970 working-class discourse contained too many invocations of democracy and the rule of law, and too few appeals to white supremacy and violence. This made it difficult to dismiss blue-collar arguments as racist, but liberal intellectuals and politicians succeeded in doing so.

"White backlash" offered an easy way to understand these perplexing challenges to the liberal order by providing a caricature: "Joe Six-Pack," insecure about his own social standing, was lashing out against the blacks, using thinly veiled code words to substitute for his true white supremacist leanings. And so, as the long arc of postwar liberalism peaked and plummeted sharply, dragged down by the destruction not only of its urban coalition, but also of the cities themselves, it was easy to pretend that no one had seen the trouble coming.

CHAPTER 6

The Not-So-Silent Majority

On 14 June 1976 Gloria Aull went to Washington, D.C., to tell a Senate subcommittee about her neighborhood. Mrs. Aull, fifty-one years old, of German descent, and the third generation to live in her family's Southeast Baltimore row house, claimed to be typical of those who had "remained in the city by choice." By then much had changed. With the early integrationist goals of the civil rights movement having been met yet found lacking, black leaders were now regularly making appeals to racial solidarity instead. People like Aull, on the other hand, were making broad claims in the interest of "working" people rather than whites. But more than the message had changed: for a brief time it seemed as if the very nature of working-class activism might have been transformed. Blue-collar political protest had always been short-lived, narrowly focused, and, most of all, rare. This spurred Richard Nixon, in a 1969 speech requesting support for the war in Vietnam, to dub white working people the "great silent majority." Then suddenly in the early 1970s, some blue collarites became activists, supporting sustained community efforts to gain and keep broad-based political power.

One precondition for this change was generational. Aull was firmly within the first postwar generation, but many of her strongest allies were blue-collar baby boomers, who, like their counterparts nationwide, were questioning the institutions and traditions they inherited from their parents. For some, the answer seemed to lie in making a new start in the suburbs; for others, the city still held promise. Those who remained, said Aull, were the "the hope for the future of southeast Baltimore."[1]

The radical politics of their campus cohorts was disdained by the young people who stayed in blue-collar Baltimore, but by the late 1960s Baltimore's working whites were developing an alternative community-based politics that was radical enough for them. Inspired by the civil rights movement, it was ignited by a full realization of what working-class whites had been suspecting for years. "Our problems were not with the people of our neighborhood," said Gloria Aull. "The source of our dilemma was with government policymakers. . . . We were written off. We were supposed to be the silent majority."[2]

In the early 1970s Baltimore's Southeast Community Organization became nationally known as one of the most successful of the new grassroots, ethnically based community organizations. SECO and groups like it empowered white working-class people when they were experiencing mounting economic and social distress and searching for a new voice in local and national politics. The new neighborhood organizations were overtly political—they accumulated and used power to effect social change, yet their politics is hard to classify. Some of the social conservatism that marked traditional neighborhood protective associations remained, but in its early period SECO was unequivocally antiestablishment, encouraging working Baltimoreans to seek change outside of the traditional channels of urban politics. It enunciated a neighborhood populism that depicted the community as the only legitimate repository of urban power.

Although it was centered in white working-class Southeast Baltimore, SECO's base was broad. Middle-class gentrifiers and longtime working-class residents, socially conservative Catholics, and radical militants all mingled in SECO. In the end this broad coalition broke down into two groups, each with conflicting visions of community activism derived from differing urban experiences. A largely middle-class group chose to create a centralized economic institution to strengthen Southeast Baltimore. A working-class group pursued a more purely democratic vision, believing that power should derive from the community and not be vested in a large, unaccountable organization. That unity of opinion carried over to the subject of race, on which most working whites shared a well-defined position. History taught them that compulsory integration, the main liberal solution to urban racial inequities, was ineffective, destructive, and, most important, unfair. Middle-class liberals practiced a politics of ideas and ideals, but white working-class politics was grounded in experience—it derived from, and sought to protect, the white working-class community.

Generations

In December 1949 the *South Baltimore Enterprise* ran an editorial on citizenship. "It is in the home that children 'grow into' the rights, privileges, and responsibilities of citizenship," the columnist wrote. "When members of a family are not made aware of their responsibilities to the community and go wrong, the whole neighborhood gets a black eye."[3] This statement not only underscored the importance of family and neighborhood to working whites' view of citizenship in the postwar years, it also affirmed a communal investment in child rearing. Working whites, the *Enterprise* suggested, had a community obligation to raise responsible children. White working-class Baltimore experienced its share of youthful rebellion in the 1940s and 1950s, but it was usually ritualistic and never a challenge to community institutions. When, in the years after World War II, Canton and Highlandtown youths formed rival gangs, adults launched the Canton Area Council to see to the proper stewardship of the community's "basic raw material, the children."[4] In the mid-1950s local teenagers, to the distress of parents, divided themselves into "drapes" (a term describing a type of dress) and "squares" and engaged in small contests over community space.[5] A generalized concern over juvenile delinquency that was typical nationwide during these years was eclipsed, however, as serious crime grew more prevalent.[6]

One consequential difference between the younger and older generations was the former's familiarity with black culture. By the mid-1950s Buddy Deane, the first Baltimore disc jockey to play black rhythm and blues records, was, according to one native, "just about every Baltimore kid's hero." White parents tolerated their children's picking up *Deane's Disc Digest* at local music stores and attending his sock hops, and they did not mind when, in 1957, Deane took his show to television. For six years local teens danced on the air, but then the show gave way to the same pressures that had already swept the city at large. Although he held an "all-black hop" once a month, Buddy Deane's show was white, and in the early 1960s black activists began picketing and holding rallies outside the WJZ studios. In January 1964 Deane integrated his TV dance floor. WJZ, overwhelmed by an outpouring of white anger, canceled the show. Deane had challenged more than white institutions, he had threatened white culture in general. "Integrated dancing is more delicate than schools or jobs," Deane observed.[7]

Although this incident can be seen as another example of the staunch defense of whiteness, it was mostly an older generation doing the defending. A younger generation of Baltimore whites embraced black culture as their own—an important early indication that blue-collar institutions need not be white in the future.

By the 1960s many grown children were engaging in a more palpable rebellion: they were among the first to abandon blue-collar neighborhoods for the suburbs. Between 1960 and 1970 the white population in Southeast

A new generation of working-class citizens. Third graders at Holy Rosary School, Southeast Baltimore, in the late 1950s. (Courtesy of the *Baltimore News-American* Photograph Collection, Special Collections, University of Maryland, College Park, Libraries)

Baltimore declined by about 20 percent. In South Baltimore and Locust Point the loss was smaller at around 11 percent.[8] As young adults fled, blue-collar Baltimore aged. In 1963 the median age in the Third Congressional District, covering white working-class Baltimore, was well below the state average. Over the next ten years the median age in the Third District increased 46 percent. By 1973 it had the most aged population in the state.[9] "All I got is old people," complained city councilman Dominic "Mimi" DiPietro in 1977, stressing the political consequences of the exodus. "It used to be four or five votes to a family," he said, but "now it's one."[10]

Older residents believed that young people had lost "the love of family and the love of neighbors" that had characterized earlier generations.[11] Many older residents despaired that Baltimore children had decided that a row house "wasn't good enough for them" and abandoned the city for the suburbs.[12] By 1971 Jim Clarke, a crane operator born and raised in Canton, was in a minority of "thirtyish" people content to stay. It is telling that the *Baltimore Evening Sun* reporter who interviewed Clarke described him as "completely neighborhood-oriented."[13]

A Baltimore working-class upbringing did much to inculcate the kind of neighborhood loyalty that Clarke displayed. George O'Connor remembered that, as children, he and his friends would "try to think of what it would be like to work at General Motors or Sparrows Point."[14] By the 1970s, though, unionists had their doubts about this new generation. Older workers—those who had lived through the struggles of the 1930s—knew well what the union had accomplished. Young people were more likely to take for granted the high wages and generous benefits that union activism had made possible. What was worse, they assumed that management provided those benefits "out of the goodness of their heart," according to veteran steelworker James Butterfield. "The only time he hears about the union is when they take his dues out," Butterfield said.[15]

There were political implications to the younger generation's indifference toward organized labor. Throughout the 1960s the AFL-CIO Committee on Political Education (COPE) had never been very successful at mobilizing working-class votes. But heavily unionized Southeast Baltimore still voted more consistently Democratic than did South Baltimore. By the end of the decade, however, Frederick Gress, a veteran of Local 2610, was convinced that the failure of young people to get involved, "not only in COPE, but in the union," was one of organized labor's main problems. "I know we have a few [younger union activists]," he said, "but there are not enough."[16] As union loyalty declined, labor's already nominal political clout could only deteriorate further.

Arthur Vogel, a longtime shop steward at Bethlehem Steel, saw another change in the generation of workers that started in the mills around 1970. "The older men took pride in making a real quality product," he said. As new workers came into the plant, Vogel believed, the pride had "slipped away." "They're there to make money now." Nevertheless, a few younger blue collarites still treasured both the union and the job. Steelworker Carl Tergis grew up in the 1950s and, like George O'Connor, went to Baltimore's Mergenthaler Vocational School. A crane operator at Sparrows Point, Tergis took pride in his work, studied labor history, and became a shop steward in Local 2610.[17]

Some blue-collar parents entertained hopes of social mobility for their children. When Jack Maeby was growing up in Southeast Baltimore, his father, a wire maker, used to tell him: "Use this," pointing to his head, "instead of these," holding out his factory-grimed hands.[18] Maeby took his father's advice. For others, blue-collar life held an attraction that parental faith in upward mobility could not change. Wayne Browning's parents wanted him to be a "doctor or a lawyer" and saved for his education. Instead, he preferred to work with his hands and dropped out of high school to be an electrician.[19]

Still, working-class parents' faith in upward mobility can be overstated. Steelworker Ed Listopad believed that "life would be easier and more secure" for his son if he were to become a doctor but was not troubled by his son's lack of interest in school. "He loves working with tools and he's happy. That's all I care about," said Listopad.[20] This attitude was not unreasonable given that, for many working-class children, college remained financially out of reach. One autoworker was proud that his son had done well at Patterson High School and had interned as a draftsman for a time. But both father and son understood that a college education—which they could not afford—would have been necessary to continue. Instead, the UAW veteran told the union that his nineteen-year-old son's "one ambition has been to work at Fisher Body."[21]

Even for the blue-collar children who did not abandon the old neighborhood and the industrial workplace, the social upheavals of the 1960s were keenly felt. George O'Connor sensed a complacency among Southeast Baltimore youth in the 1950s, but in the next decade that changed. By the late 1960s he and his friends in Highlandtown were asking the same questions about society as were suburban youth. This fostered a new sense of independence among the blue-collar young, but at least a few still recognized that the working-class community offered an opportunity to use both head and hands.[22]

Working-class women were the greatest beneficiaries of this generational change. In the postwar years, with wages rising and families growing, most blue-collar women in Baltimore, as elsewhere, opted to stay at home and raise children. At the beginning of the 1950s, the number of women in the labor force in white working-class wards 1, 23, and 24 was 4.8 percent lower than the city average; by 1960 it was 8.6 percent lower. These working-class women were never entirely homebound. They were at the forefront of community-based initiatives, active in neighborhood and religious organizations, and leaders in the school desegregation protests of the 1950s. By the 1970s they were still playing activist roles, but in organizations that were far different in scope and nature.

Unlike the Fulton Avenue Improvement Association, community organizations in white South and Southeast Baltimore had avoided controversy in the postwar years. Their community councils were essentially conservative organizations with limited goals, guided by a handful of mostly middle-class leaders who worked within, rather than around, Baltimore's political system. Local politicians representing white working-class Baltimore, after all, vigilantly guarded their constituents' interests when it came to social change.[23] It took powerful outside forces to rouse blue-collar Baltimore's community groups from their complacency.

Protesting the Road

The first plans for an expressway linking East and West Baltimore were laid in the 1940s. These stalled due to financial problems, but the 1956 Interstate Highway Act's promise of 90 percent federal funding revived the project.[24] By the early 1960s city planners had settled on a route that cut through working-class South Baltimore and spanned the harbor. Citizen's groups had opposed highway plans since the 1940s, but this one drew the first sustained resistance. In early 1962 a crowd of thirteen hundred, described by the *Sun* as "East Baltimore steelworkers and west Baltimore housewives," confronted city planners at an East Baltimore high school. A spokesman for three East Baltimore improvement associations argued against the proposed demolitions. "Our property is good tax property, not slum property," he said. A local city councilman contrasted middle-class highway supporters from suburban Baltimore County with working-class urban dwellers. City residents, he said, "are the people who ought to be heard. . . . Not those who live in the county."[25]

   The issue soon slipped out of the headlines but gained momentum in the neighborhoods. In early 1965 one councilman warned Mayor Theodore McKeldin that opposition to the expressway was deep and growing; it would soon "awaken the city."[26] Later that year an ordinance initiating the seizure of land in Southeast Baltimore for the road cleared the city council. Within the condemned areas real estate deteriorated and once-vital neighborhoods were gutted. In Canton's St. Casimir Parish, two hundred Polish families living within sight of the church packed to leave.[27] Tensions building for twenty-five years in Baltimore's working-class neighborhoods began to find release, touching off an efflorescence of neighborhood activism that crested in the 1970s. Blue-collar Southeast Baltimore was not alone in fighting Baltimore's expressway plans. Residents of white, upscale Bolton Hill, black middle- and working-class Rosemont, and tightly knit, white ethnic

Locust Point all fought the road.[28] But in Southeast Baltimore, fighting the road was a beginning, not an end.

The first major organization to oppose the road was started by newly arrived middle-class gentrifiers rather than longtime blue-collar residents. They founded the Society for the Preservation of Federal Hill, Montgomery Street, and Fells Point in early 1967. The first leader of the SPFH, a suburbanite, had recently acquired six properties in Fells Point, the eighteenth-century port area favored by the first Baltimore gentrifiers. The group advocated moving the route north, away from the historic waterfront and through a blue-collar residential area.[29] The SPFH was more interested in safeguarding members' investments than in preserving urban neighborhoods: its goal was to create "the showplace of our city."[30] The group had deep pockets and generated a great deal of fast publicity, but it just as quickly alienated blue-collar locals.

In May 1967 more than five hundred residents packed into a standing-room-only meeting of the SPFH. Most opposed the society's plans, and they "hooted down" its members' speeches. A First District councilman assured residents that "the society are not interested in you people, they never were interested in you people." After twenty minutes of this, about three hundred people walked out. "Let's let the silk stockings hold their own meeting," one of them said. The majority of those residents, the councilman later commented, did not oppose the highway. Instead, they had already decided to cut their losses and get out.[31]

Others, including Gloria Aull, were not as ready to abandon their homes and neighborhoods. Aull lived in a Canton row house that her German grandmother had bought for five dollars down at the turn of the century. While doing volunteer church work she met Barbara Mikulski.[32] Mikulski was also a third-generation East Baltimorean. Then in her early thirties, she was the granddaughter of Polish immigrants and the daughter of a local grocer. A college-educated social worker living in Highlandtown, she had just been named Maryland's "outstanding young woman of the year."[33] Mikulski shared Aull's outrage against the highway, and in early 1969 the two joined with Jack Gleason, a newcomer to Fells Point and the new president of the SPFH, to form the Southeast Committee against the Road.[34] SCAR set to work mobilizing the residents of Southeast Baltimore through educational campaigns, press releases, and the Catholic Church.[35]

Building a movement around the issue of the road posed some major difficulties. The anger that the activists sought to harness was directed more against the way in which the highway was being built—especially the prices being paid for property—than against the construction of the highway itself. One Southeast Baltimore woman who complained to President Lyndon Johnson about the "mental anguish" of having to leave her home, was most angry about "being robbed" of her property by "rich politicians" who, in her view, refused to pay what the property was worth.[36] For those determined to sell out quickly, the highway opponents were a problem rather than a solution. Residents of a condemned Lithuanian neighborhood took their case to the secretary of transportation. No longer able to sell their houses on the open market, they said that their "only hope has been the expressway." The "expressway dissidents," they complained, were too often outsiders. Those wanting to remain in the condemnation area "hardly constitute a neighborhood."[37] A final problem was residents' apathy. Many living within a few blocks of the condemnation line, activists observed, considered it "someone else's problem."[38] Moreover, because of its protracted nature, the highway fight engendered little feeling of accomplishment.

Although blue-collar Baltimore was hardly united against the road, SCAR brought together a larger and more diverse group of Southeast Baltimoreans than ever before. The group was committed to working toward change by confronting, rather than petitioning, political leaders. The road acted as a catalyst, but issues that affected more Southeast Baltimoreans and could be resolved quickly were key in building support. SCAR helped defeat a zoning ordinance that would have opened much of the area to heavy industry, blockaded truck routes through neighborhoods with baby carriages, and kept the city from closing a local branch library. Meanwhile, according to activists, SCAR had "became the planning committee for the Southeast Community Organization." SECO was not officially founded for another year, but the name was in common use by early 1970 and in the fall the group hired an organizer.[39]

By then, both the issues and the tactics that would propel SECO's rise had emerged. The activists discovered that the city had essentially "written off" Southeast Baltimore. With the exception of the road, no capital improvements were projected for the area during the next twenty years.[40] SECO's main objective became reversing urban policies that, in Gloria Aull's words, showed "insensitivity to, and bias against the older neighborhoods of our cities."[41] Blue-collar Baltimoreans were not used to making noise or crusading on issues. Usually they appealed quietly to local politicians for employment or city services. The politicians' helpfulness, in turn, depended on the reliability of their vote.[42] Previously, city council members from blue-collar districts and their constituents had been in agreement on issues that deeply concerned working whites. The road changed that.

For those opposed to the road, their chief opponent was William Donald Schaefer, city council president under Thomas D'Alesandro III and mayor after 1971. A canny politician and a determined highway advocate, Schaefer made building the road at all costs as much a personal as a political goal. By using all the plums and punishments at his disposal, he ensured that only the most dire and direct threats to their own constituencies would keep city councilmen from backing his plans.[43] Opponents of the road also had to fight the local businesses that backed the road. Baltimore's manufacturers, not surprisingly, had never pressured the city council either way on issues like open housing or school desegregation. Now they had more at stake. The road promised to make urban industries more accessible to truck traffic and cut shipping costs. Employers, therefore, brought a great deal of political pressure to bear in favor of it.[44]

The controversy also set neighborhood against neighborhood. Councilmen who rejected plans involving their own districts did not hesitate to support schemes affecting other areas. As a result, residents of Baltimore's two white working-class districts—the First and Sixth—grew mutually suspicious and combative. In 1972, for example, Southeast Baltimore's First District politicians tried to push through a resolution ensuring that the Fort McHenry route across the Sixth District's Locust Point was given first priority for construction.[45] City politics, which had usually guarded blue-collar Baltimoreans in the past, effectively sidetracked antiroad initiatives.

But an alternative to urban politics as usual was emerging. The highway fight dealt some decisive blows to Baltimore's club-based political system. In September 1970 Paul Sarbanes unseated one of Maryland's oldest and most powerful congressmen, House Public Works Committee chairman George Fallon. Fallon was Baltimore's strongest highway advocate, Sarbanes one of its most resolute opponents.[46] In November 1971 Barbara Mikulski campaigned on "ethnic unity" and won a First District city council seat.[47] Both Mikulski and Sarbanes established their careers independent of the city's old-line political clubs. Instead, they built their electoral bases largely on the invigorated neighborhood groups emerging from the road fight.[48]

Despite these challenges, the gravitational pull of the party organization was still strong in blue-collar wards. After going it alone initially, even Mikulski eventually made peace with the political clubs.[49] But once the possibility of political alternatives became clear, working Baltimoreans grew increasingly critical of the club system. "People in Southeast Baltimore are the city's biggest taxpayers," lithographer Frank Jablonski claimed in 1971, "but politicians have always looked at our neighborhood as kind of locked up. For minimum effort they have reaped a maximum harvest."[50] The neighborhood populism unleashed by SECO promised not only to force city officials to pay attention but also to do away with the indignities of the club system. "Why should we go hat in hand to the b'hoys in the political organizations, begging for handouts?" asked a Southeast Baltimore activist.[51]

In their quest to build a power base independent of existing political structures, Southeast Baltimore's activists turned to the Alinskyite model of community organization, then enjoying a resurgence of popularity. Saul Alinsky's career as a neighborhood organizer had begun with his "Back of the Yards" campaign organizing meatpacking workers and their families in 1930s Chicago. The key to his method was creating an "organization of organizations"—a coalition of labor, religious, and neighborhood groups.[52] In the 1960s the Woodlawn Organization, a mostly African American group, brought Alinsky's ideas back into the Chicago headlines. Late in the decade, middle-income Northeast Baltimoreans started the Northeast Community Organization (NECO) to fight large-scale residential turnover.[53] In the Alinskyite renaissance that followed, the Calumet Community Congress (CCC), which successfully pushed for pollution abatement at the Gary, Indiana, steel mills, was the first ethnic, blue-collar Alinskyite organization. SECO was the second.[54] One of SECO's first organizers was a veteran of the Gary effort and had been trained at Alinsky's Industrial Areas Foundation in Chicago.[55]

In Gary there had been substantial and, at times, shrill opposition to the Calumet Community Congress, and in Baltimore not all working whites shared an enthusiasm for a broad-based community organization.[56] Locust Point, for example, home to historic Fort McHenry, was a highly insular working-class community. Its residents were proud that it was "the only place left in Baltimore where people can walk the streets at night without being afraid."[57] But now the area was threatened by highway plans that included an elevated bridge across the peninsula. Locust Point residents were also appalled by city leaders' seeming arrogance and callousness. The final straw came, observed one local woman, "when this big shot from the city" called Locust Point "an industrial wasteland." "Locust Point leaders prepared for war," she said, and, as in Southeast Baltimore, the unwillingness or inability of city politicians to turn back the challenges led working whites to depart from accustomed channels.[58]

In fighting their "war," the residents of Baltimore's most isolated working-class community opted for a time-honored working-class tradition—a parade—rather than legal action. In March 1971 residents gathered outside a local tavern. Capitalizing on the Point's most important historical resource, they dressed in outfits of the War of 1812 period and some beat drums. The *South Baltimore Enterprise* wistfully observed that the occasion brought back memories of long-gone Fourth of July celebrations "when everyone supported their country and was proud to be patriotic."[59] On Locust Point, Alinskyite ideas had little currency. This overtly patriotic protest allowed residents to resist without a hint of radicalism. The next year there was another wave of protest from the Locust Point Civic Association, including regular picketing—in full 1812 regalia—of city council meetings.[60] After South Baltimoreans had set up the Coalition of Peninsula Organizations (COPO) on the model of SECO, Locust Point residents maintained their independence. "We don't want anybody telling us what to do," pronounced the president of the Locust Point Civic Association. He especially disliked the use of paid organizers. "They bring in outsiders to run COPO," he pointed out.[61]

The Southeast Community Organizes

In the early 1970s working-class Americans everywhere rediscovered their ethnic roots. One of the leading proponents of this "new ethnicity" was SECO's Barbara Mikulski. After giving up social work, Mikulski earned a master's degree and joined the faculty of the Community College of Baltimore. She became nationally known after appearing at a meeting of the Urban Task Force of the U.S. Catholic Conference in June 1970.[62] There she delivered a stinging rebuke to "phony white liberals, pseudo black militants and patronizing bureaucrats" on behalf of ethnic Americans "sick and tired of institutions not being responsive to the people they were instituted to serve" and feeling "powerless in our dealings with these monoliths." Working-class whites, she declared, did not like being blamed for the problems of black Americans, "and [what was] perhaps the key, we anguish at all of the class prejudice that is forced upon us." Her statement, printed in full by the *New York Times* and much excerpted elsewhere, was the rallying cry for what was soon dubbed "ethnic power."[63]

Mikulski's unapologetic championing of her immigrant roots, a heritage downplayed by a generation that had felt obliged to "Americanize," evoked pride among Southeast Baltimore residents who felt patronized by Baltimore's establishment. City council president Walter Orlinsky lauded Mikulski's "clear voice." "She made Polish as beautiful as black," he said.[64] As Orlinsky realized, the ethnic resurgence that powered SECO owed much to the civil rights movement.[65] Gloria Aull confirmed that the black freedom movement encouraged white Baltimoreans to "look back with pride" on their ethnic heritage.[66]

This resurgence of ethnicity in blue-collar Baltimore was a direct result of generational change. Previous generations had been taught by the "dominant culture," as Mikulski put it, that with the exceptions of church and fraternal organizations, Americanism meant assimilation. But a new generation, having grown tired of the sterility of mainstream American culture, was reclaiming an ethnic heritage partly lost.[67] Mikulski believed that she and other working whites were, in some way, reaching into the past, beyond the culture embraced by their "American-oriented parents" to that of their grandparents.[68]

In becoming nationally known as a spokesperson for ethnics in general, Mikulski drew heavily on her own experience as a member of Baltimore's large Polish population. That group, like others in the city, was reviving old associational ties in the early 1970s. The Sons of Italy, its vigor drained as older members aged, had been living a tenuous existence. But in the early 1970s younger Italians began joining, its ranks began to grow again, and by the end of the decade there were forty Sons of Italy lodges in Maryland, thirty of them new.[69] Another indicator of the vitality of the new ethnicity was the resurgence of ethnic festivals. In 1973 Baltimore's Italian and Polish communities both launched festivals that soon became popular annual events. In 1974 seventy-five different organizations participated in a Polish festival grown so large that it filled Baltimore's War Memorial building and the plaza outside. The Italian festival the same year sprawled along the inner harbor.[70] Before this tide crested at the end of the decade, Baltimore had hosted festivals for Estonians, Greeks, Hispanics, Irish, Lithuanians, and Ukranians as well.[71] The "new ethnicity" never became the mass cultural and political movement that proponents like Michael Novak predicted. For the majority of blue-collar ethnics—in Baltimore as nationwide—family, food, and festivals marked the boundaries of purely ethnic identity.[72] It was a political resource for a time, but only one among many.

SECO's founding congress, attended by one thousand representatives of some ninety community organizations in April 1971, revealed characteristic strengths and weaknesses. One source of strength was the support of working-class institutions like the churches and the labor unions. Working-class Baltimore's generation of experience with industrial unionism served

SECO well: "Our people know what it means to be organized," Mikulski said.[73] A search for a meeting chairman who could unite and command respect from the disparate groups led SECO to call upon a former president of United Steelworkers Local 2610.[74] But then the avowedly blue-collar, ethnic organization inexplicably elected as its first president a man who was neither: Jack Gleason, the most active of the Fells Point gentrifiers.[75] Gleason's vantage point was that of Baltimore's urban middle class rather than the ethnic working class. The residents of Fells Point manipulated the system—they got their neighborhood listed in the federal government's register of historic places, sued on those grounds, and kept their lawyers working until the city gave up. Southeast Baltimore's working-class residents used less sophisticated means—they applied unrelenting public pressure on city planners. These differing methods would ultimately lead each group to separate conclusions as well.

Despite the fanfare, there was strong opposition to SECO from within as well as outside the working-class community. The founding congress, noted the *Evening Sun,* touched off a debate over "whether [SECO] genuinely represents community interests." Some of the most vocal opponents were politicians and community leaders who felt threatened. Attacking Mikulski's aspirations to elected office, they dismissed SECO as an upstart's attempt to build a constituency.[76] Mimi DiPietro, city councilman from Ward 26, backed the highway and was irritated by what he called SECO's "damned 'goodguys' image." "All they did was fight concrete," he complained. Perhaps most insulting to DiPietro, who could still turn out his precinct's vote on demand, was SECO's failure to treat politicians with respect. In the Democratic clubs, DiPietro said, the president "rules with an iron hand," and strangers are not "shoved around," "cussed at," or "insulted." "The neighborhood organizations," he lamented out of experience, "they treat you like dirt."[77]

One improvement association president charged SECO with exploiting community problems rather than genuinely seeking remedies to them. Others accused it of overemphasizing ethnicity to "create sides," a practice one critic called "akin to racism."[78] The groups opposing SECO were long-standing, conservative community organizations, usually run by local small business interests who were mostly pro-road. But they were on firm ground when they called SECO's antitruck campaign unrealistic in an area that depended on industry. There was also some justification in questioning the rediscovery of ethnicity that SECO exploited. For Southeast Baltimore residents, ethnicity had long been a private, rather than public, resource.

The old and the new urban politics: Barbara Mikulski and Dominic "Mimi" DiPietro confer in the early 1970s. (Courtesy of the *Baltimore News-American* Photograph Collection, Special Collections, University of Maryland, College Park, Libraries)

SECO's status as a working-class organization must be judged by its reputation among "average" working-class people as well as activists, and there was a great deal of blue-collar mistrust. Southeast Baltimoreans, like the Locust Pointers, were genuinely troubled by SECO's reliance on paid organizers. In blue-collar Baltimore, "work" was the primary indicator of worth, and those who got paid for activities that did not fit within traditional conceptions of work were suspect. "These 'PAID' glory seekers are always jumping on somebody's band-wagon," complained one resident. "I am sick and tired of hearing about what SECO does for the community, only when they receive a grant to pay their leaders with."[79] It was also hard to believe that outsiders could truly have the interests of the community at heart. "Around Canton, the SECO staff was all thought to be from Washington," said one local politician.[80] A city councilman heard rumors that SECO was a communist front. "The organizers were dressed in a foreign uniform of jeans and flannel shirts," he said. The older residents, he recalled, "saw SECO as radicals coming into their neighborhood."[81] It is revealing that locals seemed to loathe Washingtonians and foreign radicals equally.

But SECO's biggest problem was with race. The *Evening Sun* noted that "at times SECO has been charged with being too ethnic and bypassing the blacks in their area."[82] SECO was not an all-ethnic organization, and it was nearly all white. This may seem curious given that one of the most notable things about Mikulski's 1970 speech was its call for "an alliance of white and black" as well as of "white collar and blue collar."[83] SECO, however, reflected Mikulski's view of race relations more than it first appears.

Mikulski rejected the liberal vision of integration as an overall remedy for social inequality caused by racism. She argued instead for the primacy of the neighborhood. If a neighborhood was integrated, she believed, then its neighborhood organization should be. If not, she told an interviewer, "groups should get together separately, and then, where there are common causes, join together."[84] Mikulski liked to point out that SCAR had worked with black antiroad groups, relying on coalition building between strong, but separate racial communities rather than on integration. This solution clearly appealed to blue collarites who still placed a high premium on white neighborhoods and institutions. Equally important, it respected a belief that there were limitations to the possibilities of social change. Blue collarites wanted to fix neighborhoods first and society second—not the other way around.

The resurgence of ethnic power that drove SECO was a legitimate outgrowth of the rights revolution of the 1960s and not, as some black activists charged, "simply undercover racism."[85] It is not surprising though, that Mikulski, the product of a working-class community ill-disposed to abstract moralizing and suspicious of sweeping change, adopted a practical and limited view of race relations. She well understood that much of Southeast Baltimore's strength lay in its whiteness. "If blockbusters had come in here," she boasted, "they would have gotten the hell beat out of them."[86]

This kind of sentiment disturbed liberals, who hoped to avoid the contradiction between community preservation and racial inclusion by saying nothing at all. In 1976 liberal journalist Robert Kuttner noted that "on the race issue, SECO treads a necessarily narrow line."[87] By the time he wrote, however, SECO's leaders may have felt that they had already made a misstep or two over the issue of busing.

Busing and the Southeast Coalition

In the decade and a half after the *Brown v. Board of Education* decision, controversy over school desegregation was confined mostly to the South. By the early 1970s the federal government had begun to seek remedies to the de facto segregation that resulted when whites fled the inner cities of the North. From 1969 to 1976 federal courts ordered desegregation in half of the nation's one hundred largest school districts. In every one of those cities, white enrollments dropped precipitously over the same period as residents elected to move rather than comply. Only those too poor to move or too committed to their neighborhoods to abandon them resisted. This culminated in the protracted and highly publicized Boston busing controversy of the mid-1970s, when the fanatic desperation of local whites was captured in a Pulitzer Prize–winning photograph of blue-collar Boston youths using an American flag to spear a black lawyer.[88] The Boston busing controversy, the high-water mark of white outrage against liberal integration efforts, forced the American public to reexamine the nation's approach to the problem of racial segregation. Boston's working-class whites spoke to the nation at large, but in other cities, equally impassioned, if less desperate, voices were being heard.

Southeast Baltimore, having escaped large-scale neighborhood transition and possessing a higher concentration of Catholics than elsewhere, was not as dependent on public schools as some other areas. But most Baltimore Catholics still attended public schools, and by the late 1960s parochial school enrollments were declining.[89] It was not until 1963, when the Baltimore schools took a step away from purely voluntary desegregation and Highlandtown parents gathered in protest, that Southeast Baltimore was affected at all. In 1971 the Supreme Court issued a decision that pushed the city, and blue-collar Baltimore, much further.

In an April 1971 case growing out of desegregation in Charlotte, North Carolina, the *Swann v. Mecklenberg* decision approved the use of busing to integrate schools that remained segregated because of residential patterns.[90] This was precisely the situation in Baltimore. As whites fled the city in the 1960s, the number of segregated schools rose. By 1970, of the 215 schools in the system, 70 were all black and 12 were all white.[91] In early 1974 the civil rights office of the Department of Health, Education, and Welfare (HEW) instructed Baltimore City School Board officials to draw up a desegregation plan. The board complied, adopting a system used widely in other cities in which white and black schools were "paired" and their students redistributed.[92]

Proponents of the plan dismissed the concerns of parents as "merely emotional" and confidently predicted that "they will get over it." But in early April 1974, 1,200 parents packed Patterson High School auditorium in Southeast Baltimore to protest what they called "forced busing." In populist tones, a city councilman condemned the schemes of "liberal social planners in Washington" and "left-wing do-gooders" who advocated busing yet sent their own children to private schools. He warned the crowd that the city's plan was "just another code word for busing." SECO's Betty Deacon was more direct. "That [pairing] won't work over here. It would mean busing and I'm against busing."[93]

In 1974 Deacon was thirty years old and living with her husband and two children in a Highlandtown row house that she had bought from her grandmother. Her mother lived across the street, her in-laws around the corner.[94] While she was growing up, she remembered, it was expected that a girl "went to school but not too far, got married, and tended to [her] family."[95] Deacon had watched her mother follow this track, but she wanted something different. She found a more satisfying role model in her grandmother, who had worked and was, in her view, "a progressive lady."[96]

In 1971 Deacon joined an improvement association because "the neighborhood was going down and nobody was doing anything about it."[97] Her group became part of SECO at its founding congress, and she rose quickly to head up SECO's Truck Route Task Force. When a son was diagnosed with dyslexia, she organized a tutoring program at his school. She also formed a group that, funded by a small corporate grant, reorganized the local Parent-Teacher Association and pressured the city into replacing two of Highlandtown's aging school buildings. By 1972 Deacon was considered SECO's "education leader in South Baltimore."[98] As she later told a feminist journalist, "housewives who had only a high school education or less" developed much greater feelings of effectiveness and self-worth in the process.[99] Their success also contributed to SECO's growing prestige.[100]

The federal government's 1974 guidelines on desegregation called for the establishment of a citywide Desegregation Task Force, and Deacon became SECO's representative. Previously, Deacon acknowledged, she would have "very idealistically" backed busing, but her experience on the task force led her to change her mind. "I became realistic in my views," she said. Deacon was convinced that many blacks did not really want their children bused and supported it only "to get hold of power in the city." She thought that Southeast Baltimore "was being ridiculed" because its residents opposed busing, and "that it needed a spokesman to articulate the feelings of the people."[101]

As she abandoned what she considered an unquestioning idealism and adopted a perspective that she believed was better suited to the realities of urban life, Deacon became a confident proponent of the "community first" approach to race relations enunciated by Mikulski. In some ways, Deacon's attitude toward the problem echoed that long taken by Baltimore's working whites. Ten years earlier, feeling threatened by blockbusting, Highlandtown residents had placed "we won't sell" signs in their front windows. In June 1974 the *Evening Sun* carried a photograph of Deacon standing by the front window of her row house which displayed a sign that read "we're staying" in large bold letters, and in smaller script, "at school #215." Despite the continuity this indicates with an older, more forthrightly race-based protest, Deacon insisted that blue-collar Southeast Baltimore's quest for respect had little to do with racism. She was comfortable enough with her views to put up with being labeled a white racist, but SECO had a harder time with the issue.

In the spring of 1974, as school officials grappled with a succession of desegregation plans, Baltimore parents grew increasingly vocal in opposition. Mobilization around busing, Ronald Formisano has pointed out in his study of Boston, was largely "a continuation of wars waged in recent years against the depredations of highway construction, urban renewal, and airport expansion promoted by civil engineers, bureaucrats, and above all, outsiders"—particularly highly placed outsiders.[102] Throughout the 1950s and 1960s, white working-class people had seen a host of institutions that had once mediated between the neighborhood and the federal government fall away; they were especially sensitive about the loss of control over educational institutions.[103] At a 26 April meeting, five hundred mostly white parents urged the school board to resist the HEW directive that they labeled "federal blackmail." Instead, they said, "let the communities run the schools."[104]

Meanwhile, Betty Deacon was assembling a group called the Southeast Desegregation Coalition. Some members were longtime activists, but busing drew much additional support. "East Baltimore housewives," previously uninvolved in community affairs, "suddenly identified with this emotional issue," observed one SECO official. Most important, they showed no reservations about standing behind a strategy devised by Deacon and Stan Holt, SECO's lead organizer, that crossed the color line. They argued that the black elementary schools designated for local children were inferior. Black children were welcome at local schools, but the Southeast coalition opposed busing white children out.[105] In their efforts to take back control over their children's educations, Southeast Baltimoreans threw open their "defended neighborhoods" to outsiders. Moves like this undermine a still-too-prevalent tendency to dismiss antibusers as motivated by white skin privilege and confirm that, as Formisano discovered about Boston, "racism is too simple an explanation."[106]

Busing's new recruits invigorated SECO as well. One hundred and seventy different organizations, nearly double the eighty-seven SECO member organizations, gathered at the Fourth Annual Congress, and officials unequivocally attributed the heavy turnout to "strong anti-busing sentiment." Acting on what the *Evening Sun* called "an overwhelming mandate," SECO passed a firm antibusing resolution.[107] The "We're Staying" resolution pronounced neighborhood schools "a way of life" and laid out the Southeast coalition's plan to combat busing. "Pre-registration days" were announced for each Southeast area school. Parents, acting outside of school system channels, were encouraged to preregister their children at the school of their choice.[108]

On the night of 28 May, the school board unveiled what was touted as its final desegregation plan. Southeast Baltimore learned that Patterson High School was designated a "magnet school" for courses in the construction trades. The board's action fanned smoldering class resentment. Residents believed that the board, in tracking Southeast Baltimore children away from academic pursuits by making their neighborhood school a trade school, had taken Southeast Baltimore's blue-collar status for granted. SECO's office was flooded with indignant calls. At Patterson High, 95 percent of the 1,200 students assigned to the second shift walked out, initiating six days of protest.[109] On 30 May 750 students, most of them from Patterson High, protested at city hall. The next day, the crowd reached 2,000.[110] On Sunday night, 2 June, Southeast Baltimore residents rallied in Patterson Park, vowing to fight the magnet plan. The next morning 2,000 high school students blocked traffic outside of city hall for an hour.[111]

At a public hearing on 4 June, the school board gave in, allowing Patterson to remain a comprehensive high school. Many in attendance ultimately blamed HEW, and two children displayed a banner asking, "What Happened to Democracy?"[112] At a hearing the next evening, the board adopted a much-diluted plan. Barbara Mikulski, now on the city council, took the opportunity to accuse HEW of discriminating against urban working-class whites, demanding to know why it did not force suburban school districts to desegregate.[113] Mikulski had brought up a glaring contradiction in the politics and geography of American race relations—one that blue-collar Balti-

Southeast Baltimore parents and children protest the school board's busing plans in May 1974. (Courtesy of the *Baltimore News-American* Photograph Collection, Special Collections, University of Maryland, College Park, Libraries)

moreans had been sensitive to at least since 1964, when the *South Baltimore Enterprise* condemned the hypocrisy of suburbanites "segregated by sheer wealth." Urban whites, it seemed, had long been expected to pay for the racism of the nation as a whole. Suburbanites, effectively insulated from the urban black poor by real estate prices, could remain above the fray and even condemn "racist" whites in the city. The Supreme Court made this exemption the law of the land less than a month after Mikulski spoke, excluding surrounding counties from urban desegregation plans in the *Milliken v. Bradley* decision that grew out of a Detroit case.

The highway fight divided communities and their representatives on the city council. But busing was an easy issue, and politicians capitalized on it. When school opened in the fall, the Southeast Baltimore Coalition moved into stage two of its plan, holding "sit-ins" at local elementary schools. Parents, grandparents, and neighbors accompanied children to the schools at which they had "pre-registered." In Canton, local politicians "adopted" children whose parents could not attend. Most conspicuous was Mimi DiPietro, one of SECO's leading detractors.[114]

Pressure from without was tremendous, but the blue-collar opponents of busing resolutely stood their ground. The school board circulated statistics refuting claims that blacks also opposed busing and demonstrating that they were complying in greater numbers than whites. As charges of white racism, tacitly encouraged by the board, grew louder, Betty Deacon took on her critics. At a press conference in Canton, she denounced "fringe groups" bent on creating racial confrontations. She insisted that busing was not an issue of race, but one of class. "Black and white working class communities seem to be constantly set upon by demagogues of the right and left," she said.[115] In late September the board further modified its plan, enabling more elementary students to attend local schools. The board also began granting transfer requests, most of which had been made by Southeast Baltimoreans.[116] By 1 October most Southeast Baltimore elementary schoolchildren were officially enrolled in schools of their choice.[117]

The victory of the Southeast Desegregation Coalition boosted Betty Deacon's profile to the point that her group was garnering headlines instead of SECO. The coalition requested, and got, a meeting with Baltimore's Archbishop William Borders where Deacon laid out plans to fight busing in secondary schools. The archbishop praised the coalition for its "broad base of participation" and suggested that it assist groups in other areas. In an embarrassing turn, Elaine Lowrey, speaking for SECO, could do little but point out that the aims of SECO and the church were the same.[118] At the coalition's suggestion, the school board assembled a Southeast Secondary Education Task Force to study the problem of secondary schools. This move drew new attacks from black politicians, who charged that the task force did not adequately represent blacks. The task force had more whites, Deacon countered, "because there are more whites in Southeast Baltimore." "Dunbar [a black neighborhood] is a different community and they're not going to plan my child's future."[119] Deacon, like Mikulski, emphasized that whites and blacks should work within their own communities first; she also warned that each group had a right to decide what constituted "common ground."

SECO and the coalition, however, had just about run out of common ground. The coalition's success boosted its members' confidence in the power of community activism. But SECO, having determined that it was money—not militancy—that got things done, was moving away from activism and toward "community development." In late 1973, due to the efforts of Jack Gleason, SECO had won a $100,000 Ford Foundation grant to bankroll the development of projects for improving health, housing, and transportation in East Baltimore.[120] An important result of this turn toward community development was that SECO now had to work in concert with, rather than against, local government.

By 1974 SECO had a staff of fifteen and a budget of $200,000. Three years earlier some Southeast Baltimoreans had suspected SECO of harboring communists. Now, in the eyes of many of its own members, SECO had become part of the establishment it had once fought. Early that year, several neighborhood improvement associations seceded from the organization that they said was becoming "too powerful and too uncontrollable."[121] In April an influential member angrily urged the SECO senate to remember that it was "created by the people, for the people" and warned that among a growing number of groups "there are rumbles of pulling out of SECO for good."[122]

The busing controversy irritated SECO officials, who sought to project a less militant, less blue-collar, and more professional image. One coalition member said that SECO had opposed its efforts from the start on the grounds that the coalition was "being racial."[123] For her part, Deacon was fully aware that her role in Baltimore's antibusing movement "created some tension" within SECO.[124] In December 1974, as it prepared for the founding of Southeast Development Incorporated, a platform for further community development work, the SECO senate moved to resolve the conflict between community activism and community development by firing Stan Holt. Holt, the group's organizing director since late 1973, was, by SECO's description, "a 'pure' Alinsky-style organizer who was experienced in confrontation organizing."[125] But Holt, who had begun his organizing career in Chicago's racially divided South Austin community in the 1960s, had become one of Betty Deacon's closest allies.[126]

Deacon charged that a "liberal clique" had taken over, led a fifth of SECO's constituent groups out of the meeting, and formed a steering committee for a new organization. Her explanation of the split was simple. "It's a class thing," she said. "We are working-class people, and most of the concern is in the neighborhood. . . . They are middle class professionals who don't have to worry about these things."[127] Others called it "another case of big money winning out over the little people, the big money being

Elaine Lowrey [and] the elite executive board of SECO."[128] In early January 1975 SECO fired more neighborhood organizers and announced the formation of the Southeast Development Corporation. Deacon's group, now comprised of forty organizations, took in five of SECO's fired organizers and became Neighborhoods United. The new group intended, in the words of one participant, to keep power "where it belongs—in the neighborhoods."[129] Through the rest of 1975 SECO, afraid that "taking a stand on an issue might invite an attack by Neighborhoods United" that it could not withstand, kept a low profile.[130]

Failure, Success, and Working-Class Organizations

SECO is usually depicted as a working-class organization or a grassroots ethnic movement. Certainly in its formative period it gained attention and strength by brandishing both of these images, but in the end it was neither. As Baltimore city leaders at the time agreed, the organization moved from assuming a moderately radical stance to acting as a partner of city government.[131] SECO's ambitious agenda relied on community resources accumulated through the activities of SCAR and the early SECO campaigns, even as SECO's directors realized that more intractable problems required financial and political resources that were unavailable to a "radical" group. With growing financial backing and newfound capital at city hall, the directors forgot how important the grassroots were. The late 1974 split reminded them, but in moving from ethnic power to foundation grant power SECO ceded its claim to the powerful neighborhood populism that it had so skillfully wielded previously.

Betty Deacon and the antibusers took up the very arguments that SECO was discarding and used them to great effect. By 1974 the Southeast Desegregation Coalition, not SECO, was much more the grassroots working-class organization. In contrast, Neighborhoods United, begun amid pro-democratic, populist fanfare, lacked a unifying issue and could not weld together its constituent groups.[132] By 1978 Deacon had gone on to make an unsuccessful run for city council and manage a gubernatorial campaign.[133] If her roots were in the community, her heart, like Mikulski's, was in politics.

To an impressive degree, women figured heavily in both controversies. Deacon once ventured that she received her greatest support from women "because they were around a lot more." She was convinced as well that "women naturally become more involved in community issues faster than men."[134] Although the first explanation is too flip and the last too vague, both contain a kernel of truth. With some exceptions, the most prominent male activists in SECO and the Southeast Desegregation Coalition were paid organizers and clergymen—men who were indeed "around a lot more." Women drew more sustenance from the neighborhood, and those of Mikulski and Deacon's generation, especially, were willing to work harder to protect it.[135] Furthermore, women were more likely to be excluded from preexisting channels of power. In the neighborhood, if not at work, working-class women in Baltimore were more apt, out of choice and necessity, to seek new means of change.

It would have been inconceivable for working whites of the 1940s or 1950s to have organized broadly and in such an overtly antiestablishmentarian manner. The kind of protest practiced by Locust Point residents hewed closer to long-established patterns. Although it is true that plenty of Southeast Baltimoreans were suspicious of SECO, many of those opponents tended to be older. Ultimately, it was a new generation's willingness to "question," as one man put it, that made the new working-class organizations of the early 1970s possible.

Historians and policymakers are just beginning to consider that the "integration first" approach toward social justice championed by Great Society liberals and the mainstream civil rights movement in the 1960s may have carried serious liabilities.[136] From a practical standpoint, integration alone did not accomplish what its proponents hoped it would. Working people were less likely to embrace abstract ideas and more apt to respect both traditions and limits in framing solutions than were liberal policymakers. In 1970, while integration was still the reigning philosophy, white working-class voices called for an interracial alliance—but one in which both races drew strength from their distinctive neighborhoods, be they integrated or homogeneous. Although this viewpoint, which sought to legitimize segregated urban communities, gained little attention from those in power, blue-collar concerns about busing did.

A defining feature of the school desegregation fight of the early 1970s was how much it differed from those of twenty years before. In 1954 protesting parents were condemned by nearly all community leaders, who could easily discount their arguments on the grounds of racism. By the early 1970s, though, racial language had been effectively removed from white-working class protests. Even though the issue of busing ultimately revolved around race, opponents effectively argued that the real problems were class bias and the insensitivity of bureaucrats. Most important, only the most uncompromising civil rights advocates leveled charges of racism. Leaders like Betty Deacon expected such accusations but anticipated that they would not stick. With the "racist" label removed, white working-class arguments gained new legitimacy, not only in Baltimore but also nationwide: suddenly even federal legislators were interested in hearing about blue-collar communities.

But if "the silent majority" was not silent, neither was it capable of maintaining a sustained, powerful voice. Working-class Baltimoreans had learned to mistrust those who made noise. They had grown used to liberal politicians, civil rights advocates, and student protesters demanding things they had not earned and asking for sacrifices they themselves were not willing to make. It took the plans for an expressway linking East and West Baltimore to rouse Southeast Baltimore, where, in the words of one politician, "let's not make waves" was a motto and controversy was anathema.[137] Busing further energized the community, and, like the road fight, it spawned a more ambitious organization. But SECO grew away from its working-class base to take nourishment in the exalted atmosphere of foundation grants and government partnership. Neighborhoods United sank its roots into the community, withered, and died, suggesting that, ultimately, blue collarites distrusted large, permanent, political organizations of any kind. Even Gloria Aull had to admit, "I've never been successful in organizing my own block."[138]

The working-class movements against the road and busing both floated on a tide of populist sentiment, and although there were continuities, the targets of this sentiment changed subtly. In the highway fight, the enemies were usually city planners. Some opponents blamed the federal government, but their charges rarely stuck. In contrast, although antibusers protested to school board officials, their criticisms were ultimately leveled at HEW. In the highway fight, local politicians and officials were divided. On busing they were not—all could place the blame on Washington. At one point Mayor Schaefer did just that, telling Southeastern Baltimore parents to stop pressuring him and concentrate on HEW.[139]

Although Baltimoreans criticized HEW's intractability, they eventually got concessions because the school board was able to compromise. Baltimore was no Boston: Congress put the brakes on busing before the city got its own Judge W. Arthur Garrity to singlehandedly design and enforce a far-reaching busing plan. Yet blue-collar Baltimoreans learned what they considered to be important lessons about the callousness of government bureaucrats. Gloria Aull later felt that simply having to "rattle chains" to get recognition was troubling. "It kind of changes everybody's vision of the American dream, of democracy and everybody being equal and everybody having a fair share and being able to be heard," she said.[140]

This realization led white working people down different political paths. Gloria Aull and Barbara Mikulski both wound up in Washington, Aull for a day's testimony and Mikulski for a career. Baltimore's working whites were increasingly sure that the underlying causes of some of their problems were national, and effective solutions would require support from Washington. In the years to come, blue-collar Baltimoreans were not necessarily "silent," but in matters of politics, they stuck to the ballot box to express themselves.

CHAPTER 7

Making the Reagan Democrat

In the late 1970s Hampden autoworker Albert Arnold was troubled. A Methodist whose grandparents had worked in the local textile mills, Arnold was dismayed by rising crime and the deterioration of his neighborhood; he was also surprisingly resigned. "Things had to change because of the new laws," he said, "like integrating schools and things like that." To Arnold, economic problems seemed even more pressing than social concerns. "I wish they could do something about this inflation," he remarked. "That's a horrible thing, terrible. I don't know where it's going to stop."[1]

Arnold was in many respects a model would-be "Reagan Democrat." His worldview had been shaped by the prosperity of the twenty years following World War II. He was unsettled by the cultural changes of the 1960s, bitter about the decline of the city, and frightened by the deteriorating economy of the 1970s; he held "the government" largely responsible. But Arnold's disillusionment had its limits. He did not, like more libertarian conservatives, want the government off his back. "I think this government has a lot of work to do in that area about this inflation and taking care of the sick and old," he said.[2]

Forty-five years after the New Deal began, a majority of Baltimore blue-collar voters agreed with Albert Arnold. Although disillusioned, few thought that the government had become too "active": they only wanted it to act for, rather than against, them, and most still believed it could. The turmoil of the sixties and seventies, a time when civil rights and antiwar protesters seemed to lead the city into economic decline, was fresh in their minds, and blue-collar voters had no qualms about repudiating the Democratic Party when George McGovern—more a liberal than a Democrat— was at the top of the ticket. But in 1980, despite the worst economic and social stress since the Great Depression, they stuck with the Democratic candidate because they still hoped that his was the party of the "working man."

In some respects, the 1970s brought more of that to which working whites had become accustomed: more noisy minorities making demands and more federal intervention in daily life—both of which were seldom to the benefit of blue collarites. Early in the decade, when the antiwar movement crested, white protesters appeared to be little different from the blacks who had protested and rioted in the 1960s. They were not the real problem—the liberals who tolerated and encouraged them were. It was in the 1970s that federal agencies mandated busing and compelled unions and white workers to remedy decades of shop floor discrimination. Blue collarites were acutely aware that these measures displayed class bias, and they said so in vigorous populist language. The cloud of violent crime continued to gather over the city as well, and a steady stream of whites—and blacks—who broke under the strain and could afford to leave did so.

But the 1970s also ended the postwar prosperity on which the working-class world was based. By the mid-1970s prospects for all industrial workers had diminished sharply. The postwar trajectory of blue-collar life—living standards improving from year to year and sons doing better than fathers—stalled and reversed. A political order pieced together in one economic crisis began coming apart in another forty years later.

The Wisdom of a Twenty-Year-Old

In 1969 Patrick Carter, a junior at the University of Baltimore and an avid recruit to the antiwar movement, analyzed the nation's problems for his school newspaper. "The older generation," he wrote, "perhaps blinded by degrading propaganda, just is not capable of seeing America as it really is."[3] Although Carter perceived a gulf between a "blinded" older generation and a more perceptive younger one, young people were not alone in their concern about the Vietnam War. Nor was it solely "the older generation" that resented youthful protesters. Blue-collar Baltimore's view of the war was grounded in personal experience. It rejected the wisdom of a twenty-year-old, and ultimately the war as well, out of that same experience.

At seven fifteen on the morning of 21 December 1966, Katherine Mannion, a city fireman's wife, was at home addressing Christmas cards when she heard a knock. "When I opened the door, this man in uniform stood there and I knew," she recalled. Her son had been killed in action in Vietnam. The neighbors turned off their Christmas lights, and the East Baltimore boy was buried shortly before the New Year—on his twenty-first birth-day.[4] During the Vietnam years, friends and relatives of 315 Baltimoreans killed or missing in the war shared the experience of the Mannions and their neighbors. Devastating though these losses were, to working whites Vietnam—at least at first—did not seem as exceptional as it appeared to Patrick Carter. Every generation had its war. Blue-collar Baltimoreans were saddened, but not indignant, that another generation's war had come.

By late 1966 the war was an accepted part of life in blue-collar Balti-more. The working-class weeklies featured articles, photographs, and cor-respondence from local servicemen and carried obituaries for those who had died.[5] Sorrow was inevitable, but in blue-collar communities military service was a badge of citizenship and brought with it a great deal of pride. In Hampden, where two local men had won Congressional Medals of Honor during World War II, the tradition of quitting school to work in the mills gave way in the postwar years to quitting school to join the service. In the 1960s five times more Hampden men enlisted than were drafted.[6]

Military service strengthened neighborhoods and families by linking the generations in sacrifice.[7] In early 1969 the editor of the *East Baltimore Guide* wrote: "In these days when the rallying cry of the manhood of America seems to be 'Hell, no! we won't go!' it is interesting to recall that some fami-lies have a tradition of service to their country." The story covered a local family whose men had served since the Civil War, one of whom had re-cently been involved in the Tet offensive.[8] The papers continued to feature stories like this even after the war ended. In regard to military service, one man told the *Guide* in 1975, "our family will compare to any on record."[9]

Despite the well-documented flag-waving propensities of blue-collar Americans during the Vietnam years, studies have also shown that the working class nationwide may have been somewhat less militaristic than the middle class.[10] And in Hampden, even if working people were slow to question the war, this stemmed less from acceptance of degrading propa-ganda than from the huge personal investment they had made in military service. In 1969 Ruth McDonald, whose husband was in Vietnam, did not consider antiwar demonstrations to be "responsible acts." Her commitment to the war effort was deep and beyond the persuasive powers of protesters. Should her husband not return, she wrote the mayor, who could tell their children that "it was all a terrible mistake?"[11] As Christian Appy has pointed out, Vietnam was a working-class war, and Baltimore's blue collarites knew it.[12] "It's our boys who go," explained Barbara Mikulski. "We haven't had the fancy Harvard deferments." Just as the fierce patriotism of Baltimore's working people encouraged military service, she said, it made sense of the losses they felt. "You've got to believe that death has some meaning."[13]

Blue-collar Baltimoreans had faith in military service, but they were not blind. "At first we were behind Vietnam," explained one Hampden resident, "but towards the end we were against it." He and his neighbors were convinced that the country should have either fought the war to win or have gotten out.[14] Thomas Czawlytko, who wrote the *Baltimore Sun* in 1970, believed the idea of an undeclared war to be illegitimate. "I don't see why Americans should die in a war that is not legally ours," he stated.[15] By 1970 working-class Baltimore was deeply divided over the war, a fact that goes far to explain the labor movement's problem with Vietnam.[16] With the membership so divided, Maryland AFL-CIO president Charles A. Della confessed that "we don't discuss the war in union meetings."[17] But disagreeing with the war was entirely different from protesting it. Despite his misgivings, Czawlytko insisted that he was "in no way a protester against American military policy."[18]

This caveat is crucial. Working-class perceptions of antiwar protesters were complex, involving much more than disagreements about military policy. To Baltimore blue collarites, who, on average, had not completed the ninth grade, protesters were privileged (with Johns Hopkins or University of Maryland, if not "fancy Harvard deferments") and because of that privilege, irresponsible.[19] "If these young, naive adults actually experienced hard work or hunger I'm sure their tune would change," wrote one woman.[20] Their own views were grounded in responsibility and reality, blue collarites believed; those of protesters, in selfishness and childishness. As early as 1967, the *Sun* found that while feelings on the war were mixed, "antiwar protesters got little charity from anyone."[21]

Student protest, in Baltimore as elsewhere, peaked with the 1970 Cambodian invasion. At the beginning of May one thousand students at the University of Maryland at College Park, half an hour's drive south of Baltimore, ransacked the campus ROTC office, set fires, blocked streets, and confronted state police. Within three days, the National Guard had occupied the campus.[22] Events in Ohio touched off street protests in Baltimore. On 6 May, two days after four students were killed by the Ohio National Guard at Kent State, five hundred students from Johns Hopkins, the University of Baltimore, and the Catonsville Campus of the University of Maryland marched through the city, chanting slogans, staging sit-downs, and disrupting traffic.[23] Two days later three thousand students held a demonstration at the War Memorial, then marched through downtown Baltimore. Some broke a window at the Federal Building to get at a photograph of President Richard Nixon. Twenty-seven were arrested.[24]

By the 1970s working Baltimoreans who were prone to use the label "taxpayer" to denote responsibility refused to view student protest as a legitimate critique of the war. It looked like more of what had become all too familiar since the 1960s—selfish minorities getting away with irresponsible behavior. The same adjectives that had once applied to black rioters were now applied to privileged white youth as working people voiced their resentment in the rights talk forged in racial conflicts. A Highlandtown man claimed that "the streets of Baltimore belong to the taxpayers and not a bunch of dissident campus bums, most of whom pay no taxes."[25] One woman asked why "the loud and violent" were "given all the privileges." "Do not the taxpayer and the majority have no rights?" she continued. "What do you think would happen if the silent majority would start to dissent for every little thing?"[26] A twenty-three-year-old National Guardsman's wife complained that her husband was occupied with "a hand full of bums" who were "trying to rule a state university their way" and "getting away with it."[27]

A few days after the University of Maryland protest, the Flower Mart, a springtime festival held for fifty-eight years in downtown Baltimore, was closed for good after gangs of teenagers fought—mostly black against white —in its midst. Fifty people were arrested and fifteen were hospitalized with injuries.[28] To Baltimoreans, the Flower Mart riot seemed little different from the antiwar protests. One woman blamed the fair's demise on "the undisciplined rowdies of the peace generation."[29] Tellingly, it was Flower Mart rather than the antiwar protests that finally compelled Mayor Thomas D'Alesandro to speak out against "fomenters of violence and disorder under the guise of justifiable dissent." "We have had enough of it," he said.[30] For some, however, D'Alesandro's statement came too late. The mayor's reputation for permissiveness would not die easily. "Why oh why are the loud and violent given all the privileges and the law-abiding citizen deprived of what is rightfully his," one woman wrote him after the incident.[31]

Catholic blue collarites were equally estranged from increasingly liberal church leadership. By 1969 Baltimore's laity and clergy were as split on Vietnam as on civil rights: 48 percent of the clergy favored withdrawal, whereas only 38 percent of the laity did.[32] The reforms of Vatican II had also alienated working-class Catholics. Nick Lombardi missed the dedication of "the old priests." "I don't see that nowadays," said the South Baltimore native, "because the laws of the church have changed and it's more convenient to serve a person communion in the afternoon than it is in the morning." To Lombardi as to many older Catholics, the faith was more than a matter of "convenience."[33]

Activist judges and bureaucrats seemed to have abandoned time-tested truths in favor of untried solutions to society's ills; protesters were demanding immediate redress for their "grievances;" even clergy were cutting corners, and politicians seemed oblivious to it all. Under these circumstances spoiled students became apt symbols for liberalism as a whole. "Right is right and wrong is wrong," wrote a Baltimore Catholic who described herself to the mayor as "a very indignant adult" and expressed the hope that D'Alesandro and other liberals would "grow up and face life as it is."[34]

When Wallace Won

State and national political developments seemed to confirm that the Democratic Party had become a refuge for liberals oblivious to the realities of working life. When Maryland senator Joseph D. Tydings declared for re-election in 1970, he called on America to "stop playing policeman" for the rest of the world.[35] Working-class Baltimore would have none of it. Tydings, the stepson of Millard Tydings, was among the Maryland politicians most closely associated with Great Society liberalism. In 1968, as crime rates skyrocketed and urbanites began to believe that the only protection they could count on was self-defense, Tydings pushed for gun control legislation, opening a rift between himself and working-class voters that never closed.[36] When he joined the small group of McGovern supporters at the 1968 Democratic National Convention, the *East Baltimore Guide* noted sarcastically that "everybody's out of step but Joe!"[37]

The primary campaign that began in July 1970 was the kind of contest blue-collar Baltimore relished. Tydings's challenger was George Mahoney, still a local favorite. The class dimensions of the contest were underscored when voters in the steelworkers' suburb of Dundalk booed Tydings at a Fourth of July parade.[38] Tydings, in turn, belittled Dundalk to an affluent Montgomery County audience, a gaffe that Mahoney called "a slap in the face of every hard working man in Dundalk and East Baltimore."[39]

Things got worse for Tydings when *Life* magazine charged the vocal proponent of "high ethical standards" with concealing his net worth—much of it gained through political influence.[40] Blue-collar voters were angered less by Tydings's financial misdealings than his hypocrisy. Organized labor attempted to peddle him as "the workingman's friend," but blue-collar Baltimore was not buying.[41] Tydings squeaked through the primary, but working whites voted heavily for Mahoney.[42] In the general election, Tydings lost to a Republican challenger who garnered 40 percent of the vote in Ward 1 and 51 percent in Ward 24. Tydings's problems were many, but some observers thought that what really hurt him were the patrician traits that he shared with his stepfather.[43]

The presidential race of 1972 brought an even more resounding working-class repudiation of liberal Democrats. In 1964 George Wallace had brought southern politics north, in 1968 he had prompted Richard Nixon to find an ersatz Wallace in the Maryland governor's seat, but in the 1972 primary the southerner actually won. It was a victory that ended his career. On the afternoon of 15 May 1972, the day before the primary, Wallace was gunned down at a shopping center rally in suburban Laurel, Maryland. Critically injured and paralyzed for life, Wallace swept the state the next day.[44] The black vote gave Baltimore to Hubert Humphrey, but Wallace got generous support among blue-collar voters in East and South Baltimore. There Humphrey's margins stayed in the teens while Wallace's hit 51 percent.[45]

In 1972, although to less fanfare than in 1964 and 1968, Wallace crystallized urban white issues and translated them into votes. A *Washington Post* poll found Wallace voters to be much more concerned with local problems than national issues. In the state as a whole, most voters identified Vietnam as paramount. But for Wallace voters, crime, taxes, and busing were more important.[46] For all they knew about him, Baltimore's blue-collar voters detested George McGovern. He won only 8 and 10 percent of the vote in Wards 1 and 24 respectively. More Maryland union members voted for Wallace than for any other candidate, but the party of labor nonetheless awarded the nomination to McGovern.[47]

By the fall of 1972, the leftward turn of the Democratic Party had precipitated a break with organized labor on the national level. The AFL-CIO announced that it would sit out the election, backing neither McGovern nor Nixon. Those on labor's left were outraged. Jerry Menapace, the outspokenly liberal head of the Amalgamated Meat Cutters Union with few friends among Baltimore labor leaders, withdrew his union, claiming that the ideas of labor's leadership "don't reflect the working man."[48] It is likely that more than a few white working men disagreed, however. Charles Robinson, the president of United Steelworkers Local 2610, lauded the International's decision not to support the McGovern ticket and claimed that 95 percent of his members agreed with him.[49]

Baltimore's white working class did indeed abandon the Democrats in the general election in what the *Sun*'s political analyst called a "revolt against the brand of liberalism espoused by the losing Democrat."[50] But party leaders had been convinced that George McGovern could assemble a new coalition of blacks, middle-class liberals, and the young and cynically abandoned their core blue-collar constituency.[51] The AFL-CIO's refusal to back McGovern, despite the claims of some leaders, troubled few Baltimore blue collarites. Charles Robinson suggested that electing McGovern "would only compound the nation's problems."[52] In his view, the liberal activism embodied in the 1972 Democratic slate stood a very good chance of making things worse rather than better. Robinson had a great deal of experience on which to base his opinion.

"The Price That Must Be Paid"

In the late 1960s the Department of Labor's Office of Federal Contract Compliance (OFCC) charged Bethlehem Steel with discriminating at Sparrows Point by maintaining separate white and black production units, each with its own line of seniority.[53] The OFCC recommended substituting plant seniority for unit seniority and suggested offering rate retention to aggrieved blacks.[54] "Plant seniority" allowed a worker transferring into a new unit to enter at a level reflecting seniority accrued elsewhere rather than at the bottom. A worker who was new to a unit but had fifteen years plant seniority, for example, could (once he had attained the skills to qualify for the job) take a position held by an "incumbent" worker who had been there for only ten years. This was called "bumping." Rate retention would enable transferring workers to take their existing hourly wage into the new unit.

Both labor and management resisted the OFCC's recommendations. The company charged that plant seniority would "impose an impossible and expensive burden."[55] The union used a more complicated argument—one based on more than a desire to maintain racial segregation. Plant seniority appeared likely to help black workers at the expense of many whites (and a few blacks) by devaluing the latter's seniority. With the exception of his home, seniority represented an industrial worker's largest investment. Deciding to stay in a unit or to move to another early in a career could make a huge financial difference years later, and employees tracked their status within the seniority system like investors track the performance of their stocks. The government wanted to change the whole system halfway through the game.

The OFCC case sat on Secretary of Labor James Hodgson's desk for two years. Then, on 17 January 1973, Hodgson handed down what became known as "the secretary's order."[56] Issued under the authority of Executive Order 11246, requiring government contractors to take "affirmative action" against discrimination, the order hewed closely to the OFCC plan. Blacks hired prior to 31 March 1968 into all-black or predominantly black units became members of an "affected class" and were allowed transfers with rate retention.[57] Cornell University professor George Hildebrand was charged with overseeing compliance. Hodgson acknowledged that his order would "result in some disruption on the expectations of white employees. But this is the price that must be paid."[58]

The secretary's order was unprecedented in scope. "Never has so much been granted to so many," said one Labor Department official.[59] Most of the eight thousand black workers at Sparrows Point were heartened, and some were ecstatic. The steward of a general labor gang reported that his workers were already making plans, saying "I'm going to bump this one and that one." "This ruling is going to create a lot of hostility," he concluded. Edward Bartee, the black president of Local 2609, expected that "it will be rough for a while." But he was glad that the government had made the decision instead of the union. "If there is trouble the Government will be the scapegoat," said Bartee. "I could say to a white guy, 'I didn't do it, the Government did it.'"[60] Bartee was on to something important. "It's a typical government decision," said United Steelworkers District 8 director and Sparrows Point veteran Edward Plato, favoring a "small minority" at the expense of the majority.[61] "It discriminates to end discrimination," he argued. "Two wrongs do not make a right."[62]

The secretary's order wiped out unit seniority and gave "superseniority" to 5,405 employees, who could request transfer within ninety days.[63] At that point, as one black worker remembered it, "all hell broke loose."[64] Even some whites who were previously in units with short lines of seniority benefited. "People who were never discriminated against," recalled white union official David Wilson, "started using seniority to jump around anywhere they wanted."[65] Much was made of resulting conflicts between white workers. "The feeling was more intense against other white guys that took advantage of it," said one man.[66] But it remained primarily a black and white issue, with white steelworkers complaining that "you gave blacks rate retention and a chance to take my job, but you didn't do anything for me."[67]

In November several hundred steelworkers, some of them black, gathered outside the union hall to demand that the Steelworkers International pursue grievances that members had filed against the order. "The government may have helped a few individuals but the whole plant is suffering," said a worker picketing the union hall after the rally.[68] David Wilson, now president of Local 2609, warned the International that if the union refused to fight for the rank and file, it would be hard to persuade the workers not to go elsewhere.[69]

Respite came on 12 April 1974, when the United Steelworkers and nine major producers signed a consent decree in the Alabama District Court.[70] Steel plants across the country had been embroiled in controversy like that at Sparrows Point, and employers saw the consent decree as a way to comply with federal guidelines, resolve the spate of legal suits that had cropped up, and forestall future litigation.[71] The consent decree formalized plant seniority and rate retention; provided back pay for about forty thousand affected workers; set up committees of government, business, and union officials to administer the program; and vested final authority in a district court judge in Birmingham.[72] Baltimore union officials began to breathe easier. By ending superseniority and bumping, the consent decree stopped the scramble for jobs.[73] White steelworkers were heartened by an incumbency clause allowing workers to remain in their units regardless of seniority. Black unionist Joseph Saunders recognized, however, that whites had regained, at least in part, a powerful tool of segregation and saw implementation committee members as "the same folks that discriminated saying let's make it work."[74] White steelworkers did not see things that way, though, and the bitter resentments generated in the mid-1970s hung on for years. Shop steward Arthur Vogel resigned his position due to the turmoil. In 1982, he said, many workers still were not speaking to each other.[75]

"The Government Is Running the Show"

Baltimore's waterfront workers were also subject to federally mandated affirmative action in the early 1970s. In contrast to the steelworkers, though, black and white longshoremen were not divided on the issue: both were lined up firmly against government intervention. Workers on Baltimore's waterfront, like those all along the East Coast, had been organized into racially exclusive union locals since the teens. Despite this segregated structure, the International Longshoremen's Association (ILA), according to Bruce Nelson, "achieved a biracial equilibrium that was remarkable."[76] Since its founding in 1913, Baltimore Local 829 had administered a system peculiar to Baltimore in which gangs of fifteen to twenty men worked closely together for years at a time. Companies hired gangs through the union, often requesting specific ones as a matter of course.[77]

At first, Poles predominated in Local 829. Black dockworkers, on the other hand, organized ILA Local 858, adopted the gang system, and carved out a strong bargaining position for themselves—within limits.[78] White gangs worked with "clean" freight, whereas black gangs handled "bad" cargo like potash or fishmeal. As one black longshoreman described it, "When you have to wear a mask, it's bad cargo." Whites also got more work. By 1969 a white longshoreman averaged 150 to 300 more hours of employment per year than a black dockworker.[79] This system provided many advantages to the white workers and the companies. The former seldom wore masks and could count on steady work; the latter prized the stabilizing effect that the blacks had on the labor force at the port. Black workers seldom struck, which helped discourage work stoppages by whites. They also handled cargoes that whites would take only for higher pay.[80] The system might have diminished the leverage of the longshoremen as a whole, but few whites cared. By the 1960s, in Locust Point, where the highest concentration of longshoremen could be found, the streets were filled with Cadillacs and other big American cars.[81]

In 1969 the Justice Department charged the ILA system of dual locals with violating the 1964 Civil Rights Act, demanded that Locals 829 and 858 merge, and ordered the abolition of the gang system.[82] Whites, not surprisingly, argued against the merger in federal court. But blacks, afraid that they would be outnumbered, outvoted, and sidelined in a merged local, were also skeptical. They had good reason. More than ten years earlier, after New York City's black longshoremen had been forced to merge their local into its white counterpart, half of its members had drifted away out of frustration.[83] In late 1970 the presiding judge decided that despite the desires of all those involved, the merger "could not be denied."[84]

Black workers did indeed suffer more from the decision than whites. The court, said Local 858's president, did little more than "reduce the bargaining power of black workers." "Whites," said another worker, "will elect their own officials and work the same way they always have."[85] For the next ten years irreconcilable racial conflict plagued what became ILA Local 333. It took three years to settle the merger, and union politics soon revolved solely around race.[86] In 1974 black longshoremen staged a walkout to protest the continuation of discriminatory hiring practices and demanded "nothing less than a return to racially segregated union locals."[87]

Veteran dockworkers were most troubled by what the court order did to the gang system. Like the communities of the ethnic workers who devised it—and the AFL building trades unions, which were also coming under attack at this time—the gang system functioned along informal lines and

A "black gang" works on Baltimore's docks. (Courtesy of the *Baltimore News-American* Photograph Collection, Special Collections, University of Maryland, College Park, Libraries)

depended on similar background, common experience, and mutual trust. Like working-class neighborhoods, they practiced racial exclusion, but they also worked. Both whites and blacks agreed on that. Moreover, the gang system kept Baltimore remarkably free of the corruption that plagued other ports, and it contributed to Baltimore's exceptionally low accident rates. By taking the control over replacements and temporary workers away from the gang leader and making it dependent on seniority, the court destroyed this system. When gang leaders could no longer hire, said Thomas Wilkerson, former president of Local 858, their authority disappeared. "When you don't have no authority," he concluded, "you don't have no responsibility." The autonomy that longshoremen prized had been badly eroded in Wilkerson's view. "The government is running the show," he said.[88]

The situation on the waterfront, where blacks opposed affirmative

Street life in the shadow of industry. Locust Point during the 1970s.
(Courtesy of the *Baltimore News-American* Photograph Collection,
Special Collections, University of Maryland, College Park, Libraries)

action, was clearly exceptional. But it emphasized a theme on which much of workers' criticisms were based—that of unexpected consequences. It irritated workers that bureaucrats confidently issued orders that did not work as intended and only created new, unforeseen problems. One steelworker official was amused that although the consent decree "was supposed to get us out of court," it led to even greater litigation.[89] Union leaders agreed with Edward Plato when he said that "the government infringed on our field." They felt that judges and bureaucrats had no business making the decisions they did.[90] David Wilson had little regard for the erudition of "experts" like the professor who oversaw the secretary's order. "Hildebrand, in all his wisdom, decided yes there had been discrimination," he recalled disparagingly.[91]

Drawing on the views of contemporary Labor Department officials, former NAACP labor secretary Herbert Hill, and a proliferating scholarship of "whiteness," Bruce Nelson has criticized white steelworkers, longshoremen, and their unions for having "acted to defend an employment structure that benefited them, materially and psychologically."[92] But this condemns working people for not displaying a level of altruism seldom expected of others. It also presupposes that the only way for blacks to gain historically earned privileges was for blue-collar whites to surrender theirs. According to this conception, the industrial workplace, like the urban neighborhood, becomes a container within which rights are apportioned in some kind of zero-sum game. Working whites were certainly players but hardly the masters of that game, and they keenly felt the injustice of making a few pay for the sins of a society.

Employers, not surprisingly, suffered the least. The companies doing the hiring at the port were not even targeted by the Justice Department, and the consent decree absolved the steel companies from legal claims for the bargain price of $750 per worker. In the midst of the uproar caused by the secretary's order, union officials saw a distressingly simple solution—the payment of rate retention to those bumped as well as those who did the bumping. But this potentially expensive solution was never considered.[93]

Baltimore's white working people believed that liberal advocates of affirmative action were at best ignorant and at worst duplicitous when they tried to explain away the negative effects of such programs. "There is such a thing as reverse discrimination whether we want to recognize it or not," said steelworker Neal Crowder.[94] At Sparrows Point, the secretary of labor's concern about "the price that must be paid" rang hollow. "They made career elections partly based on unit service," said William Nugent, "and there's no way you can justify what these people have lost—to them or in general."[95]

Affirmative action programs were loaded with good intentions. But between the ideal and the reality of racial equality lay the difficult problem of apportioning blame and exacting redress. Historically, white workers certainly helped exclude blacks from skilled, well-paid positions. But discrimination—the social construction of "whiteness," in academic parlance—was the product of many hands. Liberal policymakers were anxious for society to pay the price, but, unwilling and unable to challenge wealthy and even middle-class Americans, they were too content to let working-class individuals discharge the debt.

This is the fundamental flaw in affirmative action and one that sustains its opponents and hamstrings its proponents to this day. Despite the claims of ideologues, it is possible to oppose affirmative action in principle without being a racist or a determined defender of white skin privilege. As the record of the steelworkers at Sparrows Point illustrates, the streams of outright racism like those that propelled John Ruke flowed imperceptibly into a broader tide of resentment against government abrogation of individual rights and advancement by merit. The key is that whereas the former cannot be defended, the latter can.

The Economy of the 1970s

Robert Norrell has observed that a "cruel irony" of affirmative action in the steel industry was that just as black workers gained access to better jobs, those jobs disappeared.[96] But it is also important to realize that just as white industrial workers were set back by affirmative action, they lost even more ground as heavy industry declined. This was especially true for younger workers. By the early 1980s, only men with more than sixteen years' seniority still had jobs in the tin mill at Sparrows Point.[97] Longshoremen, meanwhile, were fighting their own losing battle against containerization. Black workers gained and lost in the 1970s, but white workers lost twice. When layoffs and inflation undercut the earnings and expectations of working whites, the claims of establishment experts were almost totally discredited. The New Deal coalition began unraveling faster because the Democratic Party, which had staked its reputation on providing material growth and economic justice for working people, no longer seemed willing—nor perhaps even able—to do so.

On 10 October 1973 a war in the Middle East that threatened to escalate into a confrontation between the United States and the Soviet Union was four days old, impeachment hearings for President Nixon were two weeks away, and Spiro Agnew resigned the vice presidency. The next day the *Baltimore Evening Sun* explained that Agnew had been accepting petty kick-backs from Baltimore County contractors until late 1972. Also on the front page was news of an Israeli breakthrough in the Golan Heights. But the story bound to affect white working-class Baltimoreans most was buried in the financial section. "Higher Interest and Inflation Will Persist," the head-line read.[98]

The expansive economy of the postwar years had engendered a sense of optimism among working people. From 1947 to 1962 the real hourly earn-ings of American workers increased at an average rate of 2.5 percent per year. From 1962 to 1973 earnings slowed but still increased at an average of 1.9 percent per year.[99] Baltimore's long-term industrial decline had begun years before, but few had noticed. From 1947 to 1963 the city lost 123 indus-tries and more than 17,000 manufacturing jobs. Military production helped mask this decline. From 1963 to 1967, although firms continued to leave the city, manufacturing employment actually increased 2.7 percent.[100]

Working people did expect to be inconvenienced by economic down-turns, but since the 1940s, one-year recessions had always stemmed infla-tion and started the economy on a new cycle of expansion. The one that began in 1970 did not follow the pattern, however. By mid-1971 both unem-ployment and inflation remained uncomfortably high.[101] From 1967 to 1972 Baltimore lost over 16,000 manufacturing jobs—an unprecedented drop of more than 15 percent.[102] Plant closings, relatively rare in the experience of blue-collar Baltimoreans during the fifties and sixties, were becoming a familiar occurrence. In the five years after 1967, 159 Baltimore plants shut their doors.

One of these was Canton's American Standard plant, which had pro-duced plumbing fixtures for forty-six years. In August 1972, shortly after the union won a contract that boosted now-useless fringe benefits instead of re-tirement provisions, the company announced the closing. "A lot of guys are scared to death," said William Ramsey, a native of Appalachia who moved to Baltimore in the 1950s. By the mid-1960s Ramsey had saved enough for a down payment on a house in the suburbs, but that house was now a lia-bility. "I had it all figured out," he said. "By the time I retired from the factory I'd have my house paid for." Instead, Ramsey's wife took a job in a bowling alley.[103]

Among those still working, economic security once taken for granted was steadily eroded by inflation fueled by the oil embargo resulting from the Arab-Israeli conflict. In early 1974 lines at the gas pumps annoyed Baltimoreans, but by summer skyrocketing oil costs had rippled through the economy and created more dire consequences.[104] Annual inflation of 4.7 percent had been considered high in August 1971; three years later it hit 12 percent.[105]

From the 1940s to the 1960s working people could expect their earnings to grow as they got older, and they could count on their children doing better than they did. This trend reversed abruptly in 1973.[106] By mid-decade, working whites were living close to the limit of their incomes.[107] "After I pay my rent and buy my food," reported one East Baltimore housewife, "I just don't spend any money because it's just not there to spend." "Nothing can be saved," said a saleslady, "I live from week to week."[108]

In working-class Baltimore, a second income had long been considered a luxury rather than a necessity. By mid-decade that had changed. Before, said retiree John Wiltz, "everyone seemed to get along even on low incomes . . . today a man works two jobs to get by."[109] Blue-collar husbands often resisted letting their wives work full-time, but inflation and plant closings changed that. When in 1976 the *East Baltimore Guide* asked locals if wives should work to help out their husbands, most agreed that "if he is really trying hard, his wife should help by getting a job."[110] A few found manufacturing jobs, but most, like Mrs. Ramsey, took lower-paying service-sector jobs. In Dundalk, the number of women entering the workforce increased in proportion to layoffs at Sparrows Point, and within a few years the tradition of the male "breadwinner" had become practically obsolete.[111]

Inflation affected working-class lives in less direct but equally significant ways, compounding the cultural pressures and demographic changes that were already hurting the Catholic Church, for example. From 1962 to 1977, the population of the Baltimore Archdiocese fell 15 percent and parochial school enrollments declined by half.[112] By the 1970s inflation had made the church's huge investment in property a burden rather than an asset.[113] Rising education costs and declining enrollments forced the archdiocese to close a number of schools early in the decade.[114] Parishioners did their best to help, contributing more of their shrinking incomes, but it was not nearly enough.[115]

Inflation hurt another key working-class institution, savings and loans, even more. In 1974 the supply of mortgages for city housing was drying up. Savings and loans had normally financed 70 to 80 percent of Baltimore housing, but with the government paying much higher interest on short-

term bonds, depositors abandoned savings and loans for the better investment. By the fall of 1974, most city savings and loans had stopped taking
mortgages.[116] Much of Baltimore's blue-collar housing stock, deprived of
capital, started to deteriorate, and working whites came face-to-face with
the prospect of decline in their own neighborhoods. By that time, if their
own communities were not troubling enough, the black inner city inspired
only fear.

The Urban Crisis and "the Jungle"

Blue-collar whites were hurt by the economic decline of the 1970s, but
urban blacks were devastated. As whites fled, disparities between the city's
rich and poor grew. In the 1970s the Baltimore median household income
fell from 74 to 63 percent of that of the surrounding metropolitan area.[117]
One 1975 study found that in terms of economic and social hardships, Baltimore was one of the worst major cities in the nation.[118] Its overall unemployment rate shot ahead of the national average, increasing from 4.6 to
10.3 percent in the 1970s, and by 1979 unemployment among black youth
hit 50 percent.[119] Meanwhile, 131,000 Baltimoreans were on the rolls of Aid
to Families with Dependent Children—a 31 percent increase in only eight
years.[120] In 1980, 21 percent of city residents lived below the poverty line.[121]
These hardships contributed to ever-higher rates of inner-city crime. In a
single year, from March 1969 to March 1970, violent crimes in Baltimore
rose 7.3 percent.[122] A year later the Federal Law Enforcement Assistance
Administration rated Baltimore highest in the nation in violent crime. In
1970 three-fourths of all the crime perpetrated in the state of Maryland
took place in Baltimore.[123]

By mid-decade, urbanites had lived in unrelenting fear of crime for a
decade and grim resignation had set in. Once Southeast Baltimoreans had
distinguished between safe and dangerous neighborhoods, but by 1975 they
no longer felt safe on their own streets.[124] "You can go to the best sections
and get attacked," said one woman.[125] For urban whites, the black inner
city had become an increasingly abstract and terrifying place. Few now
ventured into the city at night, and in the three years after the 1968 riots,
downtown merchants' evening business had dropped 40 to 50 percent.[126]

As stores closed, industries left, neighborhoods deteriorated, and Baltimore's tax base evaporated, the city relied increasingly on property taxes
for revenue. By 1974 Baltimore's property tax was twice the next highest
rate in Maryland.[127] Property assessments, long a touchy subject, became

bitterly contested, and Baltimoreans helped prepare the ground for the tax revolt that would help shape American politics in the late 1970s. In 1976 two tax reform groups, one affiliated with the Southeast Community Organization (SECO) and another with Neighborhoods United, garnered a great deal of support in Southeast Baltimore.[128]

It was difficult, then, for many working people to take seriously the much-publicized "Baltimore Renaissance" credited to Mayor William Donald Schaefer. In 1971 Mayor D'Alesandro, disillusioned by his turbulent term in office and his confessed "inability to close the pandora's box of urban troubles," had declined to run again.[129] Schaefer, the city council president, was a bachelor still living with his mother in what was now a nearly all-black Edmondson Village neighborhood. He had strong ties to Baltimore's black and white community groups—despite his early apprehensions about SECO—and even stronger connections to city business interests. As mayor he worked tirelessly to promote the city and revitalize its downtown.[130]

Schaefer was Maryland's most skilled politician since Theodore McKeldin, and as a Democrat in a Democratic city he could get a lot more done. D'Alesandro could not keep from making enemies, but Schaefer drained the vitriol from city politics. "He doesn't generate electricity, he grounds it," said one observer.[131] Schaefer maintained a strong biracial political base, helping to make Baltimore the last majority-black city in America to elect a black mayor. He did it by condemning black militants and avoiding civil rights causes that alienated whites but at the same time never divorcing himself from the larger black community.[132] Schaefer was popular with many of the city's neighborhood groups, especially after the highway controversy had died out. But he encouraged community leaders to "do things themselves" rather than look to the city for help.[133] This was a credo that working-class whites understood.

Baltimore's businesses, on the other hand, could count on a lot of help from the city. The revitalization of downtown was carried out by quasi-public agencies through which corporate and business leaders used public funds for mostly private gain. The first such project, an office complex called Charles Center, opened in 1970 under D'Alesandro. Schaefer expanded the scope of these activities; his crowning achievement was the Inner Harbor, a commercial showplace on the old waterfront funded publicly and managed privately.[134] Schaefer's ability as a politician was matched by his skill as a publicist. He raised Baltimore's reputation nationwide and instilled pride in residents who returned him to the mayor's office twice before electing him governor. The working whites who voted for him seemed to care little about the riches that developers were scooping up downtown. They were disturbed, however, by another aspect of the renaissance: the gentrification of their neighborhoods.

Fells Point was the site of much contention. Because one of the city's main streets terminated there, locals had long called it "the foot of Broadway." Although locals shunned the first wave of gentrifiers in the 1960s, the newcomers multiplied, intrigued by the picturesque and historic neighborhood. By the late 1970s they started to gain the upper hand. From 1970 to 1980 the proportion of professionals in Fells Point increased from 9.4 to 24.5 percent, while incomes rose from 44.6 percent of the city median to 77.5 percent. In 1970 less than 5 percent of the area's inhabitants had finished high school. Ten years later nearly 17 percent had.[135] In South Baltimore also, renovation and mounting real estate prices drove long-term residents out of the market. One row house there sold for $8,000 in 1977 but resold for $35,000 only two years later.[136]

Gentrifiers and preservationists hated the Formstone covering working-class row houses as much as blue collarites loved it. In 1980 Joseph Rosinski complained that a "loudmouth pushy lady" with "haughty stiff-necked ways" was going around telling locals to remove the offending substance. "I would like to tell these newcomers from such faraway places as Roland Park [an upper-class Baltimore neighborhood] and Boston," said Rosinski, that "these people have worked hard to put Formstone on their homes."[137] Some blamed the city for letting the interlopers in. "The city chased two-thirds of the Poles away from Fells Point to get all these fancy people in," one longshoreman complained.[138] But in 1974 working whites who felt squeezed between inner-city poor and overweening professionals had found a local champion from within their own ranks.

William Swisher was a Southeast Baltimore native and proud that his Polish grandmother had stepped off the boat at the foot of Broadway— "which snobs now call Fells Point," he liked to add.[139] Swisher grew up in Highlandtown, went to Sacred Heart school, became active in the political clubs there, and worked his way through law school driving a beer truck. His political style was in the traditional urban machine mode. Swisher was not a graceful public speaker, but he was an inveterate backslapper and buttonholer. The suspicion that he wore clip-on ties only worked in his favor.[140]

In 1974 old-line political boss Jack Pollack wanted to shore up his faltering power base at the courthouse by running a candidate for state's attorney. He had no choice but to ally with the boss of another rickety machine,

TABLE 3. Population by Race, 1940–1980

Race	1940	1950	1960	1970	1980
Black	19.3%	23.7%	34.7%	46.4%	54.8%
White	80.6	76.1	65.0	53.0	44.1
Other	0.1	0.2	0.3	0.6	1.1
N=	859,100	949,708	939,024	905,787	786,775

Sources: U.S. Bureau of the Census, *1940 Census of Population and Housing: Statistics for Census Tracts, Baltimore, Maryland* (Washington, D.C.: GPO, 1942), *Census Tract Statistics, Baltimore, Maryland, and Adjacent Area: Selected Population and Housing Characteristics, 1950* (Washington, D.C.: GPO, 1952), *1960 Census of Population and Housing: Final Report PHC(1)-13, Census Tracts, Baltimore, Maryland* (Washington, D.C.: GPO, 1962), *1970 Census of Population and Housing, Census Tracts, Baltimore, Maryland, Standard Metropolitan Statistical Area* (Washington, D.C.: GPO, 1972), and *1980 Census of Population and Housing: Census Tracts, Baltimore, Maryland, Standard Metropolitan Statistical Area, PHC80-2-82* (Washington, D.C.: GPO, 1982).

East Baltimore's Joseph Hofferbert. Hofferbert selected Swisher to carry the banner.[141] At first the campaign against a respected black incumbent did not go well. Swisher's commercials were lackluster affairs—he read crime statistics and asked for votes. Pollack's men canceled the spots and hired the Robert Goodman Agency, which had handled Spiro Agnew's campaign against George Mahoney in 1966. In the new commercial, Swisher stood amid flashing lights and sirens to declare that the city was "a jungle" and that he would do something about it. "I guess we scared a few people," said Goodman, "but if you want people to remember your name and vote for you, I guess you have to wake them up."[142]

But people were already scared, and the jungle spot, released the year that Baltimore became for the first time a majority-black city, launched Swisher from obscurity into the powerful state's attorney office. Baltimore's establishment, led by the *Sun,* heaped scorn and derision on Swisher for his machine connections as well as the racism implicit in his commercial.[143] Nevertheless, Swisher remained popular with blue-collar whites as much for his denunciations of "intellectual reformers . . . who couldn't run a nickel-and-dime candy store" as for the connotations of his jungle spot.[144] Baltimore's working white wards gave Swisher 66 percent of the vote; middle-class voters were even more generous, providing him a margin of 67 percent.[145]

Despite their majority status, Baltimore's black electorate remained split by the long-running political rivalry between the Mitchell family of the

NAACP and the Murphy family of the *Baltimore Afro-American.* Low turn-out and dissension among black leaders allowed Swisher another victory in 1978. The jungle spot anticipated George Bush's 1988 Willie Horton ad more than it reflected the race baiting of the past. Nevertheless, during the 1982 campaign, the *Sun,* in what even Swisher's detractors considered a gross overstatement, likened him to George Wallace. Swisher lost in 1982, burying the legacy of Wallace for good in the *Sun*'s estimation, as well as marking the end of black political factionalism in Baltimore. Both groups supported Rhodes scholar Kurt Schmoke against Swisher in 1982. Five years later Schmoke became the city's first black mayor.[146]

Not Over Yet

As industries closed and blue collarites settled for lower-paying jobs else-where, some grew resentful of unionized workers who seemed to make too much more than their nonunion counterparts. A streak of indigna-tion toward highly paid steel and autoworkers, long discernible in Balti-more, was intensified by the setbacks of the 1970s. In the mid-1960s the United Steelworkers negotiated an agreement giving workers thirteen-week vacations every five years. About half of Bethlehem's employees were eligible. One Sparrows Point worker, who maintained a Cadillac, an out-board motorboat, and waterfront property in suburban Essex on his wages figured that he had earned the long vacation after thirty years of ser-vice. Another said that "they ought to give it to us every year."[147] But in the inflation-ridden seventies the contract provision most prized by union members was the cost-of-living allowance. In 1968 only 2.5 million Ameri-can workers had cost-of-living allowances written into their contracts.[148] By 1976, however, 6 million workers had them.[149] Workers at Crown Cork and Seal noticed that steelworkers were getting up to 30 or 40 extra cents per year, so in 1973 they struck for a cost-of-living allowance of their own.[150]

To Baltimoreans, steelworkers epitomized the "affluent worker" of the 1960s and early 1970s. In 1974, after teachers struck for a badly needed raise, Mayor Schaefer claimed that the city did not have the money and waited them out. One exasperated teacher said, "If we were steelworkers you could believe we'd have a contract."[151] The economic crisis helped re-kindle the long-standing belief that unions helped feed inflation. An East Baltimore repairman believed that unions were "running rampant" in their demands.[152] One woman thought that unions "started out pretty good," but now, she said in the late 1970s, "they just want more and more."[153]

From 1972 to 1977 Baltimore's industrial sector continued its downward

TABLE 4. Manufacturing Firms and Employment, 1947–1977

Year	Total Firms	% Change	No. Large Firms*	% Change	Total Employed	% Change
1947	1,638	—	—	—	120,929	—
1954	1,629	−0.5	—	—	117,583	−2.8
1958	1,623	−0.4	694	—	111,757	−5.0
1963	1,515	−6.7	635	−8.5	103,852	−7.1
1967	1,396	−7.9	625	−1.6	106,700	+2.7
1972	1,237	−11.4	543	−13.1	90,600	−15.1
1977	1,101	−11.0	429	−21.0	72,900	−19.5
1982	971	−11.8	—	—	59,300	−18.7

Source: U.S. Bureau of the Census, *County and City Data Books* (Washington, D.C.: GPO, 1952–88).
*Manufacturing firms with twenty or more employees.

slide as 136 industries closed and 16,100 manufacturing jobs disappeared — a 19.5 percent loss. After the 1974 recession hit, economists waited for a recovery that never materialized.[154] Before long even the steelworkers were in trouble. The first wave of layoffs hit Sparrows Point in late 1974, and by May 1975, 7,000 of the plant's 22,000 workers were out of work.[155] In late 1979 the Organization of Petroleum Exporting Countries (OPEC) announced a fourfold increase in prices, and a too-familiar cycle started again. In the fall of 1980 inflation was at 11 percent. Unemployment hit 7.5 percent nationwide, but in Baltimore it was nearing 11 percent. Sparrows Point's full complement of workers had been cut by 3,000 by September 1979, but 3,500 of the 19,000 remaining had been laid off for a year and benefits were running out. "Things have been getting grim," said Local 2610's president.[156] At General Motors, 2,000 of 6,000 workers had been laid off since January 1980.[157]

The economy had organized labor down, and enterprising businesses issued a swift kick. Baltimore's premier anti-union law firm boasted an 80 percent success rate in 1980.[158] In 1939 industrialists had touted the "conservatism" of Baltimore labor.[159] Forty years later their successors were more candid. In its promotional packages, the Greater Baltimore Committee assured interested businesses that "union activity is not an issue."[160] In 1970 manufacturing had remained the largest of five employment sectors in Baltimore's economy. Ten years later it ranked fourth, overtaken by the service, government, and trade sectors. Baltimore was no longer an industrial blue-collar city.

But working-class Baltimore still spun on its Democratic political axis.

TABLE 5. Composition of Labor Force by Sector, 1950–1980

Sector	1950	1960	1970	1980
Manufacturing	34.1%	27.8%	25.6%	15.0%
Wholesale and retail trade	26.0	23.3	20.6	21.2
Finance, insurance, real estate	6.0	6.8	7.4	8.5
Services	7.7	8.2	11.6	22.3
Government	12.3	15.1	18.7	20.8

Source: Marc V. Levine, "Downtown Redevelopment as an Urban Growth Strategy: A Critical Appraisal of the Baltimore Renaissance," *Journal of Urban Affairs* 9 (1987): 103–23. See esp. p. 116.

In 1978 steelworker Ed Listopad confidently told a reporter that "the Democrats have been the party of the working man."[161] Two years later a young housewife expressed a similar sentiment. "The Democrats have always been for working people," said Theresa Baginski, "and the Republicans always went for the rich people." In late October 1980 obligations toward the party were more concrete, though, and Baginski appeared to have some misgivings about the coming election. "I'm a Democrat, so I *have* to vote for President Carter over Ronald Reagan," she said.[162]

Baginski was not yet among them, but a new voter had emerged within Baltimore's blue-collar electorate: the Reagan Democrat. Although they had much in common with those who remained faithful to the "party of the working man," the social changes unleashed by desegregation, the culture wars of the 1960s, and the economic shocks of the 1970s had compelled a growing number to cut old party ties. One East Baltimore woman who had "always voted the Democratic ticket" was too concerned about unemployment and inflation to back Jimmy Carter, whom she deemed "a big disappointment."[163] "I voted for the wrong man," said one South Baltimore man about Carter in 1979.[164] This feeling was so pervasive that in 1980 the *East Baltimore Guide,* with the heaviest blue-collar readership in the city, evinced a distinct pro-Reagan slant. Still others had lost faith in politics entirely. By 1980 turnout among blue-collar voters was falling sharply.[165]

On election night, 1980, locals gathered at Costa's Inn, a steelworkers' bar in Dundalk, just across the city line from Southeast Baltimore. "I don't give a damn who gets in," said a female patron, "one's as bad as the next." Across the bar, union electrician Richard Gough stared at the television in disbelief as Reagan won state after state. "I thought all the unions were with Carter," said Gough. "I can't understand how he could lose that vote." Beside him steelworker Roger Dorrier was sipping his beer and quietly backing Reagan. Dorrier had been laid off from Sparrows Point since June. "I'll bet you in two weeks I'm back to work," he said. Dorrier picked the winner, but in Costa's Inn that night, as in white working-class Baltimore, Gough was in the majority. "It's not over yet," chipped in Joe Brune, a rolling mill operator.[166]

Maryland was one of only six states the Democrats won in 1980, and Baltimore gave Jimmy Carter 71 percent of its vote. The black vote counted most, but even in blue-collar Baltimore the Democrats retained majorities. White working-class wards 1, 23, and 24 gave Reagan 36 percent of the vote—more than they had given Nixon in 1968 but much less than the Nixon and Wallace vote combined.[167]

Thousands of jobs gone, inflation nearing 13 percent on election day, the industrial city devastated, yet blue-collar Baltimore stuck with the Democrats. Why? Working-class people may not treat voting as an intellectual exercise, but they do make reasoned political decisions. Certainly there are polarizing issues, events, and candidates—George Wallace being the most notable—but long-term voting patterns and party affiliations are made on the basis of rules of thumb and generalizations drawn from experience. This may be, as Samuel Popkin has dubbed it, "low information rationality," but it is reasoning just the same.[168]

Robert Dallek was quick to take Ronald Reagan to task for his "Politics of Symbolism," but symbols have always been the stuff of politics. It is a matter of what is behind them. Blue-collar voters—and most others for that matter—do not scrutinize party platforms, but if they did they would have found a telling passage in the 1980 Republican platform: a promise to reemphasize "those vital communities like the family, the neighborhood, the workplace, and others which are found at the center of our society between government and the individual."[169] The list got the order exactly right: industrial employment had been an important blue-collar institution, but not central—that distinction belonged to the home and neighborhood. And for residents of old industrial cities, factory work—the bulwark of industrial unionism, the CIO, and the urban New Deal—was becoming a rarity.

These were not bloodless symbols. Urban whites had been preoccupied with the security of their homes and families for almost a generation. Working-class people expected and found much more autonomy in the neighborhood than on the job and acted accordingly. For many, it was simply an acknowledgment of reality when the Reagan Revolution cut the remaining links between the neighborhood and the industrial workplace by championing the former and saying little about the latter. And if the Republican commitment to the neighborhoods and families of working people was merely rhetorical, it was in any case more than seemed forthcoming from the Democrats. When evaluating the effect of symbols, it might be worthwhile to consider that the blue-collar allegiance to the party of the New Deal in 1980 stemmed more from its New Deal reputation as the party of the working man—a case of allegiance to tired old symbols if there ever was one.

In 1980 the party of the New Deal foundered nationwide, as much on the shoals of inflation and economic chaos as on ideological grounds. In Baltimore, the New Deal coalition was all but gone. But it was 1984 rather than 1980 that marked the definitive end of the Democratic New Deal coalition. Walter Mondale was no "fringe candidate" in the George McGovern mold. Instead, writes Steven Gillon, "it was the Democratic party itself, as it had come to be perceived by a strong majority of Americans" that was defeated.[170] Baltimore's working whites had backed the moderately liberal Dwight Eisenhower by a slim margin of 51 percent in 1956, although heavily unionized Ward 1 gave Adlai Stevenson 54 percent. But in 1984 the white working class—union voters included—gave a more decisive victory to a Republican bent on reversing the domestic policies of the New Deal. At the polls, activists handed out sample ballots proclaiming "Democrats are for Reagan."[171] Little Italy voted Republican, and one Hampden precinct gave Reagan a two-to-one margin.[172] South and Southeast Baltimore Wards 1, 23, and 24 gave Reagan a less resounding but still decisive 56 percent of the vote.

Were white working people "taken in" by Republicans with their unlikely concoction of lowbrow populism and elite economics? To the extent that working-class Americans—in common with their middle-class contemporaries—recurrently failed to discern the hand of government policymakers in the effects of the free market, they were. In Baltimore, the real blue-collar-job bloodbath came in the early 1980s rather than the late 1970s. But by that time, much could be forgiven if the neighborhood remained sacrosanct. That is a lesson that was learned by many Republicans and few Democrats, with the notable exception of Barbara Mikulski, a left-liberal who continued to retain her Senate seat as of 2002 more for her attention to community issues than her championing of causes highly suspect to working people.

In the end, being a Reagan Democrat was far from being a Republican: no new blue-collar bloc emerged from the wreckage of the New Deal coalition. In Costa's bar on election night, there were three groups of blue collarites: the Democratic faithful, Reagan Democrats, and nonvoters who found one party as "bad as the next." It was the nonvoter group that grew most quickly, nationwide, in every presidential election of the 1980s; more blue collarites stayed home than voted for either Republican or Democratic candidates.[173] In 1988 turnout in Baltimore hit a new low of 59 percent—down 9 percent from 1984. And those blue collarites who bothered to vote were truly willing to cross party lines only for Reagan—they swung back to vote for Michael Dukakis by a 54 percent margin.[174]

If the troubled political journey from 1940 to 1980 had a decisive effect, it was to sour a vast group of current and former urban white voters on the political system in general. This should come as no surprise. The old blue-collar city has long since been gutted, and Baltimore working-class communities like Hampden are enjoying a second life as new coffee bars and boutiques cater to young urban professionals.[175] By 1980, when blue-collar Baltimore stood up for the party of the New Deal for the last time, it had been decades since that party had stood up for them. Perhaps whatever new political order does emerge will be more attentive to these post–blue-collar Baltimoreans.

Conclusion

White working-class Baltimore was a harbor of social and cultural conservatism that the New Deal Democratic order contained for a time but
never substantially altered. The factors that precipitated its fragmentation
had been there from the start. One was the order's assumption—or, perhaps more accurately, fervent hope—that labor activists, urban intellectuals, working blacks, and blue-collar whites shared essentially similar interests. Another was the heavy reliance of New Deal Democrats on populist
images of an elite few subverting the interests of the many. This came back
to haunt them when they, rather than businesses, were on the receiving
end. A third factor was the growing use of nondemocratic administrative
and judicial, as opposed to legislative, power unleashed by the New Deal.[1]

The upheavals of the 1950s and 1960s helped discredit the social goals
of liberalism, and the events of the 1970s undermined the economic basis
of the New Deal order. Nevertheless, blue-collar loyalty to the "party of the
working man" survived until the 1980s. White working-class politics never
turned sharply to the right in these years, but blue-collar Baltimoreans
did break reluctantly but decisively with the Democratic Party. The twists
and turns of blue-collar political language mirror this watershed change.
The first postwar generation relied heavily on race-based claims to "white
rights" to express their grievances. This gave way to a language of protest
that was more explicitly grounded in populist democratic claims. "White"
rights, in effect, became "working people's" rights. In Baltimore, this shift
was most decisively made by the late 1960s. Escalating urban crime, the
decay of the inner city, urban rioting, and liberal political responses to all of
these events persuaded blue-collar Baltimoreans that race explained little.
The liberal failure to insist on responsibility and uphold the value of work
explained a great deal.

The postwar American working class, like its predecessors, was inescapably racialized. But at all times working-class white identity coexisted with convictions about democracy, responsibility, and fairness. Race-based protest had already begun to give way to more populist and less racialized language when the term "backlash" first appeared in 1964 and was virtually gone by the time it was popularized in 1970. What was popularly believed to be a resurgence of racism—or, in more contemporary terms, insistence on the preservation of "white skin privilege" through the use of code words— was, in fact, merely a change of venue as the protests of working whites followed the locus of political power that affected their lives from the local to the national arena. When not refracted through the lens of backlash, working white objections to black power, antiwar activism, busing, and highway building look like much more than fleeting and irrational outbursts. The historical roots of this protest were deep, and its message was sustained by nearly every aspect of white working-class life.

It has not been the goal of this book to diminish the liabilities of postwar white working-class politics. As contemporary critics and scholars have amply demonstrated, at various times it sustained vicious racism, fostered a narrow view of community, and justified the suppression of individual rights. But the strengths inherent in white working-class politics are worth considering. First, it encouraged humility and caution—traits rarely championed in modern political discourse. Second, as Christopher Lasch has pointed out, it recognized that there are limits inherent in human beings and in their governments.[2] Third, white working-class politics emphasized simple democracy. Blue-collar voices provided consistent reminders that in governing the nation, the will of the majority—regardless of social standing—should be as important as the opinions of experts. White working-class politics kept these concerns politically viable when they would otherwise have been excluded from American political debate.

The vast expansion of rights in the workplace and civil society for blacks, women, and other minorities was postwar America's greatest domestic accomplishment. But it should be remembered that this accomplishment was sometimes realized in less than democratic ways and that blue collarites shouldered a disproportionate share of the burden. Working whites did not want "entitlements"—they expected to work for what they got. But if they did not anticipate arbitrary rewards, neither did they expect the seemingly capricious penalties they and their communities suffered. Blue collarites were no more racist than their middle-class counterparts. True, they were preoccupied with community boundaries, but that is because, as was pointed out in 1964, they were not, as their detractors most often were, "segregated by sheer wealth."

"The cry of 'rights' has always been double-edged," Daniel T. Rodgers cautions: "radical in the hands of those with novel claims to establish, profoundly defensive in the hands of those with vested privileges to protect."[3] In the postwar years members of the white working class were a people in the middle, with little to gain and much to lose. Theirs were the claims of the defensive, but hardly the privileged, and the very existence of this group within postwar America was an unsettling—if barely heeded—reminder that there were no easy solutions. In championing a relatively unrestrained capitalism and social amelioration at the same time, liberals ensured that it was the weakest players in the economic game that would be forced to cede the most in the name of remediation. If liberal political leaders and social critics, then, like scholars now, have been overeager to dismiss the messenger along with the message, it may be because they have experienced the nagging feeling so well described by George Orwell when he wrote that for capitalism's privileged "our standard of living; and hence our 'enlightenment' demands that the robbery continue." At heart, Orwell admitted, "a humanitarian is always a hypocrite."[4]

Baltimore's working whites remained skeptical of those who championed change and thus clung to time-tested institutions. For years they wrote off a vast outside that they could not control and focused their energies and resources on small segments of physical and cultural real estate that they could protect. But the challenges to the blue-collar world did one important thing in the postwar years: they convinced working whites that their problems were much bigger than a block, a neighborhood, or a single city. National politics was changed as a result. If working whites placed more importance on "the wisdom of their ancestors" than did liberals, they also reached—if slowly, quietly, and with much encouragement—toward a wisdom of their own. That wisdom deserves to be taken seriously.[5] We should neither vilify the lawmakers, philosophers, and clergy who helped bring about social change nor the white working people who had the furthest to go in adjusting to it. One eminent Baltimorean, who would likely have washed his hands of both sides in this forty-year debate, seemed to understand this balance of continuity and change. "They change their shirts but once a day," H. L. Mencken wrote of his townsmen, "and their prejudices but once a generation."[6]

Notes

Abbreviations

ACTU	Association of Catholic Trade Unionists
ADA	Americans for Democratic Action
ALHUA	Archives of Labor History and Urban Affairs, Wayne State University, Detroit
BA-A	*Baltimore Afro-American*
BBT	Baltimore Board of Trade
BCA	Baltimore City Archives
BCD	*Baltimore City Directory* (Richmond, Va.: R. L. Polk and Co., 1928–64)
BES	*Baltimore Evening Sun*
BNHP	Baltimore Neighborhood Heritage Project, University of Baltimore Archives
BNI	Baltimore Neighborhoods Incorporated
BN-P	*Baltimore News-Post*
BSHP	Baltimore Steelworkers History Project, University of Baltimore Archives
CAA	Community Action Agency
CPHA	Baltimore Citizens Planning and Housing Association
CUA	Catholic University Archives, Washington, D.C.
EBG	*East Baltimore Guide*
HCLA	Historical Collections and Labor Archives, Pennsylvania State University, University Park
IEB	International Executive Board
IUMSWA	International Union of Marine and Shipbuilding Workers
LCMD	Library of Congress Manuscript Division, Washington, D.C.
MDCIUC	Maryland and District of Columbia Industrial Union Council
NAACP	National Association for the Advancement of Colored People
NARA	National Archives and Records Administration, Washington, D.C.

NCWC   National Catholic Welfare Conference
RG   Record Group
SBE   *South Baltimore Enterprise*
SECO   Southeast Community Organization
Sun   *Baltimore Sun*
UBA   University of Baltimore Archives
UELA   UE/Labor Archives, University of Pittsburgh
ULP   Urban League Papers, LCMD
UMA   University of Maryland Archives, College Park

Introduction

1. According to Theodore White (*Making of the President,* 233), the term "white backlash" was first coined in 1963 by economist Eliot Janeway to describe the possibility of white hostility toward blacks should automation drastically reduce industrial employment. It took on its current meaning during the Wallace primary campaign a year later. Articles that were part of the flurry of attention given to the subject late in the decade include "The Troubled American: A Special Report on the White Majority," *Newsweek,* 6 October 1969; Schrag, "Forgotten American"; and Frady, "Gary, Indiana."

2. Important works on Hispanic and black workers include Ruiz, *Cannery Women,* and Fink and Greenberg, *Upheaval in the Quiet Zone.* Works that do focus on white working-class people in the postwar period are usually studies of radicalism. Even Joshua B. Freeman's (*Working-Class New York*) otherwise exceptional study of blue-collar New York detects an incipient—but, as always, abortive—social democratic movement.

3. The most influential work on whiteness is Roediger, *Wages of Whiteness.* See also Ignatiev, *How the Irish Became White,* and T. Allen, *Invention of the White Race.* A history of postwar labor deeply influenced by this work is Nelson, *Divided We Stand.*

4. See Levison, *Working-Class Majority;* Gans, *Urban Villagers;* and Halle, *America's Working Man.*

5. See Rieder, *Canarsie;* Formisano, *Boston against Busing;* and Sugrue, *Origins of the Urban Crisis.* Sugrue focuses more explicitly on white working-class politics in his "Crabgrass-Roots Politics." A fine short overview of the subject is Rieder, "The Rise of the Silent Majority."

6. On white working-class populist language, see Kazin, *Populist Persuasion.* On the increasing importance of "rights talk" in the postwar years, see Glendon, *Rights Talk.*

7. Edsall and Edsall, *Chain Reaction.*

8. Rodgers, *Contested Truths,* 10.

9. In 1940 only 9 percent of Baltimore residents were foreign-born but 20 percent were black. In Philadelphia, the industrial city most closely resembling Balti-

more, fully 15 percent of citizens were foreign-born whereas only 13 percent were black.

10. Popkin, *Reasoning Voter,* 212. Popkin was writing when La Russa was manager of the Oakland Athletics.

Chapter One

1. One account of this incident appeared in *Life,* 14 February 1944. There, the authors of the piece remained unidentified and Cater's place of employment was given as Western Electric. A few years later the *Baltimore Evening Sun* (11 June 1947) provided more details, identifying the writers as "a group of out-of-town hands at Westinghouse."
2. J. L. Arnold, "Baltimore."
3. S. H. Olson, *Baltimore,* 238–39.
4. Ibid., 292, 304; BBT, *Second Industrial Survey,* 23.
5. Reutter, *Sparrows Poin,* 34, 127–30; BBT, *Second Industrial Survey,* 24–25.
6. BBT, *Second Industrial Survey,* 29.
7. Ibid., 39.
8. Ibid., 28.
9. Ibid., 30.
10. S. H. Olson, *Baltimore,* 179. In 1870, for example, Philadelphia's population was 14 percent Irish whereas Baltimore's was only 6 percent. See Garonzik, "Racial and Ethnic Make-up of Baltimore Neighborhoods." In 1890, 60 percent of Baltimore's foreign-born citizens were of German origin. See Crooks, *Politics and Progress,* 6.
11. See C. Phillips, *Freedom's Port,* 196–97.
12. Ibid., 239.
13. Baltimore Urban League, *Review of the Program,* 274, part I, ser. 3, box 49, ULP.
14. Neverdon-Morton, "Black Housing Patterns," 25–28; Meyer, *As Long as They Don't Move Next Door.*
15. Neverdon-Morton, "Black Housing Patterns," 35.
16. S. H. Olson, *Baltimore,* 213; Livelier Baltimore Committee, *Beyond the White Marble Steps,* 71–72; Reutter, *Sparrows Point,* 55–72.
17. Spalding, *Premier See,* 271. Canneries employed the largest number of working Baltimoreans in 1890. See Beirne, "Residential Growth and Stability." See also Rukert, *Fells Point Story.*
18. Livelier Baltimore Committee, *Beyond the White Marble Steps,* 13–16.
19. Sherman, "Study of a Neighborhood—Pigtown"; W. T. Durr, "People of the Peninsula." In the nineteenth century Pigtown, South Baltimore, and Locust Point were all dominated by the Baltimore and Ohio Railroad. See S. H. Olson, *Baltimore,* 207.
20. Beirne, "Hampden-Woodberry."

21. W. T. Durr, "People of the Peninsula," 27; *BES,* 22 March 1938.

22. Gildea, *When the Colts Belonged to Baltimore,* 51.

23. *Baltimore News-American,* 5 March 1972.

24. Spalding, *Premier See,* 271; Sandler, *The Neighborhood,* 24.

25. On the parish-centered nature of Catholic communities elsewhere, see McGreevy, *Parish Boundaries.*

26. Spalding, *Premier See,* 272–73.

27. Ibid., 287. A 1941 census found a church enrollment of more than 225,000 in the Baltimore area. *Catholic Review,* 21 February 1941.

28. Spalding, *Premier See,* 321–44 (quotation, p. 344).

29. This system was common in Maryland and Pennsylvania. See Hayward and Belfoure, *Baltimore Rowhouse,* 12–15, 114 (Wesolowski).

30. S. H. Olson, *Baltimore,* 219.

31. Argersinger, *Toward a New Deal in Baltimore,* 3.

32. Ibid., 8, 10; S. H. Olson, *Baltimore,* 333.

33. Fenton, *Politics in the Border States,* 207.

34. Ibid., 188–89.

35. Crooks, *Politics and Progress,* 11–13.

36. J. L. Arnold, "Last of the Good Old Days," 444. Among immigrants, only a minority of Germans and Jews voted Republican (p. 445).

37. *Sun,* 5 October 1951.

38. Ibid.; J. L. Arnold, "Last of the Good Old Days," 446.

39. For more on this election, see Argersinger, "Toward a Roosevelt Coalition," 291–92.

40. The margins for Smith were 63 percent and 53 percent in Wards 1 and 24 respectively. Ward 23 voted 54 percent for Hoover. *Sun,* 7 November 1928. Hoover won Baltimore by a 51.4 percent margin. Scammon, *America at the Polls,* 207.

41. In the 1932 presidential race, Baltimore City voted 64.8 percent Democrat and 31.9 Republican. Scammon, *America at the Polls,* 207.

42. Roosevelt's 1936 margin in Baltimore was 67.9 percent, and turnout was up 26 percent from 1932. Scammon, *America at the Polls,* 208. See also Argersinger, "Toward a Roosevelt Coalition," 288.

43. Argersinger, "Toward a Roosevelt Coalition," 295.

44. Ibid., 296.

45. Wright, "Baltimore's Favorite Son."

46. Argersinger, "Toward a Roosevelt Coalition," 299.

47. Ibid., 301.

48. BBT, *Second Industrial Survey,* 35.

49. S. H. Olson, *Baltimore,* 329.

50. Ibid., 282–83. See also Skotnes, "Black Freedom Movement," 119–20; Argersinger, *Toward a New Deal in Baltimore,* 168, and "'The Right to Strike,'" 305. Andor Skotnes ("Black Freedom Movement," 117–18) cautions that the BFL's

conservatism can be overemphasized and that it contained "contradictory tendencies." The BFL's conservative tendencies were clearly paramount. Skotnes offers as evidence of the BFL's engagement in "fairly radical activity" its backing of LaFollette in 1924, unremarkable given that the AFL backed the Progressives nationally.

51. Several employers, including Maryland Shipbuilding and Drydock and Bethlehem, dispatched Pinkerton agents against organizers. See Ryon, "Ambiguous Legacy," 21.

52. Argersinger, *Toward a New Deal in Baltimore,* 173.

53. BBT, *Second Industrial Survey,* 28; *BES,* 9 September 1940.

54. Manakee, *Maryland in World War II,* 389–95.

55. *Sun,* 2 January 1942.

56. Arnold interview, 22, BNHP.

57. *BES,* 30 September 1943.

58. S. Griffith, *Where Can We Get War Workers?,* 3.

59. Sanford Griffith (ibid., 25–26) notes that "in the past the Maryland Employment Service was always rather cold to union labor, averse to the employment of women and unreceptive to skilled negro labor. Its successor, the U.S.E.S. [U.S. Employment Service], kept up much the same barriers for a long time." See also U.S. Congress, House, *Hearings . . . National Defense Migration,* 6075. In mid-1941 there were no black employees out of the thousands at Martin; later in the war a small number were hired. In the shipyards during the same period there were 258 blacks out of 6,800 employed, and 240 of these were in unskilled positions.

60. Dublin to Hurley, 22 May 1941, RG 233, entry 17, box 71, NARA.

61. Harris, Mitchell, and Schecter, *Homefront,* 96. This was standard policy for the U.S. Unemployment Service. See King, *Actively Seeking Work,* 1995.

62. U.S. Congress, House, *Hearings . . . National Defense Migration,* 6066; *BES,* 13 April 1942.

63. Harris, Mitchell, and Schecter, *Homefront,* 96; Breihan, "Wings for Democracy?"

64. Dublin to Hurley, 22 May 1941, RG 233, entry 17, box 71, NARA.

65. S. Griffith, *Where Can We Get War Workers?,* 3. Some of the early migrants were skilled workers from Philadelphia and New York, and at first Marylanders, Virginians, West Virginians, and North Carolinians—typically from towns, not the countryside—took the unskilled defense jobs. See Federal Works Agency Memorandum, 14 November 1941, Maryland Council of Churches Collection, ser. 1, box 33, UBA.

66. *BES,* 14 March 1944.

67. U.S. Office of War Information, *Report on Wartime Problems,* 6.

68. Baltimore contractors built almost 17,000 private homes in 1941 and 1942. Henderson, "Local Deals and the New Deal State," 225–56. On Fairfield Trailers, see *BES,* 23 February 1943.

69. *SBE,* 30 January 1941.

70. Porach interview, 28, BNHP.

71. Memorandum: "Background of Mr. and Mrs. Harry Warfield Eisner," RG 233, entry 17, box 72, NARA.

72. *BN-P,* 24 June 1941. Names from cross-reference in the *1941 BCD.*

73. Thommen interview, 20, BNHP.

74. Response to Survey: "Are We Reaching Newcomers in Baltimore?," 18 September 1942, Maryland Council of Churches Collection, ser. 1, box 31, UBA.

75. Purdy interview, 43–44, BNHP.

76. Malone, *Country Music,* 182.

77. Purdy interview, 43–44, BNHP.

78. *Dundalk Community Press and Baltimore Countian,* 2 October 1942.

79. U.S. Congress, House, *Hearings . . . National Defense Migration,* 6036–40.

80. *BES,* 14 March 1944.

81. U.S. Congress, House, *Hearings . . . National Defense Migration,* 5951.

82. *BES,* 14 March 1944.

83. See Cabbell, "Black Invisibility and Racism in Appalachia." On "whiteness" among immigrant Americans as well as the making of white working-class consciousness generally in the nineteenth century, see Roediger, *Wages of Whiteness,* and Saxton, *Rise and Fall of the White Republic.*

84. S. Griffith, *Where Can We Get War Workers?,* 29.

85. Sexton interview, 5, HCLA.

86. Linda Zeidman, "Sparrows Point, Dundalk, Highlandtown, Old West Baltimore." See also Ryon, "Ambiguous Legacy."

87. Sexton interview, 14–15, HCLA.

88. Foner and Lewis, *The Black Worker,* 69.

89. In the 1930s the Baltimore Police Department was usually willing to assist employers in fighting organized labor. See Argersinger, *Toward a New Deal in Baltimore,* 155–57. See also Ryon, "Ambiguous Legacy."

90. DiMartino interview, 41–42, BNHP.

91. Chamberlain, "Five Largest CIO Unions," 34, 103. In 1941 the National Defense Mediation Board awarded the skilled workers at Bethlehem Steel Shipbuilding a closed shop. See Dubofsky, *The State and Labor,* 179.

92. In 1941 an organizer told the Maryland Industrial Union Council that Martin employees had "been drawn from every section of the country, particularly from areas that have no unions." He maintained that "we have to devise some method of reaching many of these boys and explain to them that the CIO is not something that has horns." MDCIUC, *Proceedings of the Fifth Annual Convention,* 154–55.

93. Chamberlain, "Five Largest CIO Unions," 82.

94. Ibid., 83.

95. MDCIUC, *Proceedings of the Seventh Annual Convention,* 5.

96. *Sun,* 29 July 1937.

97. *Sun,* 5 February 1939; MDCIUC, *Proceedings of the Third Annual Convention,* 3.

98. MDCIUC, *Proceedings of the Seventh Annual Convention,* 19.

99. *CIO News,* 18 October, 27 December 1943.

100. MDCIUC, *Proceedings of the Seventh Annual Convention,* 18; *BES,* 12 August 1943.

101. See Gillon, *Politics and Vision,* 10–11.

102. Poster: "Manpower," 29 October 1942, and Goldman to Williams, 26 August 1943, ADA Papers, ser. 3, no. 54, reel 64, LCMD.

103. See K. Olson, "Old West Baltimore." See also McDougall, *Black Baltimore.*

104. Callcott, *Maryland and America,* 149.

105. Ibid., 148.

106. Harris, Mitchell, and Schecter, *Homefront,* 98.

107. *Sun,* 4 May 1943.

108. Callcott, *Maryland and America,* 149. See Baltimore City Board of Supervisors of Elections, RG 11, ser. 1, Registration and Election Returns, 1896–1994, BCA. My calculations determine the vote for McKeldin in these wards to have been 70.6 percent. Callcott sets the figure at 74.0 percent.

109. Middle-class precincts 9 through 23 in Ward 27 gave McKeldin a 61.5 percent margin. Baltimore City Board of Supervisors of Elections, RG 11, ser. 1, Registration and Election Returns, 1896–1994, BCA.

110. MDCIUC, *Proceedings of the Eighth Annual Convention,* 43.

111. *Sun,* 7, 8 November 1944. These figures were presumably compiled from registration lists. When calculated using census figures on voting age population, the numbers are much lower at 55.3 and 48.3 percent respectively. Baltimore City Board of Supervisors of Elections, RG 11, ser. 1, Registration and Election Returns, 1896–1994, BCA, and U.S. Bureau of the Census, *Sixteenth Census of Population and Housing, . . . Census Tracts.*

112. *BES,* 8, 9 November 1944. For voting statistics, see Baltimore City Board of Supervisors of Elections, RG 11, ser. 1, Registration and Election Returns, 1896–1994, BCA.

113. Polenberg, *War and Society,* 213.

114. Loevy, "Political Behavior in the Baltimore Metropolitan Area," 90–91.

115. Fenton, *Politics in the Border States,* 189.

116. *Sun,* 9 November 1944.

117. Brinkley, *End of Reform.*

118. *Sun,* 11 June 1939.

119. *BES,* 17 June 1939.

120. *BES,* 21 June 1939.

121. Henderson, "Local Deals and the New Deal State," 240; Gardner to Triede, 14 December 1943, RG 211, entry 269, box 15, NARA.

122. Report: "Survey of Housing Requirements of War Workers in Baltimore," 1 February 1944, RG 211, entry 267, box 15, NARA; Henderson, "Local Deals and the New Deal State," 240; Gardner to Triede, 14 December 1943, RG 211, entry 269, box 15, NARA.

123. Callcott, *Maryland and America,* 148. Of 35,000 units available, 99.9 percent were occupied. Neverdon-Morton, "Black Housing Patterns," 34.

124. *BA-A,* 24 July 1943; "Recommendations of Local Baltimore Authorities on Negro Housing," July 1943, CPHA Collection, ser. 1, box 19, UBA.

125. *BA-A,* 31 July 1943.

126. MDCIUC, *Proceedings of the Seventh Annual Convention,* 22.

127. Harrison to McKeldin, 14 July 1943, RG 9, ser. 22, box 253, BCA.

128. *BA-A,* 24 July 1943.

129. Schmucker to "Dear Friends," 1 July 1943, RG 9, series 22, box 253, BCA. Luke Schmucker was pastor at St. Peters in Baltimore County, just across the city line from Highlandtown.

130. Wynn, *The Afro-American and the Second World War,* 67.

131. A few days later—on 1 August—New York City blacks rioted in the city's business district. See Polenberg, *War and Society,* 127–30.

132. These letters are in RG 9, ser. 22, box 253, BCA. The quotation is from Limpert to McKeldin, 20 July 1943, ibid.

133. Jackson to McKeldin, 14 July 1943, RG 9, ser. 22, box 253, BCA.

134. See Baltimore Urban League, *Review of the Program,* part I, ser. 3, box 49, ULP.

135. Quoted in Harris, Mitchell, and Schecter, *Homefront,* 99.

136. Allen to Ross, 9 June 1944, RG 228, entry 37, box 448, NARA.

137. MDCIUC, *Proceedings of the Seventh Annual Convention,* 16–17.

138. *CIO News,* 6 December 1943.

139. Flyer: "Attention Fellow Members of the CIO," 13 July 1938, IUMSWA Papers, ser. 5, box 68, UMA.

140. Leaflet: "Pipe Fitter Department Meeting," 10 September 1940, IUMSWA Papers, ser. 5, box 73, UMA.

141. Flyer: "Attention Ex-Coal Miners," IUMSWA Papers, ser. 5, box 91, UMA.

142. Report: "Survey of Shipbuilding Industry in Baltimore, Maryland," July 1941, RG 183, entry 89, box 165, NARA.

143. U.S. Employment Service, "Labor Market Developments Report," 9 September 1942, RG 183, entry 89, box 161, NARA.

144. One study that attributes wartime hate strikes, including the strike at Sparrows Point Shipyard, to the presence of southerners and workers with little experience of unionism is Freeman, "Delivering the Goods."

145. See *Sun,* 31 July, 2 August 1943, and *BA-A,* 7 August 1943. See also *Shipyard Worker,* 13 August 1943, IUMSWA Papers, ser. 8, subser. 1, box 5, UMA.

146. *Shipyard Worker,* 13 August 1943.

147. NAACP Press Release, 30 July 1943, NAACP Papers, group 2, box A335, LCMD.

148. MDCIUC, *Proceedings of the Seventh Annual Convention,* 4. One worker pointed out that UAW opponents argued, "if the CIO gets in, Negroes will work here!" *Aircraft Beacon,* 3 August 1943.

149. Breihan, "Wings for Democracy?"

150. Manakee, *Maryland in World War II,* 329.

151. Report: "Negro Employment Hourly Workers," 9 February 1944, RG 153, entry 188, box 28, NARA.

152. Maslow to Feinsinger, 18 December 1943, ibid.

153. Fairchild and Grossman, *The Army and Industrial Manpower,* 161–64.

154. The best overall discussion of this incident is A. J. Allen, "Western Electric's Backward Step."

155. *Sun,* 18 October 1943. By early 1945 the NLRB had deemed the PBEA a "company union" and Western Electric had been compelled to withdraw recognition. See *BES,* 23 April 1945.

156. Non-Partisan Committee of Western Electric Employees to the War Labor Board, 2 December 1943, RG 153, entry 188, box 28, NARA.

157. Bailey to PBEA, 11 August 1943, ibid.

158. Bailey to PBEA; Memorandum from Lemuel L. Foster, 17 December 1943, RG 160, entry 177, box 807, NARA.

159. *BA-A,* 18 December 1943. In 1941 the average Baltimore migrant worker was 27.5 years old. See Report: "Recent Migration into Baltimore, Maryland," 14 November 1941, Maryland Council of Churches Collection, ser. 1, box 33, UBA.

160. *Sun,* 23 December 1943.

161. According to Lewis M. Killian ("Effects of Southern White Workers"), in northern factories southern migrants "made possible the continuation of previously established discriminatory practices" but rarely tried to "change the northern interracial situation to conform to [their] southern prejudices."

162. *CIO News,* 20 December 1943.

163. FBI General Intelligence Memorandum, 29 January 1944, Maryland Manuscripts Collection 4008, UMA.

164. Memorandum: "Summary of Friday Morning Meeting," 23 June 1944, UE Yellow Dot Series, box 79, UELA.

165. Chamberlain, "Five Largest CIO Unions," 114.

166. Even in 1940, the proportion of women working in Baltimore's industries exceeded the national average—29 percent versus 25 percent nationwide. At the war's end the proportion of women employed nationwide was 34 percent. In 1940, 1,200 women worked in Baltimore's core war industries—shipbuilding, aircraft, and machinery—but by 1944, 36,200 worked in these sectors. U.S. Department of Labor, Women's Bureau, *Baltimore Women Workers,* 3–4. Most of this increase came as women took up the slack for departing migrants. After 1943, the year the production boom crested, the female workforce in Baltimore expanded 77 percent even though the number of workers overall rose only 10 percent. War Manpower Commission Report: "Recruitment and Referral of Women in Baltimore," 28 December 1943, RG 183, entry 89, box 162, NARA, 3.

167. U.S. Employment Service, "Labor Market Developments Report for Baltimore,

Maryland," September 1942, RG 183, entry 89, box 161, NARA; Manakee, *Maryland in World War II,* 329.

168. The Maryland Unemployment Compensation Board estimated that 45 percent of out-of-state workers present in 1943 remained in the spring of 1946. See *Sun,* 1 September 1946. New Orleans native Maurice Gelpi's connection with the piece and his marriage to a Baltimore native is described in *BES,* 11 June 1947.

Chapter Two

1. The *1940 BCD* lists Appell's father as a driver. In the *1942* directory he is listed as a laborer.
2. *BES,* 26 July 1951.
3. Pederson, "Red, White, and Blue," 30, 76.
4. The cosmopolitanism of sailors along with the exceptionalism of the industry—where patterns of exploitation were particularly apparent—made seamen more radical than other workers. See Nelson, *Workers on the Waterfront,* 26–27, 96–100, and Pederson, "Red, White, and Blue," 151–55.
5. An FBI General Intelligence Survey dated 3 October 1944 states, "It is known that all organizers for the UE in Baltimore are party members." Maryland Manuscripts Collection 4008, UMA. This is realistic considering that UE officials James Matles and Julius Emspak favored party members for organizer positions. Ronald L. Filippelli and Mark D. McColloch (*Cold War in the Working Class,* n. 42, p. 217) discuss how party members were designated UE organizers. Ed Peters, who organized UAW Local 738 at Glenn Martin, was a party member. FBI General Intelligence Survey, 29 January 1944, Maryland Manuscripts Collection 4008, UMA. Mike Howard came from New York to work with the Young Communist League, got a job at Eastern Rolling Mill, and became a SWOC organizer. Pederson, "Red, White, and Blue," 179–80.
6. FBI General Intelligence Survey, 29 October 1943, Maryland Manuscripts Collection 4008, UMA.
7. Pederson, "Red, White, and Blue," 229.
8. Spalding, *Premier See,* 360.
9. Ibid., 361.
10. Rosswurm, "The Catholic Church and the Left-Led Unions," 221.
11. Cogley, *Catholic America,* 72–73.
12. Cronin interview, 2, University of Notre Dame Archives.
13. Ibid., 7.
14. In many locations, particularly Detroit, a group called the Association of Catholic Trade Unionists was especially active in promoting these labor schools. There was never an ACTU chapter in Baltimore. On labor schools, see Seaton, *Catholics and Radicals.*
15. See correspondence regarding Baltimore's labor schools, NCWC Social Action Department Files, Workers Schools Series, box 40, CUA.

16. Cronin interview, 14, University of Notre Dame Archives.

17. Ibid., 7. This approximates the number mentioned in the NCWC Social Action Department Files.

18. Argersinger, *Toward a New Deal in Baltimore,* 173.

19. *Catholic Review,* 7 April 1944.

20. "At that time labor was everlastingly grateful for any help they could get from the Church," Cronin later recalled, "they needed respectability." Cronin interview, 15, University of Notre Dame Archives.

21. MDCIUC, *Proceedings of the Third Annual Convention,* 1.

22. See Cronin interview, 16, University of Notre Dame Archives, and "Confidential Report on Communist Activities, Bethlehem-Fairfield Yard," 16 November 1942, IUMSWA Papers, ser. 5, box 91, UMA. O'Brien is discussed in William Smith to Van Gelder, 22 February 1941, IUMSWA Papers, ser. 5, box 80, UMA.

23. *Sun,* 22 April 1941. Bradley had run for mayor on the communist ticket in 1931 and led Baltimore's Unemployed Council. See unsigned, undated document in June–August, 1941 folder, IUMSWA Papers, ser. 5, box 73, UMA.

24. Pederson, "Red, White, and Blue," 243–44.

25. Atkins to Van Gelder, 6 November 1939, IUMSWA Papers, ser. 5, box 68, UMA.

26. Edward Denhardt radio transcript, 4 October 1940, and Bill [Smith] to "Dear Brother," n.d., IUMSWA Papers, ser. 5, box 80, UMA.

27. See Smith to National Office, n.d., ibid.

28. *Sun,* 22 April 1941.

29. *Sun,* 15 May 1941.

30. On totalitarianism, see Morris, *American Catholic,* and Jenkins, *Cold War at Home,* 4–5.

31. In late 1939 an IUMSWA organizer wrote: "Mr. Phony Dies is certainly making his effect felt here in Balto., as far as the name CIO goes. . . . This is the damndest town for witch hunts that I ever saw." Atkins to Van Gelder, n.d., IUMSWA Papers, ser. 5, box 68. On the Industrial Union Council, see *Sun,* 15 December 1940.

32. Cronin interview, 16, University of Notre Dame Archives.

33. *BES,* 22 October 1941.

34. Flyer: "The Church Speaks Out for Unions," IUMSWA Papers, ser. 5, box 91, UMA.

35. John F. Cronin, "Report on Communist Activities," 5 November 1942, NCWC General Secretary's Files, box 23, CUA.

36. Untitled campaign flyer, IUMSWA Papers, ser. 5, box 91, UMA. On this point, see Morris, *American Catholic,* 250.

37. Parios Fleezanis, "Document Read to IUMSWA General Executive Board," 10 February 1943, IUMSWA Papers, ser. 5, box 91, UMA. See also Pederson, "Red, White, and Blue," 276–79, and Flyer from April–December 1942 folder, n.d., IUMSWA Papers, ser. 5, box 91, UMA.

38. According to UE official Harry Block, Van Gelder, after a stint in the army, ran

for IUMSWA office on a party ticket but lost. Afterward he was hired by the
UE. See Block interview by Filippelli, 16, 42, HCLA.

39. Freeman and Rosswurm, "Education of an Anti-Communist."

40. "Confidential Report on Communist Activities," April 1943, Detroit ACTU Col-
    lection, box 16, ALHUA; "Drury to Matles," 6 February 1943, UE Yellow Dot
    Series, box 79, UELA. One worker reported "a Catholic priest" visiting his
    home to encourage a slate supported by the church. See "Deposition of Italo
    Spessato," 9 February 1943, IUMSWA Papers, ser. 5, box 91, UMA.

41. *Sun,* 6 October 1944.

42. Cronin to Hayes, 17 November 1942, NCWC Social Action Department Files,
    box 8, CUA.

43. Bazinet to Curley, 1 July 1941, NCWC General Secretary's Files, box 23, CUA.
    I have found no Baltimore ties to Father Charles E. Coughlin, who was the
    church's leading proponent of these sorts of views.

44. "Confidential Report on Communist Activities," April 1943, Detroit ACTU Col-
    lection, box 16, ALHUA.

45. *Catholic Review,* 14 April 1944.

46. Cronin to Green, 29 September 1943, IUMSWA Papers, ser. 5, box 91, UMA.
    Cronin actually met with Maryland party chief Al Lannon and the FBI. See
    Freeman and Rosswurm, "Education of an Anti-Communist."

47. Cohen to IUMSWA National Office, 26 July 1943, IUMSWA Papers, ser. 5, box
    91, UMA.

48. Pechillo to Green, 12 July 1943, ibid.

49. *Catholic Review,* 28 April 1944.

50. "Confidential Report on Communist Activities, Bethlehem-Fairfield Yard,"
    16 November 1942, IUMSWA Papers, ser. 5, box 91, UMA.

51. *Catholic Review,* 28 April 1946.

52. *Sun,* 29 January 1945.

53. Pederson, "Red, White, and Blue," 328–30.

54. *Catholic Review,* 14 April 1944.

55. Report: "Communist Activities," 5 November 1942, NCWC General Secretary's
    Files, box 23, CUA.

56. John F. Cronin, "The Problem of American Communism in 1945: Facts and
    Recommendations," 29 October 1945, NCWC General Secretary's Files, box
    24, CUA, 44.

57. DeDominicis to Murray, 6 March 1945, UE Yellow Dot Series, Maryland Indus-
    trial Union Council folder, UELA.

58. In 1939 DeDominicis condemned fellow CIO leader Pat Whelan as a tool of
    the party. In December 1940 he led a walkout at the state CIO convention
    to protest the elimination of the word "Communism" from a resolution con-
    demning Nazism, fascism, and communism. See Argersinger, *Toward a New
    Deal in Baltimore,* 173, and *Sun,* 15 December 1940.

59. *Sun* and *BES,* 9 December 1944. Baltimore's Westinghouse plant was orga-

nized by Local 130 of the UE, one CIO International that was almost completely communist-dominated. But Local 130 was one of the city's strongest anticommunist unions throughout the war because its veteran leaders, allied with UE anticommunists James Carey and Harry Block, managed to exclude the left from power by winning over the wartime workers. See K. Durr, "'We Were UE a Long Time.'"

60. DeDominicis to Murray, UELA.
61. *Sun,* 15, 16 December 1944, 9, 29 January, 22 February 1945.
62. DeDominicis to Murray, UELA.
63. Zieger, *The CIO,* 275.
64. *Sun,* 21 December 1946.
65. *Sun,* 21 November 1947.
66. K. Durr, "'We Were UE a Long Time.'"
67. Spillane to Murray, 8 December 1948, International Union of Electrical Workers President's Office Files, box 2020, Rutgers University.
68. Pederson, "Red, White, and Blue," 319.
69. Callcott, *Maryland and America,* 118.
70. McKeldin spoke at a November 1943 Rally on American-Soviet Friendship with Claude Pepper. See *CIO News,* 18 November 1943; *BES,* 24 September 1946; and *Catholic Review,* 10 May 1946.
71. *Catholic Review,* 7 June 1946; Callcott, *Maryland and America,* 117–18.
72. Callcott, *Maryland and America,* 117.
73. Ibid., 119.
74. Ibid.
75. *Sun,* 21 March 1947.
76. Pederson, "Red, White, and Blue," 362; *Sun,* 11 September 1947.
77. *Sun,* 19 June 1948.
78. Heale, *McCarthy's America,* 61.
79. Callcott, *Maryland and America,* 122.
80. Prendergast, "The Ober Anti-Communist Law," 154. The Hearst papers had been using anticommunism against the Democratic Party since the mid-1930s. Heale, *American Anticommunism,* 152.
81. The dissenter, a former schoolteacher, got a standing ovation from his fellow legislators for the courageous vote but never ran for election again. See Callcott, *Maryland and America,* 123.
82. Ibid.
83. Prendergast, "The Ober Anti-communist Law," 157. See also *Labor Action,* 27 June 1949.
84. In Maryland as a whole, the margin was 77 percent. See *BES,* 8 November 1950.
85. *BES,* 29 March 1950; *1956 BCD* (husband's occupation).
86. Heale, *McCarthy's America,* 73.
87. *Baltimore Labor Herald,* 3 June 1947.

88. *Baltimore Labor Herald,* 20 June 1947.

89. Lichtenstein, *Most Dangerous Man in Detroit,* 266.

90. *Aircraft Beacon,* 3 August 1943.

91. Goertz to Murray, 4 November 1947, Murray Papers, Subject Files 47–48, Districts 1–8 folder, CUA.

92. Zucker to Matthews, 25 September 1947, UE Conference Board Series, folder 638, UELA.

93. Truman's support was greatest in Baltimore's working-class districts. *Sun,* 4 November 1948. Baltimore City Board of Supervisors of Elections, RG 11, ser. 1, Registration and Election Returns, 1896–1994, BCA.

94. The Wallace vote statewide was, not surprisingly, much smaller at 1.6 percent.

95. *Sun,* 3 November 1948.

96. See, e.g., "Membership Meeting Minutes," 8 January 1950, UAW Local 239 Collection, box 1, ALHUA.

97. Clifford to Murray, 27 March 1948, Murray Papers, Subject Files 47–48, Districts 1–8 folder, CUA.

98. Ibid.

99. *SBE,* 4 March 1948; Zieger, *The CIO,* 376.

100. Pederson, "Red, White, and Blue," 220–22.

101. Cronin, "The Problem of American Communism in 1945: Facts and Recommendations," 29 October 1945, NCWC General Secretary's Files, box 24, CUA, 37.

102. *BES,* 14 January 1975.

103. Callcott, *Maryland and America,* 12.

104. *Sun,* 22 January 1950.

105. *Sun,* 26 January 1950.

106. *BN-P,* 20 December 1948.

107. *SBE,* 16 February 1950. This statement was made by Augie Myers, a Western Electric employee, a veteran, a contributor to the *SBE,* and onetime editor of the *Brooklyn News,* a South Baltimore weekly.

108. Rovere, *McCarthy,* 145–52.

109. Heale, *American Anticommunism,* 154.

110. Rovere, *McCarthy,* 156.

111. Oshinsky, *A Conspiracy So Immense,* 174.

112. The *CIO News* (11 February 1946) called Tydings an "enemy of the people" for his opposition to FEPC.

113. Keith, *For Hell and a Brown Mule,* 85–87.

114. *Sun,* 1 September 1950.

115. Keith, *For Hell and a Brown Mule,* 88. Robert Griffith (*Politics of Fear,* 130) calls Monaghan a "thinly-veiled 'Catholic' candidate."

116. Keith, *For Hell and a Brown Mule,* 92–93.

117. Ibid., 96.

118. Ibid., 97; Fried, *Men against McCarthy,* 131.

119. Larman to "Guys and Gals," 25 October 1950, Millard Tydings Papers, ser. 3, box 7, UMA.

120. Keith, *For Hell and a Brown Mule,* 84.

121. Oshinsky, *A Conspiracy So Immense,* 175.

122. Keith, *For Hell and a Brown Mule,* 84.

123. A 15 March 1954 Gallup Poll showed that 56 percent of Catholics had a "favorable opinion" of McCarthy, compared to 45 percent of Protestants. See American Institute of Public Opinion, *Gallup Poll,* 2:1220; Rogin, *The Intellectuals and McCarthy,* 238–39; and Crosby, "Politics of Religion." Crosby emphasizes the "congruence between the Church's position and the secular anti-communism of American society at large" (p. 38).

124. Hunt to Martin, 29 April 1950, Bazinet Papers, RG 13, box 4, Sulpician Archives, Baltimore.

125. Spalding, *Premier See,* 398; Flyer: "JMJ Maryland Action Guild," Bazinet Papers, RG 13, box 4, Sulpician Archives.

126. *BES,* 14 July 1950.

127. Keough not only approved the founding of the guild, but he also provided financing and said Mass at its Annual Observances of Cardinal Mindszenty Day, held in honor of the imprisoned Hungarian prelate. See Spalding, *Premier See,* 398–99.

128. *BN-P,* 3 November 1950.

129. *Sun,* 16 September 1950; Fried, *Men against McCarthy,* 130.

130. Becker to Tydings, 16 September 1950, Millard Tydings Papers, ser. 3, box 7, UMA.

131. Larman to "Guys and Gals," 25 October 1950, ibid.

132. R. Griffith, *Politics of Fear,* 130.

133. Robert Griffith (*Politics of Fear*) credits the Catholic vote but argues nevertheless that McCarthy's effect has been overrated. Richard M. Fried ("Electoral Politics and McCarthyism," p. 213) states that the Maryland campaign "offers the clearest case for the political efficacy of McCarthy's allegations." Statistician Louis Bean (*Influences in the 1954 Mid-Term Election,* 28–30) finds a positive correlation between Maryland's Catholic population and opposition to Tydings. Shortly after the election, *Time* (13 November 1950) also stressed the Catholic factor. William E. Spillane, a strong anticommunist officer in UE Local 130, wrote to Tydings "as a Roman Catholic that voted for you in defeat and still believes in you." Spillane protested *Time*'s claim that Tydings was almost "solidly opposed" by Catholics. Spillane to Tydings, 1 January 1950, Millard Tydings Papers, ser. 3, box 8, UMA.

134. Baltimore City Board of Supervisors of Elections, RG 11, ser. 1, Registration and Election Returns, 1896–1994, BCA.

135. *BES,* 8 November 1950.

136. Powers, *Not without Honor,* 245.

137. This and subsequent information on the event is from the *Sun,* 2 May 1947.

138. Powers, *Not without Honor,* 110–11.

139. See Kazin, *Populist Persuasion.*

140. On public confidence in government, see Lipset and Schneider, *Confidence Gap.*

141. *SBE,* 8 December 1949.

Chapter Three

1. DiMartino interview, 80, BNHP; *1964 BCD* (husband's occupation). In 1956 her husband had been an employee of the City Bureau of Highways; three apparent relatives living nearby were already Bethlehem employees. See *1956 BCD.*

2. Bellah et al. (*Habits of the Heart,* 200–201) differentiate three understandings of citizenship by how they are rooted in politics. In the first, politics reflects the moral consensus of the community; in the second, politics of competing interests (roughly akin to social scientific "pluralism") predominates; the third form is "politics of the nation," expressed in terms of national purpose. Working whites in Baltimore often emphasized the first and last understandings—almost never the second.

3. Morris, *American Catholic,* 150.

4. *Sun,* 7 May 1947.

5. Ibid. In 1951 a South Baltimore journalist wrote: "You can't get away from the fact that D'Alesandro, schooled in hard knocks in East Baltimore . . . still lives down to earth with the people and has no illusions of grandeur, which has helped him." *SBE,* 28 March 1951.

6. Sergi interview, 45, BNHP.

7. Hoshall interview, 41–43, BNHP.

8. Lombardi interview, 3, BNHP. See also Purdy interview, 2, BNHP.

9. *Sun,* 7 May 1947.

10. *SBE,* 6 December 1951.

11. DiMartino interview, 38, BNHP. For blue-collar recollections of the depression in general, see the BNHP.

12. Anonymous interview, 156, BNHP.

13. Blockbusting did not become significant until the late 1950s and then affected mostly Northwest Baltimore. School desegregation was made "voluntary," and so its real impact was also limited. Both were, however, symbolically important. These issues are covered in the fourth chapter.

14. *Sun,* 5 October 1947. A feature article reconstructed the average Baltimorean's day by looking at peak gas and electricity consumption periods. The morning peak began at 6:30.

15. Josephine Purdy described these industries—excluding the railroads and the shipyards—as "foundations." Purdy interview, 9, BNHP.

16. Chamber of Commerce of Metropolitan Baltimore, *Data Profiles, 1966: Hampden-Homewood-25th Street,* 6.

17. *Sun,* 3 January 1949.

18. *BES,* 1 January 1952.

19. *Sun,* 1 January 1957. The World War II record was 210,200.

20. U.S. Department of Labor, Bureau of Labor Statistics, *Consumer Expenditures and Income.*

21. Martin UAW workers received cost-of-living benefits in their January 1952 contract. See *Sun,* 23 December 1951, and also *Aircraft Beacon,* 28 September 1956.

22. Arnold interview, 24–25, BNHP; *1956 BCD* (occupational data).

23. In the 1950s and 1960s UAW Local 239 had bowling leagues like the "toppers," the "hot rods," and the "misfits." It also sponsored baseball teams that were involved in citywide labor leagues. See programs in UAW Local 239 Collection, ser. 5, box 16, ALHUA. On the founding of a medical center for Martin Co. (formerly Glenn Martin) workers, see *Aircraft Beacon,* 18 July 1957. For the "Strengthening the Family" project sponsored jointly by the United Steelworkers and the Baltimore Urban League, see material in Hague Papers, box 6, United Steelworkers Vice Presidents Office, HCLA. United Steelworkers Local 2610 opened a $860,000 hall in December 1960; its main auditorium had seating for 1,300. *Steel Labor,* February 1962. Walter Reuther dedicated a $200,000 hall built by UAW Locals 239, 344, and 678 in May 1959. *Sun,* 31 May, 7 June 1959.

24. *BN-P and Sunday American,* 28 May 1962.

25. Levison, *Working-Class Majority,* 63.

26. Hoffman, "Changes in Housing."

27. Schiro, "Housing Surveys in 75 Cities." The 1950 census set a lower owner occupancy rate for Baltimore as a whole at 50 percent. U.S. Bureau of the Census, *Census Tract Statistics, . . . 1950.* Nationwide, home ownership rates in Baltimore were third only to Detroit and Philadelphia.

28. *BES,* 28 January 1960.

29. Hoffman, "Changes in Housing," 130; *BES,* 16 December 1949.

30. *Sun,* 17 April 1954. The FHA, in Baltimore as elsewhere, favored the suburbs. Baltimore was especially slighted by FHA minimum width requirements that eliminated most of its row houses.

31. Thommen interview, 9, BNHP.

32. Of the 13 clearly ethnic building and loans listed in the *1956 BCD,* 2 were Bohemian, 5 Polish, 2 Italian, 2 German, 1 Lithuanian, and 1 Czech.

33. These are census tracts 1–3, where Poles were 67 percent of foreign-stock residents in 1960, and 24-1, where 35 percent of foreign-stock residents were Polish in 1960. U.S. Bureau of the Census, *1960 Census of Population and Housing.* For the importance of building and loans after 1960, see Holupka, "It Was a Wonderful Life."

34. This is tract 7-1, in which 26 percent of foreign-stock residents were Czech in 1960. U.S. Bureau of the Census, *1960 Census of Population and Housing.*

35. Hampden includes census tracts 13-5 and 13-6. In tract 13-5 in 1960, only

7 percent of the population was foreign stock compared with 26 percent in tract 1-1 in Southeast Baltimore. Home ownership rates were 71 percent in tract 13-5 and 60 percent in tract 13-6. U.S. Bureau of the Census, *1960 Census of Population and Housing.* As late as 1974, according to one study, savings and loans remained "very much a part of the community fabric" in ethnic East and South Baltimore. Chaterjee, Harvey, and Klugman, "FHA Policies and the Baltimore City Housing Market," 2–7.

36. *Sun,* 5 October 1947.

37. *Sun,* 9 July 1972; Sandler, *The Neighborhood,* 13. On word-of-mouth sales in Locust Point, see *Baltimore News-American,* 24 October 1978.

38. Rich, Netherwood, and Cahn, *Neighborhood,* 41.

39. W. T. Durr, "People of the Peninsula," 47.

40. Little Italy is census tract 3-2, where in 1960, 71 percent of foreign-stock residents were Italian. Fells Point is census tract 2-3, where 68.5 percent of foreign-stock residents were Polish. U.S. Bureau of the Census, *1960 Census of Population and Housing.*

41. See Table 1.

42. McGreevy, *Parish Boundaries,* 132.

43. This refers to residents of Baltimore City as opposed to inhabitants of the entire metropolitan area, as mentioned above. Howes, *Urban Parish Study,* 14.

44. Spalding, *Premier See,* 391; Howes, *Urban Parish Study,* 14.

45. Howes, *Urban Parish Study,* 46.

46. Spalding, *Premier See,* 393–94.

47. Ibid., 397.

48. Fisher, *Let the People Decide,* 73; Arnold interview, 22–23, BNHP.

49. Fisher, *Let the People Decide,* 73.

50. "History of the Greenmount Improvement Association," n.d., RG 9, ser. 24, box 328, BCA.

51. *SBE,* 24 April 1956; *EBG,* 19 April, 31 May 1956. For a study that emphasizes the role of neighborhood groups in enforcing the color line, see Sugrue, *Origins of the Urban Crisis.*

52. Executive Secretary of the Eastern Community Council, Fourth and Fifth Annual Reports (1948 and 1949), and Southwest Community Council, First Annual Report (1949), part 1, ser. 6, box 31, ULP.

53. The *1956 BCD* lists twenty-nine clubs that can be definitely identified as political.

54. J. L. Arnold, "Last of the Good Old Days," 447.

55. *Baltimore Daily Record,* 14 December 1976.

56. *BN-P,* 19 July 1944.

57. *Baltimore American,* 37 December 1936; *Sun,* 13 August 1946; *BES,* 29 September 1950.

58. *BES,* 13 September 1950.

59. The activities of these clubs can be traced through issues of local weekly newspapers, the *SBE* and the *EBG.*

60. Freedman, *The Inheritance,* 91–97.

61. Gans, *Urban Villagers,* 177.

62. Purdy interview, 48–49, BNHP. Another South Baltimorean complained that although city hall had long promised new schools and parks for the area, "the only thing that we have received from our city fathers are large posters advertising oyster roasts, crab feasts, and Saturday night affairs." *SBE,* 29 September 1949.

63. Buhrman interview, 37, BNHP.

64. *Sun,* 7 May 1947. On machine politics as a "humanizing influence," see Jay, "Baltimore Again." Ida Esposito was proud that "Tommy's" wedding had been just two doors down from her house in Little Italy. Esposito interview, 6, BNHP.

65. *BES,* 11–19 February 1947.

66. *SBE,* 24 February 1949.

67. *Brooklyn News,* 6 January 1955.

68. The *1928 BCD* lists three German groups. In 1960, in Highlandtown census tracts 26-9 and 26-12, over 20 percent of the foreign-stock residents were German. See Map 2.

69. *BES,* 14 March 1938. The 1940 census sets the Irish proportion of foreign-born at 22 percent. But even in this neighborhood, identified by the *Evening Sun* as the "center" of Irish residence in the city, over twice as many foreign-born were Italian. See U.S. Bureau of the Census, *Sixteenth Census of Population and Housing.*

70. See C. M. Arnold, "Baltimore's Invisible Irish."

71. In Hampden census tract 13-5, 33 percent of foreign-stock residents were German and 7 percent were Irish. Overall, though, only 6 percent of residents here were of foreign stock in 1960, compared to 26 percent in tract 1-1 in Southeast Baltimore. U.S. Bureau of the Census, *1960 Census of Population and Housing.*

72. The 1960 census put Russian Jews at 18.2 percent of Baltimore's population. In 1940 Russian Jews had predominated in thirteen census tracts bordering Baltimore's 1888 boundary. By 1960 they had abandoned five of these and become the largest group in nine other tracts adjacent to the city's northwestern border. U.S. Bureau of the Census, *1960 Census of Population and Housing.* See Maps 2 and 3. On Jews and restrictive covenants in Baltimore, see Abram, *Forbidden Neighbors,* 172, 275.

73. At the 1960 census Poles accounted for 15.2 percent and Italians 13 percent of Baltimore's population. In 1950 the major ethnic communities were as follows: The Fells Point Polish community was centered around census tract 2-3, where 62.6 percent of the foreign-born were Polish. In Southeast Baltimore tract 1-3, 74.7 percent of foreign-born inhabitants were Polish. In Locust Point (tract 24-1), 38.5 percent of the foreign-born were Poles. The center of Little Italy was tract 3-2, where 60.1 percent of the foreign-born were Italian. At the heart of Southeast Baltimore's Czech neighborhood (tract 7-3), 57.5 percent

of the foreign-born were Czech. In census tract 22-2, part of South Baltimore's Lithuanian community, 44 percent of the foreign-born were Lithuanian. U.S. Bureau of the Census, *Census Tract Statistics, . . . 1950.* See also Map 2.

74. *1956 BCD.*

75. O'Connor interview, BNHP.

76. *BES,* 16 November 1950; Rich, Netherwood, and Cahn, *Neighborhood,* 105. Jonathan Rieder (*Canarsie,* 179) points out that "youthful warriors rarely operate without communal permission."

77. Rich, Netherwood, and Cahn, *Neighborhood,* 42.

78. Gildea, *When the Colts Belonged to Baltimore,* 51.

79. *EBG,* 29 May 1975.

80. Zorn interview, 4, BNHP.

81. Wuthnow, *Restructuring of American Religion,* 79–93.

82. Manning interview, 20, BNHP.

83. *Sun,* 5 June 1960.

84. Manning Interview, 20, BHNP.

85. *Sun,* 6 June 1960.

86. *BN-P,* 24 June 1941. The information from this article correlated with the *1942* and *1956 BCD.*

87. This information is from the *1956, 1958,* and *1961 BCD.* The business does not seem to have flourished, as it was not listed thereafter.

88. Burke, "From Small County Village to City Survivor." Other white Brooklynites moved southeast and settled in blue-collar Glen Burnie during the postwar years.

89. *Sun,* 7 June 1960.

90. Levering, *Baltimore Baptists,* 97–98, 166–68, 116; *SBE,* 27 October 1955.

91. *Brooklyn News,* 22 July 1954.

92. *Brooklyn News,* 28 October 1954.

93. On the predecessors to the Hillbilly Niteclub, see Burke, "From Small County Village to City Survivor."

94. Meads interview, 17, BNHP.

95. Lasson, *The Workers,* 66.

96. *BES,* 31 May 1971. A Highlandtown man used almost precisely the same words in describing the Baylis Street residents. Griffin interview, 28, BNHP.

97. In fact, the Baylis Street blacks were mostly members of one family that settled in the all-white area in the 1910s. Redd interview, 1–10, BNHP.

98. O'Connor interview, BNHP.

99. Meads interview, 14–15, BNHP.

100. *Sun,* 20 October 1954.

101. Newman, "Building in Metropolitan Areas," 691. Between 1960 and 1970 the majority of the metropolitan area population shifted from the city to the suburbs. See Table 5.

102. Jackson, *Crabgrass Frontier,* 272.

103. See, e.g., Piscopo interview, 70, BNHP. See also DeVaughn interview, 26, Purdy interview, 39, and DiMartino interview, 72, BNHP.

104. "Now where my daughter lives, you don't even see a neighbor. In the suburbs," said Grace DiMartino. DiMartino interview, 23–24, BNHP. See also Griffin interview, 22–23, BNHP.

105. *Sun,* 9 July 1972; DeVaughn interview, 25, BNHP.

106. *Sun,* 4 June 1973.

107. A photograph of this "lawn" was featured prominently in the *Sun Magazine,* 11 August 1968.

108. *Brooklyn News,* 2 November 1955.

109. *SBE,* 15 December 1949.

110. DeVaughn interview, 26, BNHP.

111. Rich, Netherwood, and Cahn, *Neighborhood,* 39. Andrew Greeley (*American Catholic,* 215) makes this point about Chicago Protestants. Eileen M. McMahon emphasizes this tendency in the title of her book, *What Parish Are You From?*

112. Howes, *Urban Parish Study,* 45.

113. See McGreevy, *Parish Boundaries.*

114. *Sun,* 9 July 1972. Still the best work on blue-collar taverns is LeMasters, *Blue-Collar Aristocrats.*

115. Rich, Netherwood, and Cahn, *Neighborhood,* 15–16, 39. Herbert J. Gans (*Urban Villagers,* 21) noted that Italian Americans in Boston, "like other working-class people," observed this stricture.

116. Rich, Netherwood, and Cahn, *Neighborhood,* 39–40.

117. Ibid., 15. On painted screens, see Eff, "Painted Screens of Baltimore."

118. Mirra Komarovsky (*Blue-Collar Marriage,* 311) has noted the insularity of working-class families when compared to middle-class families.

119. *SBE,* 14 January 1954.

120. Ibid.; *Sun,* 5 October 1947. On duckpins, see Gildea, *When the Colts Belonged to Baltimore,* 100.

121. *Sun,* 14 May 1963.

122. Hayward and Belfoure, *Baltimore Rowhouse,* 181.

123. In 1952 UAW Local 239 spent $1,385 to have the Formstone Co. cover the front of its union hall. See Vohden to Mattes, 15 April 1952, and "Membership Meeting Minutes," 7 May 1952, UAW Local 239 Collection, box 10, ALHUA. On Formstone, see Sherwood, *Maryland's Vanishing Lives,* 94–95, and Hayward and Belfoure, *Baltimore Rowhouse,* 181. Writer Samuel G. Freedman (*The Inheritance,* 172) displays this typical middle-class contempt for Formstone.

124. *Sun,* 8 August 1982; Gildea, *When the Colts Belonged to Baltimore,* 185.

125. Nast, Krause, and Monk, *Living Renaissance,* 138.

126. *SBE,* 16 September 1948. That this was a nationwide trend is indicated by a June 1949 Gallup Poll indicating that of the 44 percent of people surveyed who had seen a TV program, the largest percentage had seen it in a bar or club. American Institute of Public Opinion, *Gallup Poll,* 2:821.

127. *SBE,* 8 December 1949. The average yearly income for Baltimoreans in 1949 was $3,218. *Sun,* 18 September 1951. South Baltimore's weekly, however, set the weekly figure for blue-collarites at $40 the following fall. *SBE,* 13 September 1950.

128. *Sun,* 1 July 1951.

129. Anonymous interview, 169, BNHP.

130. Nast, Krause, and Monk, *Living Renaissance,* 144; Gildea, *When the Colts Belonged to Baltimore,* 152.

131. Kram, "A Wink at a Homely Girl," 102. The weekly was called the *News-Post* during the 1950s. In 1964 it became the *News-Post and Sunday American.* Nast, Krause, and Monk, *Living Renaissance,* 141. The paper folded in 1986 after its blue-collar audience evaporated. The *Sun* papers had surpassed it ten years earlier. See Williams, *Baltimore Sun,* 364–65. It is revealing that the *News-Post* printed a "Night Racing Edition" with racetrack results on the front-page margins, something the *Sun* would have been unlikely to consider.

132. See Nast, Krause, and Monk, *Living Renaissance,* 124. See also Gildea, *When the Colts Belonged to Baltimore,* 75.

133. These papers usually minimized conflict in the community and exploited tensions with the city at large. See Janowitz, *Community Press.* Baltimore City was home to five community papers in 1940. Detroit had twenty-two and Cleveland, eleven. Ibid., 34. In the mid-1950s, 1 percent of Baltimoreans bought appliances in suburban stores, 56 percent shopped downtown, and 36 percent patronized businesses in urban neighborhoods. Washington, D.C., residents made 23 percent of their purchases in the suburbs. "Automobile and New Appliance Purchases," *Monthly Labor Review;* Nast, Krause, and Monk, *Living Renaissance,* 125–26. See also *SBE,* 10 February 1955, and *EBG,* 29 July 1954.

134. *Sun,* 27 October 1957.

135. Kram, "A Wink at a Homely Girl."

136. Brugger, *Maryland,* 596. See esp. Gildea, *When the Colts Belonged to Baltimore,* 7, 210–11, and T. Patterson, *Football in Baltimore.*

137. Miller, "Dowager of 33rd Street," 189. See also Kram, "A Wink at a Homely Girl."

138. Nast, Krause, and Monk, *Living Renaissance,* 274.

139. Miller, "Dowager of 33rd Street," 187–200. See also Tygiel, *Baseball's Great Experiment,* 313.

140. Gildea, *When the Colts Belonged to Baltimore,* 107.

141. See, e.g., Galbraith, *Affluent Society,* and *New Industrial State.* See also Zweig, *The Worker in an Affluent Society,* and Herbert Marcuse, *One Dimensional Man.*

142. Chamber of Commerce of Metropolitan Baltimore, *Data Profiles, 1966: Highlandtown-Armistead-Colgate,* 6. Here South Baltimore refers to Ward 23, Hampden refers to census tracts 13-5 and 13-6 (part of Ward 13), and Canton and Highlandtown refers to Ward 1. Percentages calculated from U.S. Bureau of the Census, *1960 Census of Population and Housing.*

143. O'Connor interview, BNHP.

144. Nugent interview, BSHP.

145. According to the 1960 census, manufacturing employment for the residents of predominantly black Wards 5, 14, and 17 averaged only 18 percent, below the city average and far below the averages for working whites in South and Southeast Baltimore. U.S. Bureau of the Census, *1960 Census of Population and Housing.*

146. Purdy interview, 23–24, BNHP.

147. Griffin interview, 39–43, BNHP; *1956 BCD* (Griffin's occupation).

148. See, e.g., *SBE,* 21 February, 25 July 1946, and 13 September 1950.

149. *SBE,* 31 January 1946.

150. See Janowitz, *The Community Press in an Urban Setting,* 78.

151. Beirne, "Hampden-Woodberry," 17.

152. Fletcher interview, 26, BNHP; *1956 BCD* (occupational data).

153. Womer interview, BSHP.

154. Amos to Tydings, 10 October 1950, Millard Tydings Papers, ser. 3, box 7, UMA. In the letter Amos described himself as a retired union member seeking a night watchman's job. The *1942 BCD* lists him as an ironworker.

155. Slechta interview, 44–45, BNHP.

156. Duerbeck interview, BSHP.

157. Browning interview, 42, BNHP; *1956 BCD* (occupational data).

158. Lasson, *The Workers,* 74.

159. See Thomas interview, 23, BNHP.

160. Quotation reprinted in *SBE,* 3 January 1951.

161. See Maier, *City Unions.*

162. *Sun,* 12 March 1941, 18 October 1942.

163. *BES,* 29 December 1952.

164. *BES,* 1 January 1953.

165. See letters in RG 9, ser. 23, box 301, BCA

166. "One of the Strikers' Wives" to D'Alesandro, 14 January 1953, ibid.

167. Stunz to D'Alesandro, 17 January 1953, ibid. The D'Alesandro files contain over one hundred letters, about two dozen of which expressed support for the strikers (most of these were from unions). The rest, many from working-class addresses, were in opposition.

168. "We taxpayers realize that the only way you could have given them an increase was to raise our taxes," wrote "Taxpayer" to D'Alesandro, 2 February 1953, RG 9, ser. 23, box 301, BCA. For a sampling of public opinion on the municipal workers' strike, see collected correspondence in ibid.

169. From 1939 to 1945 the tax burden was extended from 3.9 million citizens to 42.6 million nationwide. Brownlee, "Tax Regimes, National Crisis, and State-Building," 93.

170. *BES,* 13 September 1950.

171. *SBE,* 26 January, 9 March 1950. On the latter date the South Baltimoreans had eight thousand signatures.

172. *Baltimore News-American,* 21 January 1968.

173. *Sun,* 1 January 1957. From 1954 to 1956 the proportion of industry in the metropolitan area built in the suburbs increased from 25 to 63 percent. Newman, "Building in Metropolitan Areas," 691.

174. *Baltimore Magazine,* May 1964.

175. Martin employed about 20,000 workers during peak periods in the 1950s but was down to a workforce of 6,700 by 1964. *Sun,* 24 November 1958; *Aircraft Beacon,* 15 March 1961; *Baltimore News-American,* 15 June 1964.

176. *BES,* 11 December 1957; W. T. Durr, "People of the Peninsula," 50.

177. *BES,* 11 December 1957.

178. *BES,* 20 May 1964.

179. Urban League Department of Industrial Relations Field Report, 21 February 1952, part 1, ser. 3, box 50, ULP.

180. U.S. Department of Labor, Bureau of Labor Statistics, *Consumer Expenditures and Income,* 11.

181. *SBE,* 13 September 1950.

182. *EBG,* 31 June 1956.

183. *Sun,* 9 July 1972.

184. Schmucker to "Dear Friends," 1 July 1943, RG 9, ser. 22, box 253, BCA. Schmucker was pastor at St. Peters in Baltimore County, just across the city line from Highlandtown.

185. Anonymous interview, 156, BNHP.

186. See, e.g., *SBE,* 26 February 1948.

187. David Halle (*America's Working Man*) argues that working people hold three identities—one at work, one in the community, and another in regard to the nation as a whole. My emphasis on the centrality of the concept of "working" here is very much in accord with Halle's. See also Katznelson, *City Trenches,* 215.

188. Suttles, *Social Construction of Communities,* 267.

Chapter Four

1. *Sun,* 28 February 1945. The notice was also published on 3 March 1945.

2. Glendon, *Rights Talk,* 4.

3. On black and white skirmishing, see, e.g., Farrell, *Studs Lonigan.*

4. On "home owners rights," see Sugrue, *Origins of the Urban Crisis,* 218.

5. Kleppner, *Chicago Divided,* 41.

6. On this point, see Levison, *Working-Class Majority,* 106.

7. *Sun,* 28 March 1945.

8. *BA-A,* 10 March 1945.

9. Ibid.

10. *BA-A,* 17 March 1945.

11. *Sun,* 28 March 1945.

12. *Sun,* 17 May 1945.
13. Cross to McKeldin, 27 July 1945, RG 9, ser. 22, box 253, BCA.
14. Kaupp to McKeldin, 18 October 1945, RG 9, ser. 22, box 259, BCA.
15. Orser, *Blockbusting in Baltimore,* 68.
16. *Sun,* 21 July 1945.
17. *Sun,* 27 July 1945.
18. FBI General Intelligence Survey, July 1945, Maryland Manuscripts Collection 4008, UMA.
19. *Sun,* 27 July 1945.
20. Orser, *Blockbusting in Baltimore,* 69. Any student of racial change in postwar Baltimore must be indebted to Professor Orser's work.
21. Unsigned letter to D'Alesandro, 3 December 1951, RG 9, ser. 23, box 282, BCA.
22. *BA-A,* 18 October 1947.
23. This account is drawn from *BES,* 12 October 1947, and *BA-A,* 18, 25 October, 1 November 1947.
24. *BA-A,* 25 October, 1 November 1947. In the Ossian Sweet case, a black Detroit doctor killed a member of a mob attacking his home. He was charged with murder but was defended successfully by Clarence Darrow on grounds that "a man's home is his castle." See Charles Abrams, *Forbidden Neighbors,* 92–93.
25. See Hirsch, *Making the Second Ghetto.*
26. Sugrue, *Origins of the Urban Crisis,* 233.
27. Callcott, *Maryland and America,* 151.
28. *Sun,* 16 March 1955.
29. *BA-A,* 16 March 1955.
30. U.S. Bureau of the Census, *Census Tract Statistics . . . 1950.*
31. In this same period, 15,000 whites left. *Sun,* 15, 14 March 1955. The black median income was $1,054 below that of whites in 1950 and $1,500 below in 1953.
32. *Sun,* 15 March 1955.
33. *Sun,* 12 February 1950.
34. Rorty, "Desegregation along the Mason-Dixon Line," 493.
35. *Sun,* 3 October 1954.
36. Pancoast, *Study on Desegregation,* 26.
37. Callcott, *Maryland and America,* 151, 244.
38. Pancoast, *Study on Desegregation,* 44–47.
39. State officials held that the incident was not racially motivated, although a few Baltimore clergymen insisted otherwise. *Sun,* 10 November 1949; *Time,* 31 October 1949.
40. *BES,* 30 September 1954.
41. Quoted in Roberts, "Pigtown."
42. Pancoast, *Study on Desegregation,* 53.
43. Ibid., 64, 55.
44. *BA-A,* 9 October 1954; *BES,* 30 September 1954.

45. Pancoast, *Study on Desegregation,* 56.

46. Callcott, *Maryland and America,* 151.

47. This was confirmed by a participant in the protests in an anonymous interview at the BCA, Summer 1995.

48. *BES,* 1 October 1954; Pancoast, *Study on Desegregation,* 59–61.

49. *Southern School News,* 4 November 1954; *Sun,* 2 October 1954.

50. *Southern School News,* 4 November 1954.

51. *Sun,* 2 October 1954.

52. *SBE,* 7 October 1954.

53. *Sun,* 4 October 1954.

54. Pancoast, *Study on Desegregation,* 67.

55. Orser, *Blockbusting in Baltimore,* 111.

56. Pancoast, *Study on Desegregation,* 68–73.

57. It is significant that Glen Burnie was considered by many Baltimore whites to have been a "safe," or unlikely to be integrated, area. A description of these safe areas is given in Anonymous to BNI, 13 April 1964, CPHA Collection, ser. 2, box 13, UBA.

58. Pancoast, *Study on Desegregation,* 72–73.

59. These statistics were compiled in ibid., 44–45.

60. Ibid., 50, 70.

61. *Sun,* 1 October 1954.

62. Pancoast, *Study on Desegregation,* 49–51, 76. The other incorporators of the Baltimore Association for States Rights were Samuel E. Oldershaw and Adam Hoffman. Oldershaw, a maintenance man from East Baltimore, had been involved in "noisy and unruly" meetings with school officials regarding crowded facilities that also had racial overtones. No picketing resulted. Oldershaw later became president of the association. Another participant in the east side meetings, Whittier Sprinkel, was a driver for Anchor Motor Freight, who later became president of the local chapter of the National Association for the Advancement of White People. Hoffman, also a driver for Anchor Motor Freight, participated in picketing and led a meeting at the Methodist church across from the school in Pigtown. Occupational data are from *1956 BCD.*

63. Maryland Council for Civic Responsibility, Inc., "Some Active Groups Advocating Extreme Political or Social Views in Maryland," May 1967, CPHA Collection, ser. 2, box 14, UBA; *Sun,* 29 November 1955, 4 January 1956.

64. *Sun,* 21 November 1954.

65. Maryland Council for Civic Responsibility, "Groups Advocating Extreme Political or Social Views."

66. Primary election returns in Maryland Secretary of State, *1960 Maryland Manual,* 467. See also *1966 Maryland Manual,* 528.

67. Templeton to Granger, 21 September 1959, part 1, ser. 1, box 80, ULP.

68. Hirsch, *Making the Second Ghetto,* 73

69. Rorty, "Desegregation along the Mason-Dixon Line," 494.

70. *BA-A,* 9 October 1954.

71. *Southern School News,* 1 December 1954.

72. Burdette, "Modern Maryland Politics," 814.

73. *BES,* 2 November 1950; *Southern School News,* 4 November 1954.

74. MDCIUC, *Proceedings of the Sixteenth Annual Convention,* 26.

75. *Sun,* 3 November 1954.

76. Loevy, "Political Behavior in the Baltimore Metropolitan Area," 75-76.

77. In precincts 8 and 9 of Ward 20, Byrd got 60 and 59 percent of the vote respectively.

78. Hamilton's vote corresponds with middle-class precincts 9 through 23 in Ward 27.

79. Burdette, "Modern Maryland Politics," 811.

80. MDCIUC, *Proceedings of the Sixteenth Annual Convention,* 15.

81. MDCIUC, *Proceedings of the Seventeenth Annual Convention,* 185-89.

82. *SBE,* 14 October 1954.

83. *BN-P,* 20 August 1958 (chronology).

84. Curran, "History of a Changing Neighborhood."

85. Orser, *Blockbusting in Baltimore,* 99.

86. Ibid., 113.

87. *Sun,* 21 July 1945.

88. Orser, *Blockbusting in Baltimore,* 6, 87.

89. Library of Congress Legislative Reference Service, American Law Division, "Civil Rights Project Report, Maryland No. 2," 24 November 1958, RG 453, A1 entry 2, box 9, NARA; Maryland Commission on Interracial Problems and Relations, "Annual Report," January 1962, RG 9, ser. 24, box 331, BCA.

90. Library of Congress, "Civil Rights Project Report."

91. This is census tract 27-10. In 1950 the tract was 61 percent professional (including clerical workers) and 39 percent blue collar. Its median income was 27 percent above the city's average, and it was 95 percent white. U.S. Bureau of the Census, *Census Tract Statistics, . . . 1950.*

92. M.E.A.A. to Baltimore Housing Authority, 4 June 1956, RG 48, ser. 13, box 5, BCA.

93. Orser, *Blockbusting in Baltimore,* 108.

94. Ibid., 90.

95. Baltimore Urban League, *Review of the Program,* part I, ser. 3, box 49, ULP.

96. Orser, *Blockbusting in Baltimore,* 91; *Sun,* 15 March 1955.

97. "Minority Occupancy and Housing Values," n.d., Baltimore Urban League, CPHA Collection, ser. 1, box 11, UBA. A good example of the continued vitality of this rationalization is Stephen Grant Meyer's *As Long as They Don't Move Next Door,* which credits neighborhood decline to the age of the housing at issue and the inordinate expense of financing, but white refusal to live with blacks to racism pure and simple.

98. "The Church and Integrated Housing—The Baltimore Story," 15 October 1959,

CPHA Collection, ser. 2, box 84, UBA; Rosen, "When a Negro Moves Next Door."

99. Crocetti to Research Advisory Committee, 12 July 1963, BNI Collection, ser. 1, box 4, UBA.
100. Colby, "Desegregation Activities," 67, 70–76.
101. Orser, *Blockbusting in Baltimore,* 94.
102. Ibid., 148 (quotation). Census tract 8-3 was 99.7 percent white in 1950 and 86 percent black in 1960.
103. See esp. Gamm, *Urban Exodus,* and McGreevy, *Parish Boundaries.* See also Sugrue, *Origins of the Urban Crisis,* 244, and Hirsch, *Making the Second Ghetto,* 193.
104. Orser, *Blockbusting in Baltimore,* 23, 7, 78, 110.
105. Suttles, *Social Construction of Communities.*
106. On protesters as ethnic working-class Catholics, see Sugrue, *Origins of the Urban Crisis,* 192, and Hirsch, *Making the Second Ghetto,* 98. On the tendency of Jews to abandon neighborhoods more readily, see Hirsch, 194, and Sugrue, 242–43.
107. Orser, *Blockbusting in Baltimore,* 99.
108. M.E.A.A to Housing Authority, 4 June 1956, RG 48, ser. 13, box 5, BCA.
109. Kaupp to McKeldin, 18 October 1945, RG 9, ser. 22, box 259, BCA.
110. M.E.A.A to Housing Authority, 4 June 1956, RG 48, ser. 13, box 5, BCA.
111. *BN-P,* 21 August 1958.
112. Lasson, *The Workers,* 67.
113. *BN-P,* 22 August 1958.
114. M.E.A.A to Housing Authority, 4 June 1956, RG 48, ser. 13, box 5, BCA.
115. Orser, *Blockbusting in Baltimore,* 99.
116. M.E.A.A to Housing Authority, 4 June 1956, RG 48, ser. 13, box 5, BCA.
117. Orser, *Blockbusting in Baltimore,* 1.
118. O'Connor interview, BNHP.
119. Baltimore Urban League, *Review of the Program,* part I, ser. 3, box 49, ULP.
120. Nelson, *Divided We Stand,* xxi.
121. Hobbs to Temko, 1 March 1961, RG 453, A1 entry 2, box 20, NARA.
122. Hobbs to Temko, 5 June 1961, ibid.
123. Gorman interview, BSHP.
124. Tucker to Thomas, 21 February 1952, part 1, ser. 3, box 50, ULP.
125. Saunders interview, BSHP.
126. Klauzenberg, according to FBI reports, was once a Communist Party member. Although this remained unknown throughout his lifetime, the report seems consistent with Klauzenberg's record in the late 1930s and early 1940s, although by the 1950s it is unlikely that he was still associated with the party. FBI General Intelligence Report, December 1944, Maryland Manuscripts Collection 4004, UMA.
127. Hobbs to Temko, 9 June 1961, RG 453, A1 entry 2, box 20, NARA.

128. Hobbs to Temko, 8 June 1961, ibid.

129. Ibid.; U.S. Department of Labor, Office of Federal Contract Compliance, Docket 102-68, 15 February 1970, RG 174, UD entry 9, box 42, NARA, 15.

130. Hobbs to Temko, 8 June 1961, RG 453, A1 entry 2, box 20, NARA.

131. Hobbs to Temko, 9 June 1961, ibid.

132. In 1958 a union official wrote that "until the last few years, Ruke was not even a member of the union local." Thompson to McDonald, 11 March 1958, United Steelworkers IEB Collection, box 16, HCLA.

133. *BN-P,* n.d., clipping from United Steelworkers IEB Collection, ibid.

134. Rowlett to McDonald, 10 April 1957, ibid.

135. Damron to McDonald, 24 May 1956, Hague Papers, United Steelworkers Vice Presidents Office, box 9, HCLA.

136. *Educator,* June 1956, ibid. The vote was 1,316 for Damron, 1,477 for Klauzenberg, and 1,917 for Ruke.

137. At first Ruke's opponents charged him with playing golf on union time and with union funds. See accounts in Simonson to McDonald, 16 April 1957, "What Are You Going to Do About It?," attached to Ruke to McDonald, 17 May 1957, and Thompson, McMorris, and Elliott to Abel, 15 April 1957, all in United Steelworkers IEB Collection, box 16, HCLA.

138. Excerpt from "Special Local Meeting, 14 May 1957," attached to Ruke to McDonald, 17 May 1957, ibid.

139. *Educator,* July 1957, Hague Papers, United Steelworkers Vice Presidents Office, box 9, HCLA.

140. Maryland historian George H. Callcott (*Maryland and America,* 127) describes public opinion as having been "distinctly unfriendly to the investigators," citing the newspapers' "reluctance" to list names. This appears to be a bit of an overstatement, however. The *Sun* and especially the *News-American* eagerly told the tale of Clifford Miller, although treating it more as a spectacle than a dire warning against subversion. The *Evening Sun* ran a three-part series on Miller, treating HUAC and the FBI with the utmost respect. See *BES,* 14–17 May 1957.

141. *EBG,* 16 May 1957.

142. On Miller's testimony, see *BES,* 14–17 May 1957.

143. See Ruke to McDonald, 8 May 1957, United Steelworkers IEB Collection, box 16, HCLA. See also *BN-P,* 6 June 1957.

144. *Sun,* 26 June 1957.

145. See five letters from Ruke supporters to the International Office, dated 11–17 June 1957, all of which claimed to speak for the "will of the majority." See also "dear member" by the "Committee for Freedom," November 1957, both in United Steelworkers IEB Collection, box 16, HCLA.

146. Baltimore Urban League, "The League Newsletter, November 1958," part 1, ser. 3, box 50, ULP.

147. Suttles, *Social Constitution of Communities,* 21. On "defensive localism," see also Sugrue, *Origins of the Urban Crisis,* 210.

148. Templeton to Mitchell, 8 March 1962, and Young to Mitchell, 2 March 1962, attached to Templeton to "all Executive Board Members," 7 March 1962, part 2, ser., 1, box 62, ULP.

149. Meier, "Successful Sit-Ins in a Border City."

Chapter Five

1. Lippman, *Spiro Agnew's America,* 18–41.
2. Meier, "Sit-Ins in a Border City."
3. Colby, "Desegregation Activities," 48–49.
4. Ibid., 50.
5. *BA-A,* 15 September 1962; *BES,* 3, 4 September 1962.
6. *BA-A,* 8 September 1962.
7. Colby, "Desegregation Activities," 93. In 1958, 88 out of 169 schools were segregated. See Crain, *Politics of School Desegregation,* 75. Blacks made up 54 percent of the total school enrollment but only 35 percent of the city's population.
8. According to one account, the school board was influenced by "the militant Baltimore NAACP waiting in the background." See Crain, *Politics of School Desegregation,* 79; Press Release: "Major Win for NAACP in Baltimore Schools" 13 September 1963, NAACP Papers, Group 3, box A102, LCMD.
9. *BES,* 5 September 1963.
10. Ibid. (Hamilton parent leader); Chamber of Commerce of Metropolitan Baltimore, *Data Profiles 1966: Hamilton-Gardenville,* 4–6. In 1960 the average years of schooling in white working-class Baltimore census tracts 1, 23, and 24 was 7.8 years; in Hamilton it was 9.8 years. U.S. Bureau of the Census, *1960 Census of Population and Housing.*
11. *BES,* 9 September 1963.
12. *BES,* 2 November 1954.
13. *SBE,* 25 January, 1 February 1962.
14. Garmatz, always backed by labor, was a "card-carrying" member of the local electricians' union. *Sun,* 22 April 1962.
15. *EBG,* 30 January 1964; Weiner to McKeldin, 4 January 1965, RG 9, ser. 25, box 382, BCA. For a measure of growing apprehension of urban crime and the tendency for citizens to depict it as a relatively new phenomenon, see letters to the mayor filed under "Crime" in ibid.
16. *EBG,* 30 January 1964.
17. *SBE,* 27 September 1962.
18. See Meier and Rudwick, *CORE,* 92, 121.
19. Ibid., 57.
20. *Sun Magazine,* 1 December 1968.
21. Meier and Rudwick, *CORE,* 223.
22. *Sun,* 5 July 1963; *Time,* 12 July 1963; Mattingly, "Gwynn Oak"; Wuthnow, *Restructuring of American Religion,* 146.

23. *BES,* 5 July 1963.

24. *BES,* 12 July 1963.

25. *BES,* 8 July 1963.

26. *BA-A,* 22 September 1962.

27. *BES,* 5 July 1963.

28. Mattingly, "Gwynn Oak," 136.

29. On divisions between clergy and laity nationally, see McGreevy, *Parish Boundaries.*

30. Mattingly, "Gwynn Oak," 137.

31. The best work on this widening split between orthodox and progressive within religious groups is Hunter, *Culture Wars,* and Wuthnow, *Restructuring of American Religion,* 146.

32. *Sun,* 27 October 1960.

33. Howard, "Madalyn Murray," 94.

34. *BES,* 17 June 1963. Murray's case was considered jointly with *Schempp.* See *BES,* 27 February 1963.

35. In 1959, 69 percent of Americans participated in organized religion. J. T. Patterson, *Grand Expectations,* 329. Eisenhower's nondenominational approach was revealed in his conclusion to that phrase, which was "—and I don't care what it is."

36. *SBE,* 27 February 1964.

37. *Towson (Md.) Jeffersonian,* 12 July 1963.

38. *BES,* 18 June 1963.

39. Jones, *Wallace Story,* 260.

40. U.S. Congress, House, *Hearings before the Committee on the Judiciary on Proposed Amendments to the Constitution Relating to Prayers,* 845.

41. Jones, *Wallace Story,* 259.

42. *BES,* 13 September 1963.

43. *BES,* 10 March 1964.

44. *Catholic Review,* 20 March 1964.

45. Jones, *Wallace Story,* 272.

46. *BES,* 18 March 1964.

47. *SBE,* 23 April 1964.

48. Jones, *Wallace Story,* 263; Makay, "The Speaking of . . . Wallace," 59.

49. *BES,* 1 May 1964.

50. Makay, "The Speaking of . . . Wallace," 97.

51. Kazin, *Populist Persuasion,* 236.

52. Carlson, *Politics of Powerlessness,* 64–65, 63–64, 66.

53. *BES,* 5 May 1964.

54. *BES,* 12 May 1964.

55. Jones, *Wallace Story,* 268.

56. *SBE,* 14 May 1964.

57. *EBG,* 14 May 1964.

58. *BES,* 18 May 1964.

59. Maryland State and District of Columbia AFL-CIO, *Proceedings of the Sixth Convention,* 56.

60. *EBG,* 14 May 1964. Devlin touted his union membership when he campaigned for a Maryland House of Delegates seat in 1966. See *EBG,* 25 August 1966.

61. McDonald to Attalah, 6 May 1964, McDonald Papers, United Steelworkers Presidents Office, box 47, HCLA.

62. *BES,* 13 May 1964; Carter, *Politics of Rage,* 213.

63. McDonald, *Union Man,* 315; Carlson, *Politics of Powerlessness,* 36.

64. Carter, *Politics of Rage,* 215.

65. Jones, *Wallace Story,* 302.

66. *U.S. News and World Report,* 1 June 1964, 31.

67. *BA-A,* 30 May 1964.

68. Conway, "White Backlash Re-examined," 719.

69. Baltimore City Board of Supervisors of Elections, RG 11, ser. 1, Registration and Election Returns, 1896–1994, BCA.

70. *BA-A,* 30 May 1964.

71. Jones, *Wallace Story,* 309.

72. Carter, *Politics of Rage,* 12.

73. Edsall and Edsall, *Chain Reaction,* 10.

74. Chamber of Commerce of Metropolitan Baltimore, *Negro Market Data Handbook,* 15.

75. Orser, *Blockbusting in Baltimore,* 4; Anonymous Edmondson Village resident (name removed) to BNI, 13 April 1964, CPHA Papers, ser. 2, box 13, UBA.

76. Chamber of Commerce of Metropolitan Baltimore, *Negro Market Data Handbook,* 24.

77. Orser, *Blockbusting in Baltimore,* 93–94.

78. Zorn interview, 15, 18 BNHP. Zorn recalled the signs going up in 1964 or "around the time of [John] Kennedy's death" (p. 9).

79. Griffin interview, 59, BNHP.

80. Colby, "Desegregation Activities," 77, 84.

81. *Sun,* 14 January 1966.

82. A. J. Mattes letter to editor, *Sun,* 20 January 1966. Mattes was a UAW International staff representative.

83. Fornaro to Stockton, 7 August 1964, UAW Local 239 Collection, box 4, ALHUA.

84. Bachrach and Baratz, *Power and Poverty,* 113.

85. When Sixth District councilman Dominic Leone (for whom Riverside Park is now named) voted for a rent subsidy bill on the highly principled ground that "I don't want people to think I'm a racist," he met with general revulsion; some threatened to bomb his home. *Baltimore News-American,* 21 January 1968.

86. *Sun,* 18 January 1966.

87. *Sun,* 24 January 1966.

88. *Sun,* 19 January 1966.

89. Meier and Rudwick, *CORE,* 304, 359, 409–410, 358.

90. See Goldberg, "CORE in Trouble."

91. Lynch to McKissick, 25 April 1966, CORE Papers, King Library Collection, reel 24, LCMD.

92. Butler to McKeldin, 19 April 1966, RG 9, ser. 25, box 382, BCA.

93. Eaton to McKeldin, 22 April 1966, ibid.

94. Meier and Rudwick, *CORE,* 377; Goldberg, "CORE in Trouble," 51, 94.

95. *Sun,* 2 May 1966.

96. On 15 May CORE protests at the Horizon House apartment building were televised nationally on NBC. Goldberg, "CORE in Trouble," 73. CORE also made the 6 June 1966 issue of *Newsweek.*

97. Bachrach and Baratz, *Power and Poverty,* 71; Goldberg, "CORE in Trouble," 77.

98. Goldberg, "CORE in Trouble," 99 (quotation), 104–5; *BES,* 30 May 1966.

99. *BES,* 31 May 1966.

100. Goldberg, "CORE in Trouble," 101 (first quotation), 122.

101. *Sun,* 30 July 1966; Maryland Council for Civic Responsibility, Inc., "Some Active Groups Advocating Extreme Political or Social Views in Maryland," May 1967, CPHA Papers, ser. 2, box 14, UBA.

102. The Vinland bookstore was the NSRP headquarters. It occupied a prominent site on Eastern Avenue across from Haussner's, Highlandtown's most renowned restaurant.

103. *Sun,* 26 July 1966.

104. Goldberg, "CORE in Trouble," 162.

105. *Sun,* 28 July 1966.

106. *Sun,* 29 July 1966.

107. *Sun,* 30 July 1966.

108. Ibid.

109. Ibid.

110. O'Connor interview, BNHP.

111. *EBG,* 4 August 1966.

112. See Lippman, *Spiro Agnew's America,* 74–75.

113. Callcott, *Maryland and America,* 141.

114. *BES,* 18 August 1966.

115. Lippman, *Spiro Agnew's America,* 76.

116. *Sun,* 17 August 1966.

117. Burdette, "Modern Maryland Politics," 855.

118. *BES,* 18 August 1966.

119. *EBG,* 4 August 1966.

120. *EBG,* 18 August 1966.

121. *EBG,* 25 August 1966.

122. Garmatz ran half-page advertisements in the *East Baltimore Guide* every week in the month before the primary. See *EBG,* 18, 25 August, 1, 8 September 1966.

123. *Sun,* 18 September 1966.

124. *New York Times,* 15 September 1966.

125. "Minutes of the Regular Membership Meeting," 10 October 1966, UAW Local 678 Collection, box 2, ALHUA.

126. *BES,* 20 September 1966.

127. *Sun,* 10 November 1966.

128. On party problems, see *Sun,* 16 September 1966. On Districts 1 and 6, see *Sun,* 22 August 1966, and *BN-P,* 9 September 1966.

129. Halle, *America's Working Man,* 197–98.

130. *BA-A,* 9 October 1954.

131. Smith to McKeldin, 17 June 1963, RG 9, ser. 25, box 428, BCA.

132. Lowe to McKeldin, 2 September 1964, RG 9, ser. 25, box 425, BCA. Emphasis in the original.

133. Miller to McKeldin, 14 September 1966, RG 9, ser. 25, box 414, BCA.

134. *Sun,* 4 November 1966.

135. Lippman, *Spiro Agnew's America,* 82.

136. "Mahoney on the Issues and Some of the Issues on Mahoney" (brief compiled by 1970 Tydings for Senator campaign), Agnew quotation dated 27 October 1966, Joseph Tydings Papers, ser. 5, box 3, UMA. The Baltimore NSRP did back Mahoney, although he officially rejected its support. See *Sun,* 4 November 1966. The article is provocatively titled "Racists Back Mahoney."

137. *Catholic Review,* 28 October 1966; *Sun,* 9 November 1966. Walter Dean Burnham (*Critical Elections,* 152) found a +0.917 correlation between the 1964 Wallace vote and the 1966 Mahoney vote. For voting statistics, see Baltimore City Board of Supervisors of Elections, RG 11, ser. 1, Registration and Election Returns, 1896–1994, BCA.

138. *Baltimore Magazine,* January 1967.

139. *BES,* 13 February 1967.

140. *EBG,* 15 February 1968.

141. An important work on the role of crime in discrediting Democratic liberalism in the 1960s is Flamm, "Law and Order."

142. Of more than a thousand addicts tracked by Baltimore police in 1964, over 75 percent were black. At the time, heroin was mostly unavailable to whites. Jonnes, *Hep-Cats,* 248–52.

143. Baltimore burglaries rose from 7,393 in 1965 to 19,041 in 1970. Robberies rose from 2,109 to 10,965 during the same period. Jonnes, *Hep-Cats,* 247, 251.

144. In 1961 the U.S. murder rate was 4.7 per 100,000; in Maryland it was 4.5 per 100,000. In 1968 the national rate was 6.8 per 100,000, whereas the Maryland rate was 9.3 per 100,000. U.S. Bureau of the Census, *Statistical Abstract of the United States.*

145. *Baltimore News-American,* 24 June 1968, 9 February 1969. Baltimore police officials argued that these high crime figures were the result of improvements in record keeping.

146. *EBG,* 15 February 1968.

147. Rosenthal, "Cage of Fear."
148. Brown to McKeldin, 20 August 1966, RG 9, ser. 25, box 414, BCA. Brown's husband ran a plumbing and heating business.
149. Ross to McKeldin, 3 November 1966, RG 9, ser. 25, box 376, BCA.
150. Ibid. She called herself a "firm believer in soap and water."
151. Davis to McKeldin, 23 July 1964, RG 9, ser. 25, box 376, BCA. Emphases in the original.
152. Schluter to McKeldin, 11 December 1967, RG 9, ser. 26, box 455, BCA.
153. Callcott, *Maryland and America,* 136.
154. Curran, "History of a Changing Neighborhood," 774.
155. Lane to D'Alesandro, 6 February 1968, RG 9, ser. 26, box 455, BCA.
156. The property tax burden was becoming especially heavy for Baltimoreans by 1965. See Burdette, "Modern Maryland Politics," 854.
157. *BES,* 27 May 1966.
158. *BES,* 11 April 1968.
159. Helen Wilensky, letter to the editor, *BES,* 4 February 1967. According to the *1964 BCD,* Mrs. Wilensky was a secretary.
160. Fisher to D'Alesandro, 17 June 1968, RG 9, ser. 26, box 459, BCA. In 1964 Fisher was a laborer for the Baltimore City Parks Department. *1964 BCD.*
161. Jonnes, *Hep-Cats,* 250.
162. CAA funds were 90 percent federal and 10 percent city. Callcott, *Maryland and America,* 204. By the beginning of 1968, according to one study, Baltimore's Community Action Agency was "operating at full tilt, practically out in the open, to organize power bases for the poor." Bachrach, "Power Analysis," 177.
163. *EBG,* 31 March 1966.
164. Lippman, *Spiro Agnew's America,* 105–8.
165. *Sun,* 8 April 1968.
166. O'Connor interview, BNHP; Zorn interview, 11, BNHP. For another strong statement against restrictions on police and soldiers and in favor of letting "the citizenry handle things in their own way," see Clayton to Brewster, 11 May 1968, RG 9, ser. 26, box 453, BCA.
167. Zorn interview, 12, BNHP.
168. O'Connor interview, BNHP; Zorn interview, 10, BNHP.
169. O'Connor interview, BNHP.
170. *EBG,* 8 January 1969. In contrast, said the editorialist, the *Baltimore News-American,* blue-collar Baltimore's preferred paper, gave the proper front-page treatment to crime stories "that used to call for the blackest type in the shop, and [got] the posse out on the trail of the criminal."
171. *Sun,* 8 April 1968.
172. Callcott, *Maryland and America,* 163–64.
173. Wills, *Nixon Agonistes,* 265–66.
174. *Sun,* 7 April 1969; Wills, *Nixon Agonistes,* 269.

175. Wills, *Nixon Agonistes,* 269.

176. Lippman, *Spiro Agnew's America,* 112–13.

177. *Baltimore Labor Herald,* 19 April 1968.

178. Burdette, "Modern Maryland Politics," 872.

179. Backert to D'Alesandro, 20 March 1968, RG 9, ser. 26, box 453, BCA.

180. Chatfield to D'Alesandro, 11 April 1968, ibid.; *1964 BCD* (husband's occupation).

181. Gray to D'Alesandro, 11 April 1968, RG 9, ser. 26, box 453, BCA; *1964 BCD* (occupational data).

182. Lippman, *Spiro Agnew's America,* 113.

183. Wills, *Nixon Agonistes,* 264–65, 270.

184. Lippman, *Spiro Agnew's America,* 135.

185. Mary E. Murphy interview, 1, Friends of the Catonsville Area Library Oral History Program, Catonsville, Md.

186. Phyllis Morsberger interview, 1–2, ibid.; *BES,* 18 April 1968. In a 1967 case that was less sensational, Philip Berrigan had been convicted of pouring blood over draft records in Baltimore.

187. Wills, *Nixon Agonistes,* 50.

188. *Sun,* 7 October 1968.

189. Wills, *Nixon Agonistes,* 53–54.

190. *Sun,* 8 October 1968. On Glen Burnie, see *BES,* 25 June 1968.

191. Wills, *Nixon Agonistes,* 57.

192. See Chester, Hodgson, and Page, *American Melodrama,* 705–6.

193. Maryland State and District of Columbia AFL-CIO, *Proceedings of the Tenth Convention,* 41.

194. See *Baltimore Labor Herald,* 20, 27 September 1968.

195. *EBG,* 26 September, 3 October 1968; *1964 BCD* (Murawski's occupation).

196. *EBG,* 31 October 1968. The Agnew fan is Wayne Browning, the son of Jeanette Browning. See Browning interview, 34, BNHP.

197. See Baltimore City Board of Supervisors of Elections, RG 11, ser. 1, Registration and Election Returns, 1896–1994, BCA. In Wards 23 and 24, Humphrey got 49.9 and 44.0 percent respectively.

198. Chester, Hodgson, and Page, *American Melodrama,* 496.

199. *BES,* 18 May 1964; *1964 BCD* (husband's occupation).

200. Lasson, *The Workers,* 76.

201. American Institute of Public Opinion, *Gallup Poll,* 2231.

202. *Sun,* 9 July 1972.

203. On the growing importance of backlash late in the decade, see, e.g., "The Troubled American: A Special Report on the White Majority," *Newsweek,* 6 October 1969; Schrag, "Forgotten American"; and Frady, "Gary, Indiana." For a synthetic account, see Ehrenreich, *Fear of Falling,* 97–146.

Chapter Six

1. U.S. Congress, Senate, Committee on Banking, Housing, and Urban Affairs, *Neighborhood Preservation,* 72.
2. Ibid.
3. *SBE,* 15 December 1949.
4. *BES,* 16 November 1950.
5. See Orser, *Blockbusting in Baltimore,* 80–82, and *Brooklyn News,* 26 August 1954.
6. *Brooklyn News,* 6, 13 January 1955. Community councils during this period always regarded combating delinquency to be one of their main tasks. See "First Annual Report of the Southwest Community Council, Inc.," 31 August 1949, part 1, ser. 6, box 31, ULP.
7. Sutton, "Buddy Deane Show," 12; Gildea, *When the Colts Belonged to Baltimore,* 152–60 (quotations, pp. 152, 160). For a fictionalized version of the "Buddy Deane Show" controversy, see the 1988 motion picture *Hairspray* by Baltimore native John Waters.
8. The white population drop from 1960 to 1970 was as follows: Ward 1, 20.1 percent; Ward 23, 11.1 percent; Ward 24, 11.6 percent. Maryland Department of State Planning, *Maryland Population Data.*
9. In 1963 the state median age was 24.0 years and the Third District median age was 21.4 years. In 1973 the state median age was 27.3 years, whereas the Third District median age was 31.3 years. U.S. Bureau of the Census, *Congressional District Data Book, 88th Congress* and *93rd Congress.*
10. Edsall, *Power and Money,* 86.
11. Lombardi interview, 24, BNHP.
12. Litzinger interview, 20, BNHP.
13. *BES,* 31 May 1971.
14. O'Connor interview, BNHP.
15. Butterfield interview, BSHP. See also Gorman and Nugent interviews, BSHP.
16. AFL-CIO, *Proceedings of the Tenth Convention,* 66.
17. *Sun Magazine,* 5 September 1982.
18. Freedman, *The Inheritance,* 173.
19. Browning interview, 34, BNHP.
20. *Sun,* 21 March 1978.
21. Beayhan to union, 27 September 1968, Local 239 Collection, box 4, ALHUA.
22. O'Connor Interview, BNHP.
23. Fisher, *Let the People Decide,* 72.
24. Haeuber, *Expressway Controversy,* 4–7.
25. *Baltimore Sun,* 31 January 1962.
26. Ward to McKeldin, 31 March 1965, RG 9, ser. 25, box 417, BCA.
27. *Sun,* 4 June 1973.
28. Brugger, *Maryland,* 661–62.

29. *BES,* 27 February 1967.
30. SPFH flyers, 15, 19 May 1967, SPFH vertical file, Maryland Room, Pratt Free Library, Baltimore.
31. *Sun,* 24 May 1967.
32. *Sun Magazine,* 13 November 1977.
33. *EBG,* 29 August 1968.
34. J. P. Sweeney, "Mikulski: Representing the Neighborhood," 105–6; Lee Trulove, "SECO History," September 1977, SECO Collection, ser. 1, box 2, UBA, 24 (hereafter cited as Trulove, SECO History).
35. Trulove, SECO History, 25.
36. Gauthreaux to Johnson, 30 July 1968, RG 406, entry 1A, box 177, NARA.
37. Bird to Volpe, 16 July 1970, RG 406, entry 1B, box 74, NARA.
38. Trulove, SECO History, 24.
39. Ibid., 30–31, 26 (quotation), 32–33.
40. *New York Times Magazine,* 9 May 1976, 21.
41. U.S. Congress, Senate, Committee on Banking, Housing, and Urban Affairs, *Neighborhood Preservation,* 72.
42. Edsall, *Power and Money,* 82–90.
43. Haeuber, *Expressway Controversy,* 29–30. On Schaefer's tendency to make the political personal, see O'Keeffe, *Baltimore Politics.*
44. Haeuber, *Expressway Controversy,* 45–55.
45. Ibid., 36–37.
46. *BES,* 24 May 1971. See also *Nation,* 21 December 1970, 652–53.
47. *BES,* 3 November 1971.
48. Edsall, *Power and Money,* 87.
49. Ibid.
50. *Sun,* 16 April 1971.
51. *BES,* 3 May 1971. The archaic expression "b'hoys" was commonly used in Baltimore as late as the 1950s. Its significance was no doubt still understood by blue collarites in the early 1970s.
52. On Alinsky and his influence in the "new" community organizing, see Boyte, *Backyard Revolution,* 49–57.
53. See Klugman, "The FHA and Home Ownership," 171–88. NECO, based primarily on local church membership, held its first congress in April 1970—its first organizer had studied under Alinsky. Like SECO, NECO had its share of critics who claimed it was "disruptive, anti-establishment and racially antagonistic." NECO's agenda remained restricted, though. It focused primarily on reducing slum housing and opening up areas to blacks. Before 1972 the organization had significant black membership. This changed when NECO's critics charged it with trying to exclude blacks under the guise of "orderly integration." Ibid., 173–74.
54. See Krickus, "Organizing Neighborhoods."
55. *Sun,* 16 April 1971.

56. Krickus ("Organizing Neighborhoods"), unfortunately, gives a shallow depiction of the CCC's opponents, suggesting that they were inevitably Klansmen, red-baiters, or big businessmen.

57. *SBE,* 1 March 1971.

58. W. T. Durr, "People of the Peninsula," 52.

59. *SBE,* 1 March 1971.

60. See Haeuber, *Expressway Controversy,* 58–59.

61. *Baltimore News-American,* 24 October 1978.

62. *Baltimore Magazine,* December 1970, 8.

63. *New York Times,* 17 June 1970.

64. Orlinsky quoted in Trulove, SECO History, 94.

65. It is interesting to note that Mikulski had a direct link with the Baltimore civil rights movement. She was at one time a member of CORE, something that she seems, understandably, to have downplayed in her community activist phase. See *EBG,* 29 August 1968.

66. *Baltimore News-American,* 11 May 1973.

67. *Baltimore Magazine,* December 1970.

68. Mikulski, "Growing Up Ethnic," 226.

69. *Sun,* 4 September 1975, 30 June 1979.

70. *EBG,* 25 July, 2 August 1974.

71. Nast, Krause, and Monk, *Living Renaissance,* 70.

72. See Novak, *The Rise of the Unmeltable Ethnics.* Another important work in this genre is Krickus, *Pursuing the American Dream.*

73. *Baltimore Magazine,* 10 December 1970.

74. *EBG,* 22 April 1971.

75. Trulove, SECO History, 38–39.

76. *BES,* 18 April 1971.

77. Trulove, SECO History, 101; DiPietro interview, 15, BNHP; Edsall, *Power and Money,* 87.

78. *EBG,* 22 April 1971.

79. *EBG,* 2 May 1974. This tendency seems to closely resemble the oft-commented-on working-class resentment toward union "pie-carders" who no longer worked on the shop floor.

80. American Joe Medusiewski, quoted in Trulove, SECO History, 100.

81. Donald Hammen, quoted in Trulove, SECO History, 102.

82. *BES,* 31 May 1971.

83. *New York Times,* 17 June 1970.

84. *Baltimore Magazine,* December 1970, 56.

85. *Baltimore News-American,* 13 November 1977.

86. *New York Times Magazine,* 9 May 1976, 30.

87. Ibid.

88. Formisano, *Boston against Busing,* 150.

89. Howes, *Baltimore Urban Parish Study,* 14.

90. Metcalf, *From Little Rock to Boston,* 106–7.
91. *Sun,* 18 November 1970.
92. *Sun,* 3 March 1974. "Pairing" was used in Queens as early as 1963 and in Buffalo during the mid-1970s. See Sanjek, *The Future of Us All,* and Goodman, *City on the Lake.*
93. *EBG,* 11 April 1974.
94. *BES,* 10 June 1974.
95. Quoted in Fahey, "Block by Block," 27.
96. Quoted in Rich, Netherwood, and Cahn, *Neighborhood,* 107.
97. Fahey, "Block by Block," 24.
98. Trulove, SECO History, 43, 47–49.
99. Rich, Netherwood, and Cahn, *Neighborhood,* 132.
100. Trulove, SECO History, 47–49.
101. *BES,* 10 June 1974.
102. Formisano, *Boston against Busing,* 3.
103. See Gelfand, *A Nation of Cities,* and Ravitch, *Troubled Crusade,* 322.
104. *BES,* 26 April 1971.
105. Trulove, SECO History, 65.
106. Formisano, *Boston against Busing,* xi.
107. *BES,* 6 May 1974.
108. "SECO Resolution 14," 4 May 1974, SECO Collection, ser. 2, box 1, UBA.
109. *BES,* 30 May 1974.
110. *BES,* 31 May 1974.
111. *BES,* 3 June 1974.
112. *BES,* 4 June 1974.
113. *BES,* 5 June 1974.
114. *BES,* 5 September 1974.
115. *EBG,* 12 September 1974.
116. *BES,* 21 September 1974.
117. Trulove, SECO History, 66.
118. *EBG,* 26 September 1974.
119. *EBG,* 28 November 1974.
120. *Sun,* 20 November 1973.
121. *BES,* 18 March 1974.
122. Matilda Koval, "Statement to SECO Senate," 23 April 1974, SECO Collection, ser. 4, box 1, UBA.
123. *EBG,* 6 February 1975.
124. *BES,* 18 December 1974.
125. Quoted in Trulove, SECO History, 58.
126. Melvin, *American Community Organizations,* 68.
127. *Sun,* 18 December 1974.
128. *EBG,* 26 December 1974.
129. *EBG,* 16 January 1975.

130. Trulove, SECO History, 71–72.
131. Ibid., 92.
132. On the demise of Neighborhoods United, see Cunningham and Kotler, *Building Neighborhood Organizations,* 76.
133. Fahey, "Block by Block," 28.
134. Quoted in ibid., 24.
135. One study finds activist women's "emotional attachment to their neighborhood" to be a an important factor in explaining their activism. See McCourt, *Working-Class Women,* 220.
136. For this position, see Lasch, *The True and Only Heaven,* 566.
137. Donald Hammen, quoted in Trulove, SECO History, 102.
138. Quoted in Rich, Netherwood, and Cahn, *Neighborhood,* 133.
139. *BES,* 12 September 1974.
140. Quoted in Rich, Netherwood, and Cahn, *Neighborhood,* 132.

Chapter Seven

1. Arnold interview, 4–6, BNHP.
2. Ibid., 6.
3. *Student Press,* 9 May 1969.
4. *Maryland Magazine,* Summer 1989.
5. See, e.g., *EBG,* 11 December 1966. On 4 January 1968 the *EBG* paid its respects to two local youths, both of whom had enlisted at the Highlandtown recruiting station.
6. *BES,* 28 May 1970.
7. Appy, *Working-Class War,* 57.
8. *EBG,* 27 March 1969.
9. *EBG,* 13 March 1975.
10. See Levison, *Working-Class Majority.*
11. McDonald to D'Alesandro, 14 November 1969, RG 9, ser. 26, box 518, BCA.
12. Appy, *Working-Class War,* 17–38.
13. *Baltimore Magazine,* December 1970.
14. *BES,* 28 May 1970.
15. *Sun,* 5 May 1970.
16. The labor movement split over Vietnam. For a synopsis, see Brody, *Workers in Industrial America,* 225. See esp. P. B. Levy, *The New Left and Labor,* 46–63.
17. *Baltimore Magazine,* February 1971.
18. *Sun,* 5 May 1970.
19. In 1970 the median school years completed among the blue-collar residents of Wards 1, 23, and 24 was 8.4. U.S. Bureau of the Census, *1970 Census of Population and Housing.*
20. *Sun,* 17 May 1970.
21. *Sun,* 27 December 1967.

22. *Sun,* 2, 5 May 1970.

23. *Sun,* 7 May 1970.

24. *Sun,* 9 May 1970.

25. Lipinski to D'Alesandro, 7 May 1970, RG 9, ser. 26, box 519, BCA.

26. Weslowski to D'Alesandro, 16 May 1970, ibid.

27. Dibbern to D'Alesandro, 14 May 1970, ibid.

28. *Sun,* 14 May 1970.

29. *Sun,* 7 May 1970.

30. *Sun,* 15 May 1970.

31. Weslowski to D'Alesandro, 16 May 1970, RG 9, ser. 26, box 519, BCA.

32. A *Catholic Review* poll found that by 1969, 43 percent of area Catholics thought that the church was too active in the area of civil rights while 16 percent believed that the church was not active enough. At the same time, only 14 percent of the clergy thought that the church was too active in civil rights and 43 percent considered that it was not active enough. *Catholic Review,* 11 April 1969.

33. Lombardi interview, 26, BNHP.

34. Martin to D'Alesandro, 15 May 1970, RG 9, ser. 26, box 519, BCA.

35. *Sun,* 10 May 1970.

36. *EBG,* 13 July 1968.

37. *EBG,* 5 September 1968.

38. Press Release, 17 July 1970, Joseph Tydings Papers, ser. 5, box 3, UMA.

39. Mahoney to Tydings, 16 July 1970, Joseph Tydings Papers, ser. 5, box 3, UMA.

40. *Life,* 28 August 1970.

41. *AFL-CIO Affiliate,* September 1970.

42. East Baltimore's Ward 1 gave him 73 percent of the vote and South Baltimore's Ward 24, 70 percent.

43. *Sun,* 5 November 1970.

44. *Washington Post,* 17 May 1972.

45. In Ward 1, Wallace got 49 percent of the vote to Humphrey's 14 percent. In Ward 24, Humphrey garnered 16 percent. Baltimore City Board of Supervisors of Elections, RG 11, ser. 1, Registration and Election Returns, 1896–1994, BCA.

46. *Washington Post,* 18 May 1972.

47. Ibid.

48. *Sun,* 19 January 1973. On Menapace and his troubled relations with black activists, see Flug, "Organized Labor and the Civil Rights Movement." See also P. B. Levy, *The New Left and Labor,* 64–65.

49. Robinson to Abel, 17 July 1972, Abel Papers, United Steelworkers Presidents Office, box 3, HCLA.

50. *Sun,* 9 November 1972.

51. See Gillon, *The Democrat's Dilemma.*

52. Robinson to Abel, 17 July 1972, Abel Papers, United Steelworkers Presidents Office, box 3, HCLA.

53. For CORE's prodding, see Griffin and Brooks to Wirtz, 3 February 1967, RG 174, UD entry 2 (Willard Wirtz Files), box 479, NARA; *Sun,* 3 February 1967.
54. "The plantwide seniority and rate retention position of OFCC continues to dominate the OFCC program," wrote Steelworkers official Ben Fischer to I. W. Abel. See Fischer to Abel, 8 April 1969, United Steelworkers Civil Rights Department Collection, box 18, HCLA.
55. *Sun,* 18 November 1969.
56. For narrative, see "Decision of the Secretary of Labor," OFCC Docket No. 102–68, 16 January 1973, RG 174, UD entry 4, box 201, NARA, 1–4.
57. See ibid., 67–75.
58. U.S. Department of Labor Press Release, 17 January 1973, Kotelchuck Papers, box 5, Baltimore Museum of Industry Archives. See also "Decision of the Secretary of Labor," OFCC Docket No. 102–68, 16 January 1973, RG 174, UD entry 4, box 201, NARA, 51.
59. *Sun,* 17 January 1973.
60. *New York Times,* 22 January 1973.
61. *BES,* 17 January 1973.
62. *New York Times,* 22 January 1973.
63. *BA-A,* 3 March 1973.
64. Saunders interview, BSHP.
65. Wilson interview, BSHP.
66. Crowder interview, BSHP.
67. Gorman interview, BSHP.
68. *Sun,* 14 November 1973.
69. Wilson to Johns, 15 November 1973, Abel Papers, United Steelworkers Presidents Office, box 9, HCLA.
70. The case is *United States v. Allegheny-Ludlum Industries, Inc., et al.*
71. Matera, "Consent Decree on Seniority."
72. Powell to Mitchell, 18 April 1974, RG 403, entry 3, box 1, NARA.
73. Butterfield interview, BSHP.
74. Saunders interview, BSHP.
75. Since the consent decree, Vogel claimed, some men had lost $5,000 a year in income. *Sun Magazine,* 5 September 1982.
76. Nelson, *Divided We Stand,* 50.
77. On the Baltimore gang system, see U.S. Congress, Senate, Committee on Interstate and Foreign Commerce, *Waterfront Investigation,* 46. See also *Sun,* 18 December 1952.
78. *BA-A,* 10 October 1970.
79. *Sun,* 29 September 1970.
80. *Sun,* 18 December 1952.
81. *Washington Post,* 4 June 1979.
82. *Sun,* 29 September 1970.
83. See "United States of America, Plaintiff v. International Longshoremen's Asso-

ciation (ILA) and Locals 829 and 858, Defendants," 6024–33, *Employment Practices Decisions* 4, no. 6 (18 May 1972); Nelson, *Divided We Stand,* 84.

84. Ibid., 6194, *Employment Practices Decisions* 3, no. 59 (20 January 1971).

85. *BA-A,* 10 October 1970.

86. *Sun,* 29 October 1973.

87. *Sun,* 10 June 1974.

88. Wilkerson interview, 30, BNHP.

89. Nugent interview, BSHP.

90. *New York Times,* 22 January 1973.

91. Wilson interview, BSHP.

92. Nelson, *Divided We Stand,* xx.

93. David Wilson and Edward Gorman make these arguments. See Wilson and Gorman interviews, BSHP.

94. Crowder interview, BSHP.

95. Nugent interview, BSHP.

96. Norrell, "Caste in Steel," 690.

97. *Sun,* 14 October 1982.

98. *BES,* 11 October 1973.

99. Doughty, "Slowdown in Real Wages."

100. See Table 5.

101. F. Levy, *Dollars and Dreams,* 60.

102. See Table 5.

103. *Sun,* 30 January 1973.

104. *EBG,* 17 January 1974. On the belief that the gas shortage was rigged, see *EBG,* 28 February 1974.

105. F. Levy, *Dollars and Dreams,* 62.

106. Ibid., 78.

107. *EBG,* 8 May 1975.

108. *EBG,* 10 July 1975.

109. *EBG,* 12 June 1975.

110. *EBG,* 26 February 1976.

111. See K. Olson, "When a Woman Has a Working Life," 85–109.

112. *Sun,* 12 May 1978.

113. *Baltimore News-American,* 28 November 1976.

114. *BES,* 30 January 1973.

115. *Sun,* 12 May 1978.

116. *BES,* 26 September 1974.

117. Levine, "Downtown Redevelopment," 107.

118. Of fifty-four cities with a population over 500,000, Baltimore placed seventh from the bottom. *BES,* 23 December 1975.

119. *BES,* 31 May 1978. The unemployment rate for young whites was much lower at 7.7 percent. *BES,* 17 July 1981.

120. *BES,* 31 May 1978.

121. *Baltimore Magazine,* December 1980.

122. *Baltimore Magazine,* June 1970.

123. *Baltimore Magazine,* March 1971.

124. *EBG,* 12 June 1975.

125. *EBG,* 12 February 1976.

126. *Baltimore Magazine,* June 1970.

127. *Washington Post,* 5 March 1974.

128. *EBG,* 5, 12 February 1976.

129. Teaford, *Rough Road to Renaissance,* 201.

130. See O'Keeffe, *Baltimore Politics.*

131. *Baltimore Magazine,* July 1976.

132. See Joseph, "The Sleeping Giant Remains Asleep," 115.

133. O'Keeffe, *Baltimore Politics,* 11; J. L. Arnold, "Baltimore," 36.

134. See Levine, "Downtown Redevelopment," and Harvey, "A View from Federal Hill."

135. Levine, "Downtown Redevelopment," 115.

136. Hayward and Belfoure, *Baltimore Rowhouse,* 178.

137. *EBG,* 4 September 1980.

138. *Sun,* 6 July 1978.

139. *Sun,* 1 January 1978.

140. Ibid. On clip-on ties, see *Sun,* 8 December 1979.

141. *Sun,* 1 January 1978.

142. *Sun,* 12 September 1974. Goodman also did spots for George Bush in the 1980 presidential primary race. See Diamond and Bates, *The Spot,* 250.

143. See *Sun,* 12 September 1974.

144. *Sun,* 25 June 1978.

145. Baltimore City Board of Supervisors of Elections, RG 11, ser. 1, Registration and Election Returns, 1896–1994, BCA.

146. O'Keeffe, *Baltimore Politics,* 61–88.

147. *Baltimore News-American,* 27 March 1966.

148. The United Steelworkers had bargained theirs away in 1964 and put a great deal of effort into getting it back in 1971. Gorman interview, BSHP.

149. Doughty, "Slowdown in Real Wages," 10.

150. Griffin interview, 56, BNHP.

151. *BES,* 5 February 1974.

152. *EBG,* 12 June 1975.

153. Thomas interview, 23, BNHP.

154. *BES,* 31 May 1978.

155. *EBG,* 18 December 1975.

156. *EBG,* 4 September 1980; *Sun,* 1 November 1980.

157. *EBG,* 26 September 1980.

158. *Baltimore Magazine,* December 1980.

159. BBT, *Second Industrial Survey,* 23.

160. *Baltimore Magazine,* December 1980.

161. *Sun,* 21 March 1978.

162. *EBG,* 10 August 1980. My emphasis.

163. *EBG,* 30 October 1980.

164. Block interview, 50, BHNP.

165. For national trends, see Halle and Romo, "Blue-Collar Working Class," 158–61. Among voters in Baltimore blue-collar wards 1, 23, and 24, turnout hit a postwar low of 41 percent in 1972, bounced to 50 percent in 1976, and remained in the 40 percent range thereafter. Baltimore City Board of Supervisors of Elections, RG 11, ser. 1, Registration and Election Returns, 1896–1994, BCA; U.S. Bureau of the Census, *1970 Census of Population and Housing, 1980 Census of Population and Housing,* and *1990 Census of Population and Housing.*

166. *Sun,* 15 November 1980.

167. Baltimore City Board of Supervisors of Elections, RG 11, ser. 1, Registration and Election Returns, 1896–1994, BCA.

168. Popkin, *The Reasoning Voter.*

169. J. K. White, *New Politics of Old Values,* 50.

170. Gillon, *Democrat's Dilemma,* xiv.

171. *Sun,* 7 November 1984.

172. *Sun,* 8 November 1984.

173. See Halle and Romo, "Blue-Collar Working Class."

174. *BES,* 9, 10 November 1988. These turnout figures are presumably compiled from voter registration rolls. When calculated from census voter age population statistics, the numbers are much lower.

175. *Washington Post,* 14 July 2001.

Conclusion

1. On the significance of the growth of administrative government, see Milkis, *The President and the Parties,* and Rohr, *To Run a Constitution.*

2. Lasch, *The True and Only Heaven.*

3. Rodgers, *Contested Truths,* 13.

4. "Rudyard Kipling," in Orwell, *Decline of the English Murder,* 49.

5. This phrase, as "the wisdom of *our* ancestors," is attributed to Russell Kirk by George H. Nash. See Nash, *Conservative Intellectual Movement,* 191.

6. H. L. Mencken, "Good Old Baltimore," *Smart Set,* May 1913, reprinted in Bode, *The Young Mencken,* 268.

Bibliography

Archives

Baltimore, Md.
  Baltimore City Archives
    Administrative Files of the Mayor of Baltimore, Record Group 9
    Baltimore City Board of Supervisors of Elections, Record Group 11
    Files of the Baltimore Housing Authority, Record Group 48
  Baltimore Museum of Industry Archives
    Joseph Kotelchuck Papers
  Sulpician Archives
    John L. Bazinet Papers
  University of Baltimore Archives
    Baltimore Citizens Planning and Housing Association Collection
    Baltimore Neighborhoods Incorporated Collection
    Maryland Council of Churches Collection
    Southeast Community Organization Collection
College Park, Md.
  University of Maryland Archives
    International Union of Marine and Shipbuilding Workers Papers
    Maryland Manuscripts Collection 4008
    Joseph Tydings Papers
    Millard Tydings Papers
Detroit, Mich.
  Archives of Labor History and Urban Affairs, Wayne State University
    Detroit Association of Catholic Trade Unionists Collection
    UAW Local 239 Collection
    UAW Local 678 Collection
New Brunswick, N.J.
  International Union of Electrical Workers President's Office Files, Rutgers University

Pittsburgh, Pa.
  UE/Labor Archives, University of Pittsburgh
    United Electrical Workers Union
      Conference Board Series
      Red Dot Series
      Yellow Dot Series
University Park, Pa.
  Historical Collections and Labor Archives, Penn State University
    United Steelworkers Civil Rights Department Collection
    United Steelworkers International Executive Board Collection
    United Steelworkers Presidents Office
      I. W. Abel Papers
      David McDonald Papers
    United Steelworkers Vice Presidents Office
      Howard Hague Papers
Washington, D.C.
  Catholic University Archives
    Philip Murray Papers
    National Catholic Welfare Conference Papers
  Library of Congress Manuscript Division
    Americans for Democratic Action Papers. Microfilm.
    CORE Papers, King Library Collection. Microfilm.
    CORE Papers, Wisconsin State Historical Society Collection. Microfilm.
    National Association for the Advancement of Colored People Papers
    Urban League Papers
  National Archives and Records Administration
    Record Group 107, Records of the Secretary of War
    Record Group 153, Records of the Army Judge Advocate General
    Record Group 160, Records of the Army Service Forces
    Record Group 174, Records of the Department of Labor
    Record Group 183, Records of the Bureau of Employment Security
    Record Group 211, Records of the War Manpower Commission
    Record Group 228, Records of the Fair Employment Practices Commission
    Record Group 233, Records of the U.S. House of Representatives, Select Committee Investigating National Defense Migration
    Record Group 403, Records of the Equal Employment Opportunity Commission
    Record Group 406, Records of the Federal Highway Administration
    Record Group 453, Records of the U.S. Commission on Civil Rights

Interviews

BALTIMORE NEIGHBORHOOD HERITAGE PROJECT,
UNIVERSITY OF BALTIMORE ARCHIVES

Anonymous. Interview by Linda Shopes, 15 July 1978. Interview 19, transcript.

Arnold, Albert. Interview by Susan Hawes, 11 May 1979. Interview 51, transcript.

Block, Harry. Interview by Christine Green, 19 July 1979. Interview 121, transcript.

Browning, Jeanette. Interview by Thomas Jacklin, 17 March 1978. Interview 1, transcript.

Buhrman, Melvyn. Interview by Christine Green, 10 August 1979. Interview 127, transcript.

DeVaughn, Myrtle. Interview by Michael Tiranoff, 29 July 1979. Interview 82, transcript.

DiMartino, Grace. Interview by Linda Shopes, 17 April 1978. Interview 9, transcript.

DiPietro, Mimi. Interview by Rosewyn Sweeney, 29 July 1979. Interview 120, transcript.

Esposito, Ida. Interview by Holly Gordon, 28 June 1979. Interview 78, transcript.

Fletcher, Margie Mae. Interview by Susan Hawes, 22 May 1979. Interview 52, transcript.

Griffin, Daniel. Interview by Michael Tiranoff, 1 August 1979. Interview 115, transcript.

Hoshall, Fenton. Interview by Bill Harvey, 13 April 1979. Interview 71, transcript.

Litzinger, James. Interview by Susan Hawes, 27 June 1979. Interview 86, transcript.

Lombardi, Nick. Interview by Areta Kupchyk, 15 May 1979. Interview 60, transcript.

Manning, Joe. Interview by Areta Kupchyk, 13 May 1979. Interview 61, transcript.

Matthews, Dorothy. Interview by Chuck Andreatta, 27 November 1978. Interview 36, transcript.

Meads, Richard. Interview by Susan Hawes, 6 April 1979. Interview 43, transcript.

O'Connor, George. Interview by Michael Tiranoff, 10 September 1979. Interview 199, no transcript.

Piscopo, Vincent. Interview by Linda Shopes, 30 June 1978. Interview 15, transcript.

Porach, Louise. Interview by Thomas Jacklin, 28–30 July 1979. Interview 16, transcript.

Purdy, Josephine. Interview by Areta Kupchyk, 11 October 1979. Interview 179, transcript.

Redd, Bernard. Interview by Lucy V. Peebles, 17 September 1979. Interview 161, transcript.

Sergi, Joseph. Interview by Jean Scarpaci, 21 August 1979. Interview 139, transcript.

Slechta, Mildred. Interview by Michael Tiranoff, 24 July 1979. Interview 109, transcript.

Thomas, Ruth. Interview by Susan Hawes, 19 July 1979. Interview 97, transcript.

Thommen, Joe. Interview by Areta Kupchyk, 28 August 1979. Interview 180, transcript.

Wilkerson, Thomas. Interview by Benjamin Primer, 16 October 1981. Interview 224, transcript.
Zorn, Greg. Interview by Michael Tiranoff, 19 July 1979. Interview 102, transcript.

BALTIMORE STEELWORKERS HISTORY PROJECT

Butterfield, James. Interview by Linda Zeidman, 17 May 1979. No transcript.
Crowder, Neal. Interview by Linda Zeidman, 29 March 1979. No transcript.
Duerbeck, John. Interview by Linda Zeidman, 15 March 1979. No transcript.
Garvin, Leroy. Interview by Linda Zeidman, 10 May 1979. No transcript.
Gorman, Ed. Interview by Linda Zeidman, 17 April 1979. No transcript.
Nugent, William. Interview by Linda Zeidman, 15 May 1979. No transcript.
Saunders, Joseph. Interview by Linda Zeidman, 8 May 1979. No transcript.
Watson, Preston, and William C. Bland. Interview by Linda Zeidman, 3 May 1979. No transcript.
Wilson, David. Interview by Linda Zeidman, 16 April, 22 May 1979. No transcript.
Womer, Ben. Interview by Linda Zeidman, 24 April 1979. No transcript.

OTHER

Block, Harry. Interview by Ron Filippelli, 25 September 1967. Transcript. Pennsylvania State University, Historical Collections and Labor Archives, University Park.
Cronin, John F. Interview by Thomas Blantz, 17 March 1978. Transcript. University of Notre Dame Archives, Notre Dame, Ind.
Morsberger, Phyllis. Interview by Charlotte French, 25 October 1976. Transcript. Friends of the Catonsville Area Library Oral History Program. Catonsville, Md.
Murphy, Mary E. Interview by Dorothy Beaman, 2 November 1972. Transcript. Friends of the Catonsville Area Library Oral History Program. Catonsville, Md.
Sexton, Brendan. Interview by Don Kennedy, 6 November 1978. Transcript. Steelworkers Oral History Collection. Pennsylvania State University, Historical Collections and Labor Archives, University Park.

Newspapers and Magazines

AFL-CIO Affiliate (Maryland and D.C. AFL-CIO), September 1970
Aircraft Beacon (UAW Local 739), 1943–61
Baltimore Afro-American, 1940–80
Baltimore Daily Record, 14 December, 1976
Baltimore Evening Sun, 1940–84
Baltimore Labor Herald, 1940–68
Baltimore Magazine, 1964–80
Baltimore News-Post, 1940–62
Baltimore News-Post and Sunday American (*News-American*), 1962–80
Baltimore Sun, 1949–84
Brooklyn News, 1954–56

Catholic Review (Baltimore), 1940–80
CIO News (Maryland and D.C. editions), 1943–44
Dundalk Community Press and Baltimore Countian, 1942–64
East Baltimore Guide, 1954–80
Educator (USWA Local 2610), 1954–57
New York Times, 1966–73
New York Times Magazine, 9 May 1976
Shipyard Worker (IUMSWA), 1943
South Baltimore Enterprise, 1941–64
Southern School News, 1954–58
Steel Labor, February 1962
Student Press (University of Baltimore), May–October 1969
Sun Magazine, 1968–82
Towson (Md.) Jeffersonian, 12 July 1963
UE News, 1946–48
Washington Post, 1972–79

Published Primary Sources

Baltimore Board of Trade. *Second Industrial Survey of Baltimore: A Quarter Century of Progress in the City of Industrial Advantages.* 2d ed. Baltimore: Baltimore Board of Trade, 1939.
Baltimore City Directory. Richmond, Va.: R. L. Polk and Co., 1928–64.
Baltimore Urban League. *A Review of the Program and Activities of the Baltimore Urban League and a Brief Analysis of Conditions in the Community Which It Serves, Part II.* Baltimore, 1949. Located in Urban League Papers, Library of Congress Manuscript Division.
Chamber of Commerce of Metropolitan Baltimore. *Data Profiles, 1966: Hamilton-Gardenville.* Baltimore: Chamber of Commerce of Metropolitan Baltimore, 1966.
———. *Data Profiles, 1966: Hampden-Homewood-25th Street.* Baltimore: Chamber of Commerce of Metropolitan Baltimore, 1966.
———. *Data Profiles, 1966: Highlandtown-Armistead-Colgate.* Baltimore: Chamber of Commerce of Metropolitan Baltimore. 1966.
———. *Negro Market Data Handbook: Metropolitan Baltimore.* Baltimore: Chamber of Commerce of Metropolitan Baltimore. 1968.
Maryland Department of Employment Security Research and Analysis Division. *The Story of the Labor Force: Baltimore Metropolitan Area, 1950–1965.* Baltimore: Department of Employment Security Research, 1967.
Maryland Department of State Planning. *Maryland Population Data: State, County, Minor Civil Divisions and Municipal Traits through 1980.* Baltimore: Department of State Planning, 1981.
———. *1980 Census Profile: Social, Economic, and Housing Characteristics for Maryland, Volume 1.* Baltimore: Department of State Planning, 1981.

Maryland and District of Columbia Industrial Union Council. *Proceedings of the Third Annual Convention*. Baltimore: IUC, 1939.

———. *Proceedings of the Fifth Annual Convention*. Baltimore: IUC, 1941.

———. *Proceedings of the Seventh Annual Convention*. Baltimore: IUC, 1943.

———. *Proceedings of the Eighth Annual Convention*. Baltimore: IUC, 1944.

———. *Proceedings of the Sixteenth Annual Convention*. Baltimore: IUC, 1954.

———. *Proceedings of the Seventeenth Annual Convention*. Baltimore: IUC, 1955.

Maryland Secretary of State. *Maryland Manual: A Compendium of Legal, Historical, and Statistical Information Relating to the State of Maryland*. Baltimore: Secretary of State, 1960–66.

Maryland State and District of Columbia AFL-CIO. *Proceedings of the Sixth Convention*. Baltimore: Maryland State and D.C. AFL-CIO, 1965.

———. *Proceedings of the Tenth Convention*. Baltimore: Maryland State and D.C. AFL-CIO, 1969.

"United States of America, Plaintiff v. International Longshoremen's Association (ILA) and Locals 829 and 858, Defendants." *Employment Practices Decisions* 3, no. 59 (also vol. 4, no. 6). Washington, D.C.: Commerce Clearing House, Inc., 1972.

U.S. Bureau of the Census. *Congressional District Data Book, 88th Congress*. Washington, D.C.: GPO, 1963.

———. *Congressional District Data Book, 93rd Congress*. Washington, D.C.: GPO, 1973.

———. *County and City Data Books*. Washington, D.C.: GPO, 1952–88.

———. *1940 Census of Population and Housing: Statistics for Census Tracts, Baltimore, Maryland*. Washington, D.C.: GPO, 1942.

———. *1940 Census of Population: Characteristics of the Population: United States Summary*. Washington, D.C.: GPO, 1943.

———. *1940 Census of Population, 3rd Series: The Labor Force, Occupation, Industry, Employment, and Income, Maryland*. Washington, D.C.: GPO, 1943.

———. *Census Tract Statistics, Baltimore, Maryland, and Adjacent Area: Selected Population and Housing Characteristics, 1950*. Washington, D.C.: GPO, 1952.

———. *1950 Census of Population: Characteristics of the Population: United States Summary, 1950*. Washington, D.C.: GPO, 1953.

———. *1950 Census of Population and Housing: General Characteristics, P-B20*. Washington, D.C.: GPO, 1953.

———. *1960 Census of Population and Housing: Final Report PHC(1)-13, Census Tracts, Baltimore, Maryland*. Washington, D.C.: GPO, 1962.

———. *1960 Census of Population: Final Report PC(1)-22C, General Social and Economic Characteristics, Maryland*. Washington, D.C.: GPO, 1962.

———. *1960 Census of Population: Characteristics of the Population: United States Summary*. Washington, D.C.: GPO, 1963.

———. *1970 Census of Population and Housing: Census Tracts, Baltimore, Maryland, Standard Metropolitan Statistical Area*. Washington D.C.: GPO, 1972.

————. *1970 Census of Population, PC(1)-C22: General Social and Economic Charac-*
teristics. Washington, D.C.: GPO, 1972.

————. *1980 Census of Population and Housing: Census Tracts, Baltimore, Maryland,*
Standard Metropolitan Statistical Area, PHC80-2-82. Washington, D.C.: GPO,
1982.

————. *1990 Census of Population and Housing: Characteristics for Census Tracts and*
Block Numbering Areas, Baltimore, Maryland, Standard Metropolitan Statistical
Area, 1990 CPH-3-80. Washington, D.C.: GPO, 1993.

————. *Statistical Abstract of the United States.* Washington D.C.: GPO, 1963–70.

U.S. Congress. House. *Hearings before the Committee on the Judiciary on Proposed*
Amendments to the Constitution Relating to Prayers and Bible Reading in the Public
Schools, Part 1. 88th Cong., 2d sess., 3 June 1964.

————. *Hearings before the Select Committee Investigating National Defense Migra-*
tion, Part 15. 77th Cong., 1st sess., 1 and 2 July 1941.

U.S. Congress. Senate. Committee on Interstate and Foreign Commerce. *Waterfront*
Investigation: New York—New Jersey. 83d Cong., 1st sess., 27 July 1953.

————. Committee on Banking, Housing, and Urban Affairs. *Neighborhood Preser-*
vation: The Cause of Neighborhood Decline and the Impact, Positive or Negative, of
Existing Programs Policies and Laws on Existing Neighborhoods. 94th Cong., 2d
sess., 14 June 1976.

U.S. Department of Labor. Bureau of Labor Statistics. *Consumer Expenditures and*
Income, Baltimore, Maryland, 1960. Report No. 237–16. Washington, D.C.: GPO,
1963.

U.S. Department of Labor. Women's Bureau. *Baltimore Women Workers in the Post-*
war Period, 1948. Typescript, U.S. Department of Labor Library.

U.S. Office of War Information. *Report on Wartime Problems and Conditions in the*
City of Baltimore, Maryland, 1943. Typescript, U.S. Department of Labor Library.

Secondary Works

Abrams, Charles. *Forbidden Neighbors: A Study of Prejudice in Housing.* Port Washington, N.Y.: Kennikat Press, 1971.

Allen, Alexander J. "Western Electric's Backward Step." *Opportunity: Journal of*
Negro Life (Summer 1994): 108–43.

Allen, Theodore. *The Invention of the White Race: Volume One, Racial Oppression and*
Social Control. London: Verso, 1994.

American Institute of Public Opinion. *The Gallup Poll: Public Opinion, 1935–1971.*
2 vols. New York: Random House, 1972.

Appy, Christian G. *Working-Class War: American Combat Soldiers and Vietnam.*
Chapel Hill: University of North Carolina Press, 1993.

Argersinger, Jo Ann E. "'The Right to Strike': Labor Organization and the New Deal
in Baltimore." *Maryland Historical Magazine* (Winter 1983): 299–318.

————. "Toward a Roosevelt Coalition: The Democratic Party and the New Deal in
Baltimore." *Maryland Historical Magazine* (Winter 1987): 288–305.

———. *Toward a New Deal in Baltimore: People and Government in the Great Depression.* Chapel Hill: University of North Carolina Press, 1988.

Arnold, Christine M. "Baltimore's Invisible Irish: Patterns of Assimilation and Mobility, 1850–1929," 1973. MS in vertical file: "Irish in Baltimore." Pratt Free Library, Baltimore.

Arnold, Joseph L. "The Last of the Good Old Days: Politics in Baltimore, 1920–1950." *Maryland Historical Magazine* (Fall 1976): 443–48.

———. "Baltimore: Southern Culture and a Northern Economy." In *Snowbelt Cities: Metropolitan Politics in the Northeast and Midwest since World War II,* edited by Richard M. Bernard, 25–39. Bloomington: Indiana University Press, 1990.

"Automobile and New Appliance Purchases in Six Cities, 1953–56." *Monthly Labor Review* (March 1957): 336–41.

Bachrach, Peter. "A Power Analysis: The Shaping of Antipoverty Policy in Baltimore." *Public Policy* (Winter 1970): 155–86.

Bachrach, Peter, and Morton S. Baratz. *Power and Poverty: Theory and Practice.* New York: Oxford University Press, 1970.

Bean, Louis. *Influences in the 1954 Mid-Term Election.* Washington, D.C.: Public Affairs Institute, 1954.

Beirne, D. Randall. "Residential Growth and Stability in the Baltimore Industrial Community of Canton during the Late Nineteenth Century." *Maryland Historical Magazine* (March 1978): 39–51.

———. "Hampden-Woodberry: The Mill Village in an Urban Setting." *Maryland Historical Magazine* (Spring 1982): 6–26.

Bell, Daniel, ed. *The Radical Right: The New American Right Expanded and Updated.* Garden City, N.Y.: Anchor Books, 1964.

Bellah, Robert N., Richard Madsen, William M. Sullivan, Ann Swindler, and Steven M. Tipton. *Habits of the Heart: Individualism and Commitment in American Life.* New York: Harper and Row, 1985.

Binzen, Peter. *Whitetown U.S.A.* New York: Vintage Books, 1970.

Bode, Carl. *The Young Mencken: The Best of His Work.* New York: Dial Press, 1973.

Boyte, Harry. *The Backyard Revolution: Understanding the New Citizen Movement.* Philadelphia: Temple University Press, 1980.

Breihan, John R. "Wings for Democracy?: African-Americans in Baltimore's World War II Aviation Industry." Paper presented at the 1996 Baltimore History Conference, Coppin State College.

Brinkley, Alan. *The End of Reform: New Deal Liberalism in Recession and War.* New York: Knopf, 1995.

Brody, David. *Workers in Industrial America: Essays on the Twentieth-Century Struggle.* New York: Oxford University Press, 1980.

Brownlee, W. Elliot. "Tax Regimes, National Crisis, and State-Building in America." In *Funding the Modern American State, 1941–1995: The Rise and Fall of the Era of Easy Finance,* edited by W. Elliot Brownlee, 37–104. Washington, D.C.: Woodrow Wilson Center Press, 1996.

Brugger, Robert J. *Maryland: A Middle Temperament, 1634–1980.* Baltimore: Johns Hopkins University Press, 1988.

Burdette, Franklin L. "Modern Maryland Politics and Social Change." In *Maryland: A History, 1632–1974,* edited by Richard Walsh and William Lloyd Fox, 773–904. Baltimore: Maryland Historical Society, 1974.

Burke, Carol. "Brooklyn: From Small County Village to City Survivor," 1992. MS in Local History Research Papers Collection, University of Baltimore Archives.

Burnham, Walter Dean. *Critical Elections and the Mainsprings of American Politics.* New York: Norton, 1970.

Cabbell, Edward J. "Black Invisibility and Racism in Appalachia: An Informal Survey." In *Blacks in Appalachia,* edited by William H. Turner and Edward J. Cabbell, 3–10. Lexington: University Press of Kentucky, 1985.

Callcott, George H. *Maryland and America, 1940–1980.* Baltimore: Johns Hopkins University Press, 1985.

Carlson, Jody. *George C. Wallace and the Politics of Powerlessness: The Wallace Campaigns for the Presidency, 1964–1976.* New Brunswick, N.J.: Transaction Books, 1981.

Carter, Dan T. *The Politics of Rage: George Wallace: The Origins of the New Conservatism and the Transformation of American Politics.* New York: Simon and Schuster, 1995.

Chamberlain, Vivian Edwards. "The Five Largest CIO Unions in Baltimore, Maryland, with Special Reference to the Negro." M.A. thesis, Howard University, 1945.

Chaterjee, Lata, David Harvey, and Lawrence Klugman. "FHA Policies and the Baltimore City Housing Market." Johns Hopkins Center for Metropolitan Planning and Research, April 1974.

Chester, Lewis, Godfrey Hodgson, and Bruce Page, *An American Melodrama: The Presidential Campaign of 1968.* New York: Viking Press, 1969.

Cogley, John. *Catholic America.* Garden City, N.Y.: Image Books, 1973.

Colby, Ann R. "Desegregation Activities in Baltimore: 1954–1968." M.A. thesis, University of Maryland, 1972.

Conway, M. Margaret. "The White Backlash Re-examined: Wallace and the 1964 Primaries." *Social Science Quarterly* (December 1968): 710–19.

Crain, Robert L. *The Politics of School Desegregation.* Garden City, N.Y.: Anchor Books, 1969.

Crooks, James B. *Politics and Progress: The Rise of Urban Progressivism in Baltimore, 1895 to 1911.* Baton Rouge: Louisiana State University Press, 1968.

Crosby, Donald F. "The Politics of Religion: American Catholics and the Anti-Communist Impulse." In *The Specter: Original Essays on the Cold War and the Origins of McCarthyism,* edited by Robert Griffith and Athan Theoharis, 20–38. New York: New Viewpoints, 1974.

Cunningham, James V., and Milton Kotler, *Building Neighborhood Organizations.* Notre Dame, Ind.: University of Notre Dame Press, 1983.

Curran, Robert Emmett. "History of a Changing Neighborhood." *America,* 15 June 1968, 773–75.

Diamond, Edwin, and Stephen Bates. *The Spot: The Rise of Political Advertising on Television* Cambridge: MIT Press, 1992.

Doughty, H. M. "The Slowdown in Real Wages: A Postwar Perspective." *Monthly Labor Review* (August 1977): 7–12.

Dubofsky, Melvyn. *The State and Labor in Modern America.* Chapel Hill: University of North Carolina Press, 1994.

Durr, Kenneth. "'We Were UE a Long Time': The Left, the Right, and Baltimore Electrical Workers." MS, 1996.

———. "When Southern Politics Came North: The Roots of White Working-Class Conservatism in Baltimore, 1940–1964." *Labor History* (Summer 1996): 309–31.

Durr, W. Theodore. "People of the Peninsula." *Maryland Historical Magazine* (Spring 1982): 27–53.

Edsall, Thomas Byrne. *Power and Money: Writing about Politics, 1971–1987.* New York: Norton, 1988.

Edsall, Thomas Byrne, and Mary Edsall. *Chain Reaction: The Impact of Race, Rights, and Taxes on American Politics.* New York: Norton, 1991.

Eff, Elaine. "The Painted Screens of Baltimore, Maryland: Decorative Folk Art, Past and Present." Ph.D. diss., University of Pennsylvania, 1984.

Ehrenhalt, Alan. *The Lost City: Discovering the Forgotten Virtues of Community in the Chicago of the 1950s.* New York: Basic Books, 1995.

Ehrenreich, Barbara. *Fear of Falling: The Inner Life of the Middle Class.* New York: HarperCollins, 1989.

Fahey, Maureen. "Block by Block: Women in Community Organizing." *Women: A Journal of Liberation* 6 (1978): 24–28.

Fairchild, Byron, and Jonathan Grossman. *The Army and Industrial Manpower.* Washington, D.C.: U.S. Department of the Army, 1959.

Farrell, James T. *Studs Lonigan: A Trilogy Comprising Young Lonigan, The Young Manhood of Studs Lonigan, and Judgment Day.* 1935. Introduction by Ann Douglas, Reprint, New York: Penguin, 2001.

Fenton, John H. *Politics in the Border States: A Study of the Patterns of Political Organizations, and Political Change Common to the Border States—Maryland, West Virginia, Kentucky, and Missouri.* New Orleans: Hauser Press, 1957.

Fields, Barbara J. "Ideology and Race in American History." In *Region, Race, and Reconstruction: Essays in Honor of C. Vann Woodward,* edited by J. Morgan Kousser and James M. McPherson, 143–77. New York: Oxford University Press, 1982.

Filippelli, Ronald L., and Mark D. McColloch. *Cold War in the Working Class: The Rise and Decline of the United Electrical Workers.* Albany: State University of New York Press, 1995.

Fink, Leon, and Brian Greenberg, *Upheaval in the Quiet Zone: A History of Hospital Workers' Union, Local 1199.* Urbana: University of Illinois Press, 1989.

Fisher, Robert. *Let the People Decide: Neighborhood Organizing in America.* Boston: Twayne Publishers, 1984

Flamm, Michael William. "'Law and Order': Street Crime, Civil Disorder, and the Crisis of Liberalism." Ph.D. diss., Columbia University, 1998.

Flug, Michael. "Organized Labor and the Civil Rights Movement of the 1960s: The Case of the Maryland Freedom Union." *Labor History* (Summer 1990): 322–46.

Foner, Philip S., and Ronald L. Lewis. *The Black Worker from the Founding of the CIO to the AFL-CIO Merger, 1936–1955.* Philadelphia: Temple University Press, 1983.

Formisano, Ronald P. *Boston against Busing: Race, Class, and Ethnicity in the 1960s and 1970s.* Chapel Hill: University of North Carolina Press, 1991.

Frady, Marshall. "Gary, Indiana." *Harper's Magazine,* August 1969, 35–45.

Freedman, Samuel G. *The Inheritance: How Three Families and America Moved from Roosevelt to Reagan.* New York: Simon and Schuster, 1996.

Freeman, Joshua B. "Delivering the Goods: Industrial Unionism during World War II." *Labor History* (Fall 1978): 570–93.

———. *Working-Class New York: Life and Labor since World War II.* New York: New Press, 2000.

Freeman, Joshua B., and Steve Rosswurm. "The Education of an Anti-Communist: Father John F. Cronin and the Baltimore Labor Movement." *Labor History* (Spring 1992): 217–47.

Fried, Richard M. "Electoral Politics and McCarthyism: The 1950 Campaign." In *The Specter: Original Essays on the Cold War and the Origins of McCarthyism,* edited by Robert Griffith and Athan Theoharis, 192–222. New York: New Viewpoints, 1974.

———. *Men against McCarthy.* New York: Columbia University Press, 1976.

Galbraith, John Kenneth. *The Affluent Society.* New York: New American Library, 1958.

———. *The New Industrial State.* New York: New American Library, 1967.

Gamm, Gerald. *Urban Exodus: Why the Jews Left Boston and the Catholics Stayed.* Cambridge: Harvard University Press, 1999.

Gans, Herbert J. *The Urban Villagers: Group and Class in the Life of Italian-Americans.* New York: Free Press, 1962.

Garonzik, Joseph. "The Racial and Ethnic Make-up of Baltimore Neighborhoods, 1850–1870." *Maryland Historical Magazine* (Fall 1976): 394–95.

Gelfand, Mark I. *A Nation of Cities: The Federal Government and Urban America, 1933–1965.* New York: Oxford University Press, 1975.

Gildea, William. *When the Colts Belonged to Baltimore.* New York: Ticknor and Fields, 1994.

Gillon, Steven M. *Politics and Vision: The ADA and American Liberalism, 1947–1985.* New York: Oxford University Press, 1987.

———. *The Democrats' Dilemma: Walter F. Mondale and the Liberal Legacy.* New York: Columbia University Press, 1992.

Glendon, Mary Ann. *Rights Talk: The Impoverishment of Political Discourse.* New York: Free Press, 1991.

Goldberg, Louis C. "CORE in Trouble: A Social History of the Organizational Dilemmas of the Congress of Racial Equality Target City Project in Baltimore, 1965–1967." Ph.D. diss., Johns Hopkins University, 1970.

Goodman, Mark. *City on the Lake: The Challenge of Change in Buffalo, New York.* New York: Prometheus Books, 1990.

Greeley, Andrew M. *The American Catholic: A Social Portrait.* New York: Basic Books, 1977.

Griffith, Robert. *The Politics of Fear: Joseph R. McCarthy and the Senate.* Lexington: University Press of Kentucky, 1970.

Griffith, Sanford. *Where Can We Get War Workers? Results of a Manpower Survey in Baltimore.* Public Affairs Pamphlets, No. 75. New York: Public Affairs Committee, 1942.

Haeuber, Douglas H. *The Baltimore Expressway Controversy: A Study of the Political Decision-Making Process.* Johns Hopkins University Center for Metropolitan Planning and Research, 1974.

Halle, David. *America's Working Man: Work, Home, and Politics among Blue-Collar Property Owners.* Chicago: University of Chicago Press, 1984.

Halle, David, and Frank Romo. "The Blue-Collar Working Class: Continuity and Change." In *America at Century's End,* edited by Alan Wolfe, 152–84. Berkeley: University of California Press, 1991.

Hamilton, Richard F. *Class and Politics in the United States.* New York: John Wiley and Sons, 1972.

Harris, Mark Jonathan, Franklin D. Mitchell, and Steven J. Schecter. *The Homefront: America during World War II.* New York: G. P. Putnam's, 1984.

Harvey, David. "A View from Federal Hill." In *The Baltimore Book: New Views of Local History,* edited by Elizabeth Fee, Linda Shopes, and Linda Zeidman, 227–49. Philadelphia: Temple University Press, 1991.

Hayward, Mary Ellen, and Charles Belfoure, *The Baltimore Rowhouse.* New York: Princeton University Press, 1999.

Heale, M. J. *American Anticommunism: Combatting the Enemy Within, 1830-1970.* Baltimore: Johns Hopkins University Press, 1990.

———. *McCarthy's America: Red Scare Politics in State and Nation, 1935-1965.* Athens: University of Georgia Press, 1998.

Heineman, Kenneth. "The Silent Majority Speaks: Antiwar Protest and Backlash, 1965-1972." *Peace and Change* (October 1992): 402–33.

Henderson, Peter Harry. "Local Deals and the New Deal State: Implementing Federal Public Housing in Baltimore, 1933-1968." Ph.D. diss., Johns Hopkins University, 1994.

Himmelstein, Jerome L. *To the Right: The Transformation of American Conservatism.* Berkeley: University of California Press, 1990.

Hirsch, Arnold R. *Making the Second Ghetto: Race and Housing in Chicago, 1940-1960.* Cambridge: Cambridge University Press, 1983.

———. "Massive Resistance in the Urban North: Trumbull Park, Chicago, 1953-1966." *Journal of American History* (September 1995): 522–50.

Hixson, William B., Jr. *Search for the American Right Wing: An Analysis of the Social Science Records, 1955–1987.* Princeton: Princeton University Press, 1992.

Hoffman, Morton. "The Role of Government in Influencing Changes in Housing in Baltimore, 1940 to 1950." *Land Economics: A Quarterly Journal of Planning, Housing, and Public Utilities* 30 (1954): 125–40.

Holupka, Scott C. "It Was a Wonderful Life: Mortgage Lending and Neighborhood Change in Baltimore City, 1960 to 1980." Ph.D. diss., Johns Hopkins University, 1992.

Howard, Jane. "Madalyn Murray: Scrappy Atheist in a Hurry: 'The Most Hated Woman in America'." *Life,* 11 June 1964, 91–94.

Howes, Robert G. *Baltimore Urban Parish Study.* Baltimore: Archdiocese of Baltimore, 1967.

Hunter, James Davison. *Culture Wars: The Struggle to Define America.* New York: Basic Books, 1991.

Ignatiev, Noel. *How the Irish Became White.* New York: Routledge, 1995.

Jackson, Kenneth T. *Crabgrass Frontier: The Suburbanization of the United States.* New York: Oxford University Press, 1985.

James, Henry. "A Landscape Painter." *Atlantic Monthly,* February 1866, 182–202.

Janowitz, Morris. *The Community Press in an Urban Setting: The Social Elements of Urbanism.* 2d ed. Chicago: University of Chicago Press, 1967.

Jay, Peter A. "Baltimore Again: Old Myths Die Hard, New Ones Die Even Harder." *Baltimore Magazine,* July 1976, 24–25.

Jenkins, Philip. *The Cold War at Home: The Red Scare in Pennsylvania, 1945–1960.* Chapel Hill: University of North Carolina Press, 1999.

Jones, Bill. *The Wallace Story.* Northport, Ala.: American Southern Publishing Co., 1966.

Jonnes, Jill. *Hep-Cats, Narcs, and Pipe Dreams: A History of America's Romance with Illegal Drugs.* New York: Scribner, 1996.

Joseph, Matthew Harris. "The Sleeping Giant Remains Asleep: Why Baltimore Was the Last Major American City with a Black Majority to Elect a Black Mayor." B.A. thesis, Harvard University, 1988.

Katznelson, Ira. *City Trenches: Urban Politics and the Patterning of Class in the United States.* New York: Pantheon Books, 1981.

Kazin, Michael. "The Grass-Roots Right: New Histories of U.S. Conservatism in the Twentieth Century." *American Historical Review* (February 1992): 136–55.

————. *The Populist Persuasion: An American History.* New York: Basic Books, 1995.

Keith, Caroline H. *For Hell and a Brown Mule: The Biography of Senator Millard J. Tydings.* New York: Madison Books, 1991.

Killian, Lewis M. "The Effects of Southern White Workers on Race Relations in Northern Plants." *American Sociological Review* 17 (1952): 327–31.

Kimeldorf, Howard. "Bringing Unions Back In." *Labor History* (Winter 1991): 91–103.

King, Desmond. *Actively Seeking Work.* Chicago: University of Chicago Press, 1995.

Klarman, Michael J. "How *Brown* Changed Race Relations: The Backlash Thesis." *Journal of American History* (June 1994): 81–118.

Kleppner, Paul. *Chicago Divided: The Making of a Black Mayor.* DeKalb: Northern Illinois University Press, 1985.

Klugman, Laurence Stephen. "The FHA and Home Ownership in the Baltimore Housing Market, 1963–1972." Ph.D. diss., Clark University, 1974.

Komarovsky, Mirra. *Blue-Collar Marriage.* New York: Vintage Books, 1962.

Kram, Mark. "A Wink at a Homely Girl." *Sports Illustrated,* 10 October 1966, 86–103.

Krickus, Richard J. "Organizing Neighborhoods: Gary and Newark." In *The World of the Blue-Collar Worker,* edited by Irving Howe, 72–88. New York: Quadrangle Books, 1972.

———. *Pursuing the American Dream: White Ethnics and the New Populism.* Garden City, N.Y.: Anchor Press, 1976.

Lasch, Christopher. *The True and Only Heaven: Progress and Its Critics.* New York: Norton, 1991.

Lasson, Kenneth. *The Workers: Portraits of Nine American Job Holders.* New York: Grossman Publishers, 1971.

LeMasters, E. E. *Blue-Collar Aristocrats: Life Styles at a Working-Class Tavern.* Madison: University of Wisconsin Press, 1975.

Levenstein, Harvey A. *Communism, Anticommunism, and the CIO.* Westport, Conn.: Greenwood Press, 1981.

Levering, Rosalind Robinson. *Baltimore Baptists, 1773–1973: A History of the Baptist Work in Baltimore during 200 Years.* Baltimore: Baltimore Baptist Association, 1973.

Levine, Marc V. "Downtown Redevelopment as an Urban Growth Strategy: A Critical Appraisal of the Baltimore Renaissance." *Journal of Urban Affairs* 9 (1987): 103–23.

Levison, Andrew. *The Working-Class Majority.* New York: Coward Mc-Cann, 1974.

Levy, Frank. *Dollars and Dreams: The Changing American Income Distribution.* New York: Russell Sage Foundation, 1987.

Levy, Peter B. *The New Left and Labor in the 1960s.* Urbana: University of Illinois Press, 1994.

Lichtenstein, Nelson. "From Corporatism to Collective Bargaining: Organized Labor and the Eclipse of Social Democracy in the Postwar Era." In *The Rise and Fall of the New Deal Order, 1930–1980,* edited by Steve Fraser and Gary Gerstle, 122–52. Princeton: Princeton University Press, 1989.

———. *The Most Dangerous Man in Detroit: Walter Reuther and the Fate of American Labor.* New York: Basic Books, 1995.

Lippman, Theo., Jr., *Spiro Agnew's America: The Vice President and the Politics of Suburbia.* New York: Norton, 1972.

Lipset, Seymour Martin. *Political Man: The Social Bases of Politics.* Garden City, N.Y.: Doubleday, 1960.

Lipset, Seymour Martin, and Earl Raab. *The Politics of Unreason: Right-Wing Extremism in America, 1790–1970.* New York: Harper and Row, 1970.

Lipset, Seymour Martin, and William Schneider. *The Confidence Gap: Business, Labor, and Government in the Public Mind.* New York: Free Press, 1983.

Lipsitz, George. *Rainbow at Midnight: Labor and Culture in the 1940s.* Urbana: University of Illinois Press, 1994.

Livelier Baltimore Committee of the Citizens Planning and Housing Association. *Beyond the White Marble Steps: A Look at Baltimore Neighborhoods.* Baltimore: Citizens Planning and Housing Association, 1979.

Loevy, Robert D. "Political Behavior in the Baltimore Metropolitan Area." Ph.D. diss., Johns Hopkins University, 1963.

Lukas, J. Anthony. *Common Ground: A Turbulent Decade in the Lives of Three American Families.* New York: Knopf, 1985.

Maier, Mark H. *City Unions: Managing Discontent in New York City.* New Brunswick, N.J.: Rutgers University Press, 1987.

Makay, John Joseph. "The Speaking of Governor George C. Wallace in the 1964 Maryland Presidential Primary." Ph.D. diss., Purdue University, 1969.

Malone, Bill. *Country Music, USA.* 2d ed. Austin: University of Texas Press, 1985.

Manakee, Harold Randall. *Maryland in World War II.* Vol. 4. Baltimore: Maryland Historical Society, 1950.

Marcuse, Herbert. *One Dimensional Man.* Boston: Beacon Press, 1968.

Matera, Vincent L. "Consent Decree on Seniority in the Steel Industry." *Monthly Labor Review* (March 1975): 43–46.

Mattingly, Trueblood. "Gwynn Oak." *America,* 10 August 1963, 136–37.

McCourt, Kathleen. *Working-Class Women and Grass-Roots Politics.* Bloomington: Indiana University Press, 1977.

McDonald, David. *Union Man.* New York: E. P. Dutton, 1969.

McDougall, Harold A. *Black Baltimore: A New Theory of Community.* Philadelphia: Temple University Press, 1993.

McGreevy, John T. *Parish Boundaries: The Catholic Encounter with Race in the Twentieth-Century Urban North.* Chicago: University of Chicago Press, 1996.

McMahon, Eileen M. *What Parish Are You From? A Chicago Irish Community and Race Relations.* Lexington: University Press of Kentucky, 1995.

Meier, August. "The Successful Sit-Ins in a Border City: A Study in Social Causation." *Journal of Intergroup Relations* (Summer 1961): 230–37.

Meier, August Meier, and Elliott Rudwick. *CORE: A Study in the Civil Rights Movement.* Urbana: University of Illinois Press, 1975.

Melvin, Patricia Mooney, ed. *American Community Organizations: A Historical Dictionary.* New York: Greenwood Press, 1986.

Metcalf, George R. *From Little Rock to Boston: The History of School Desegregation.* Westport, Conn.: Greenwood Press, 1983.

Meyer, Stephen Grant. *As Long as They Don't Move Next Door: Segregation and Racial Conflict in American Neighborhoods.* New York: Rowman and Littlefield, 2000.

Mikulski, Barbara. "Growing Up Ethnic Means Learning Who You Are." *Redbook,* October 1971, 86–226.

Milkis, Sidney. *The President and the Parties: The Transformation of the American Party System since the New Deal.* New York: Oxford University Press, 1993.

Miller, James Edward. "The Dowager of 33rd Street: Memorial Stadium and the Politics of Big-Time Sports in Maryland, 1954–1991." *Maryland Historical Magazine* (Summer 1992): 187–200.

Morris, Charles R. *American Catholic: The Saints and Sinners Who Built America's Most Powerful Church.* New York: Times Books, 1997.

Myrdal, Gunnar. *An American Dilemma: The Negro Problem and Modern Democracy.* 25th anniversary ed. New York: Harper and Row, 1962.

Nash, George H. *The Conservative Intellectual Movement in America since 1945.* New York: Basic Books, 1976.

Nast, Lenora Heilig, Laurence Krause, and R. C. Monk. *Baltimore: A Living Renaissance.* Baltimore: Baltimore Historical Society, 1982.

Nelson, Bruce. *Workers on the Waterfront.* Urbana: University of Illinois Press, 1988.

———. *Divided We Stand: American Workers and the Struggle for Black Equality.* Princeton: Princeton University Press, 2001.

Neverdon-Morton, Cynthia. "Black Housing Patterns in Baltimore City, 1885–1953." *Maryland Historian* (Spring–Summer 1985): 25–39.

Newman, Dorothy K. "Building in Metropolitan Areas, 1954–1956." *Monthly Labor Report* (June 1957): 689–96.

Norrell, Robert J. "Caste in Steel: Jim Crow Careers in Alabama." *Journal of American History* (December 1986): 669–94.

Novak, Michael. *The Rise of the Unmeltable Ethnics: Politics and Culture in the Seventies.* New York: Macmillan, 1971; Macmillan Paperbacks Edition, 1973.

O'Keeffe, Kevin. *Baltimore Politics, 1971–1986: The Schaefer Years and the Struggle for Succession.* Washington, D.C.: Georgetown University Press, 1986.

Olesker, Michael. *Michael Olesker's Baltimore: If You Live Here, You're Home.* Baltimore: Johns Hopkins University Press, 1995.

Olson, Karen. "Old West Baltimore: Segregation, African-American Culture, and the Struggle for Black Equality." In *The Baltimore Book: New Views of Local History,* edited by Elizabeth Fee, Linda Shopes, and Linda Zeidman, 58–78. Philadelphia: Temple University Press, 1991.

———. "When a Woman Has a Working Life: The Transformation of Gender Relations in a Steelmaking Community." Ph.D. diss., University of Maryland, 1994.

Olson, Sherry H. *Baltimore: The Building of an American City.* Baltimore: Johns Hopkins University Press, 1980.

Orser, W. Edward. *Blockbusting in Baltimore: The Edmondson Village Story.* Lexington: University Press of Kentucky, 1994.

Orwell, George. *The Decline of the English Murder and Other Essays.* Middlesex, U.K.: Penguin Books, 1965.

Oshinsky, David. *A Conspiracy So Immense: The World of Joe McCarthy.* New York: Free Press, 1983.

Pancoast, Elinor. *The Report of a Study on Desegregation in the Baltimore City Schools.*

Baltimore: Maryland Commission on Interracial Problems and Relations and Baltimore Commission on Human Relations, 1956.

Patterson, James T. *Grand Expectations: The United States, 1945–1974*. New York: Oxford University Press, 1996.

Patterson, Ted. *Football in Baltimore: History and Memorabilia*. Baltimore; Johns Hopkins University Press, 2000.

Pederson, Vernon Lee. "Red, White, and Blue: The Communist Party of Maryland, 1919–1949. Volumes I and II." Ph.D. diss., Georgetown University, 1993.

Phillips, Christopher. *Freedom's Port: The African American Community of Baltimore, 1790–1869*. Urbana: University of Illinois Press, 1997.

Phillips, Kevin. *The Emerging Republican Majority*. Garden City, N.Y.: Anchor Books, 1969.

Polenberg, Richard. *War and Society: The United States, 1941–1945*. New York: J. B. Lippincott, 1972.

Popkin, Samuel L. *The Reasoning Voter: Communication and Persuasion in Presidential Campaigns*. Chicago: University of Chicago Press, 1991.

"Postwar Work Stoppages Caused by Labor-Management Disputes." *Monthly Labor Review* (December 1946): 872–92.

Powers, Richard Gid. *Not without Honor: The History of American Anticommunism*. New York: Free Press, 1995.

Prendergast, William B. "Maryland: The Ober Anti-communist Law." In *The States and Subversion,* edited by Walter Gellhorn, 140–83. Ithaca: Cornell University Press, 1952.

Ravitch, Diane. *The Troubled Crusade: American Education, 1945–1980*. New York: Basic Books, 1983.

Reutter, Mark. *Sparrows Point: Making Steel—The Rise and Ruin of American Industrial Might*. New York: Summit Books, 1988.

Ribuffo, Leo P. "Why Is There So Much Conservatism in the United States and Why Do So Few Historians Know Anything about It?" *American Historical Review* (April 1994): 438–49.

Rich, Linda G., Joan Clark Netherwood, and Elinor B. Cahn. *Neighborhood: A State of Mind*. Baltimore: Johns Hopkins University Press, 1981.

Rieder, Jonathan. *Canarsie: The Jews and Italians of Brooklyn against Liberalism*. Cambridge: Harvard University Press, 1985.

Rieder, Jonathan. "The Rise of the Silent Majority." In *The Rise and Fall of the New Deal Order, 1930–1980,* edited by Steve Fraser and Gary Gerstle, 243–68. Princeton: Princeton University Press, 1989.

Roberts, Byron. "Pigtown: Some People Left the City, Some Are Coming Back, in Pigtown They Never Moved." *Baltimore Magazine,* August 1976, 31–32.

Rodgers, Daniel T. *Contested Truths: Keywords in American Politics since Independence*. New York: Basic Books, 1987.

Roediger, David R. *The Wages of Whiteness: Race and the Making of the American Working Class*. London: Verso, 1991.

Rogin, Michael Paul. *The Intellectuals and McCarthy: The Radical Specter.* Cambridge: MIT Press, 1967.

Rohr, John A. *To Run a Constitution: The Legitimacy of the Administrative State.* Lawrence: University Press of Kansas, 1986.

Rorty, James. "Desegregation along the Mason-Dixon Line." *Commentary,* December 1954, 493–501.

Rosen, Ellsworth E. "When a Negro Moves Next Door." *Saturday Evening Post,* 4 April 1959, 32–33, 139–42.

Rosenthal, Jack. "The Cage of Fear in Cities Beset by Crime." *Life,* 11 July 1969, 16–23.

Rosswurm, Steve. "The Catholic Church and the Left-Led Unions: Labor Priests, Labor Schools, and the ACTU." In *The CIO's Left-Led Unions,* edited by Steve Rosswurm, 199–237. New Brunswick, N.J.: Rutgers University Press, 1992.

Rovere, Richard H. *Senator Joe McCarthy.* Cleveland: Meridian Books, 1959.

Ruiz, Vicky. *Cannery Women, Cannery Lives: Mexican Women, Unionization, and the California Food Processing Industry, 1930–1950.* Albuquerque: University of New Mexico Press, 1987.

Rukert, Norman G. *The Fells Point Story.* Baltimore: Bodine and Associates, 1976.

Ryon, Roderick N. "An Ambiguous Legacy: Baltimore Blacks and the CIO, 1936–1941." *Journal of Negro History* (Winter 1980): 18–33.

Sandler, Gilbert. *The Neighborhood: The Story of Baltimore's Little Italy.* Baltimore: Bodine and Associates, 1974.

Sanjek, Roger. *The Future of Us All: Race and Neighborhood Politics in New York City.* Ithaca: Cornell University Press, 1998.

Saxton, Alexander. *The Rise and Fall of the White Republic: Class Politics and Mass Culture in Nineteenth-Century America.* London: Verso, 1990.

Scammon, Richard M. *America at the Polls: A Handbook of American Presidential Election Statistics, 1920–1964.* Pittsburgh: University of Pittsburgh Press. 1965.

Scammon, Richard M., and Ben J. Wattenberg. *The Real Majority.* New York: Coward Mc-Cann, 1970.

Schiro, Bruno A. "Housing Surveys in 75 Cities, 1950 and 1952." *Monthly Labor Review* (July 1954): 745.

Schrag, Pete. "The Forgotten American." *Harper's Magazine,* August 1969, 27–34.

Seaton, Douglas. *Catholics and Radicals: The Association of Catholic Trade Unionists and the American Labor Movement from the Depression to the Cold War.* Lewisburg, Pa.: Bucknell University Press, 1981.

Sherman, Albert. "Study of a Neighborhood—Pigtown," 1965. MS in Local History Research Papers Collection, University of Baltimore Archives.

Sherwood, John. *Maryland's Vanishing Lives.* Baltimore: Johns Hopkins University Press, 1994.

Skotnes, Andor D. "The Black Freedom Movement and the Workers' Movement in Baltimore, 1930–1939." Ph.D. diss., Rutgers University, 1991.

Spalding, Thomas W. *The Premier See: A History of the Archdiocese of Baltimore, 1789–1994.* Baltimore: Johns Hopkins University Press, 1989.

Sugrue, Thomas J. "Crabgrass-Roots Politics: Race, Rights, and the Reaction against Liberalism in the Urban North, 1940–1964." *Journal of American History* (September 1995): 551–78.

———. *The Origins of the Urban Crisis: Race and Inequality in Postwar Detroit.* Princeton: Princeton University Press, 1996.

Suttles, Gerald D. *The Social Construction of Communities.* Chicago: University of Chicago Press, 1972.

Sutton, Julie. "The Buddy Deane Show," n.d. MS in Local History Research Papers Collection, University of Baltimore Archives.

Sweeney, Jane P. "Barbara M. Mikulski: Representing the Neighborhood." In *Women in Contemporary U.S. Politics,* edited by Frank P. LeVeness and Jane P. Sweeney, 105–16. London: Lynne Rienner Publishers, 1987.

Sweeney, Rosewyn. "Highlandtown Politics," n.d. MS in Local History Research Papers Collection, University of Baltimore Archives.

Teaford, Jon C. *The Rough Road to Renaissance: Urban Revitalization in America, 1940–1985.* Baltimore: Johns Hopkins University Press, 1990.

Thompson, E. P. *The Making of the English Working Class.* New York: Vintage Books, 1963.

Tygiel, Jules. *Baseball's Great Experiment: Jackie Robinson and His Legacy.* New York: Oxford University Press, 1983.

Warren, Donald I. *The Radical Center: Middle Americans and the Politics of Alienation.* Notre Dame, Ind.: University of Notre Dame Press, 1976.

White, John Kenneth. *The New Politics of Old Values.* Hanover, N.H.: University Press of New England, 1988.

White, Theodore H. *The Making of the President, 1964.* New York: New American Library, 1966.

Williams, Harold A. *The Baltimore Sun, 1837–1987.* Baltimore: Johns Hopkins University Press, 1987.

Wills, Garry. *Nixon Agonistes: The Crisis of the Self-Made Man.* New York: Houghton Mifflin, 1969; Mentor Books, 1979. (Page references in notes are to the 1979 Mentor edition.)

Wright, Todd. "Baltimore's Favorite Son." *Colliers,* 29 December 1951, 30–69.

Wuthnow, Robert. *The Restructuring of American Religion: Society and Faith since World War II.* Princeton: Princeton University Press, 1988.

Wynn, Neil A. *The Afro-American and the Second World War.* New York: Holmes and Meier, 1975.

Zeidman, Linda. "Sparrows Point, Dundalk, Highlandtown, Old West Baltimore: Home of Gold Dust and the Union Card." In *The Baltimore Book: New Views of Local History,* edited by Elizabeth Fee, Linda Shopes, and Linda Zeidman, 175–202. Philadelphia: Temple University Press, 1991.

Zieger, Robert H. *The CIO, 1935–1955.* Chapel Hill: University of North Carolina Press, 1995.

Zweig, Ferdynand. *The Worker in an Affluent Society: Family Life and Industry.* New York: Free Press, 1962.

Index